Kellom Tomlinson

The Art of Dancing
AND
Six Dances

London 1735 and 1720

Noverre Press

THESE are to certify, That the following Work, entitled, THE ART OF DANCING EXPLAIN'D, was design'd and composed by Mr. Kellom Tomlinson *in the Year* 1726 *in the same Manner in which it now appears, we having seen the said* Work *in the Year above mentioned, which he told us he intended for the Press as soon as his Subscription was full; in Witness whereof and in Justice to the Author we have hereunto set our Hands this twelfth Day of* February 1728.

JOSEPH SANDYS, *Gent.*
HENRY CAREY, *Master of Music.*

R.d V. Bleeck Pinxit. 1716.   F. Morellon la Cave Sculpsit. 1754.

Mr. Kellom Tomlinson
AUTHOR of the Original ART of DANCING, Composer, Writer of DANCES,
and their Music, for the Use & Entertainment of the Public.

THE
ART
OF
DANCING

Explained by

READING and FIGURES;

Whereby the

Manner of Performing the STEPS

IS MADE EASY

By a New and Familiar METHOD:

Being the

ORIGINAL WORK

First Defign'd in the Year 1724,

And now Publifhed by

KELLOM TOMLINSON, Dancing-Mafter.

In Two BOOKS.

——*Tulit* alter *Honores.*

LONDON.
Printed for the AUTHOR:
And are to be had of him, at the *Red* and *Gold Flower Pot* next Door to Edwards's
Coffee-Houfe, over againft the *Bull* and *Gate*, in *High-Holbourn*.
MDCCXXXV.

Published by
The Noverre Press
Southwold House
Isington Road
Binsted
Hampshire
GU34 4PH

© 2010 The Noverre Press

ISBN 978-1-906830-06-9

A CIP catalogue record for this book is available from the British Library

The FIRST BOOK treats of the beautiful Attitudes or Postures of STANDING, the different Positions from whence the STEPS of DANCING are to be taken and performed; and likewise of the Manner of WALKING gracefully. The several Sorts of Bows and COURTESIES are also fully described, and all or most of the STEPS used in Genteel DANCING, as well as many of those properly belonging to the STAGE: Illustrated with sixteen Copper Plates containing twenty nine Figures.

The SECOND BOOK contains fourteen Plates, consisting of twenty eight Figures of GENTLEMEN and LADIES, one of each in a Plate, as dancing a MINUET; beginning from the REVERENCE or Bow, and proceeding regularly on 'till the whole is finish'd; shewing the beautiful Attitudes and graceful Deportments of the Performers, in the different Figures and Circles of that celebrated DANCE; together with the Instructions for understanding and keeping Time, and Directions for the Elevation, Movement, and graceful Fall of the Arms in DANCING. To which are added at the Request of some particular Persons of Quality, some Instructions concerning COUNTRY DANCES.

The whole WORK is adorned with thirty Copper Plates, consisting of fifty seven Figures; with five other additional Plates, marked A. E. I. O. U. containing all the STEPS described in this Treatise, written in CHARACTERS; for the Amusement of the Curious, the farther Illustration of this Work, and the Instruction of such as are desirous to understand the CHARACTERS of DANCING.

To the Right Honourable

CATHERINE

Viscountess FAUCONBERG.

Madam,

THE Work I here presume to offer your *Ladyship*, treating of a Subject in which you are not only well versed, but even excel; it was natural and obvious

DEDICATION.

ous for me to *dedicate* it to you, confiding that, under so honourable a Protection, it may at least be skreen'd from such unjust Censures as Malice or Envy ordinarily produce.

It may perhaps be expected that I should say something of the Nobility and great Endowments of your Ancestors, as is usually done in *Dedicatory Epistles*; but the World is so well acquainted with your LADYSHIP's illustrious Families, both that from which you came as well as that to which you are happily ally'd, that to mention any thing of them would rather be derogating from their Praise, seeing all I could relate would be inferior, both to their Merit and to the Opinion of all those who know them. All that I will venture to say is, that your Candour, Affability, Sweetness and Charity, join'd to all your other great Qualities, give as great a Lustre to your Family, as what you receive from it.

BUT

DEDICATION.

But of all your Perfections what touches me the moſt, is your great Talent in the ART of DANCING, which I can ſpeak the more freely of, as I was not only a Spectator, but had the Honour to contribute to, for ſome Time: Not that I pretend to arrogate to myſelf the Glory of the great Proficiency you made (for that was wholly due to your natural Genius for that Science) but only think myſelf happy in having had the good Fortune to give Leſſons to a LADY that perform'd in a Manner no leſs elegant than uncommon.

Nor do I ſo much wonder at the Progreſs your LADYSHIP made in this Science, when I conſider your wonderful Genius and exquiſite Taſte for *Muſic*, which is one of the greateſt Helps to a perfect Performance in DANCING. All theſe rare Talents give me a greater

DEDICATION.

greater Title to your LADYSHIP's gracious Acceptance of this Work; at least it gives me an Occasion of assuring you how much I am, with all Respect and Esteem,

MADAM,

Your LADYSHIP's

most obliged,

most obedient, and

most humble Servant,

KELLOM TOMLINSON.

A LIST
OF THE
SUBSCRIBERS NAMES.

N. B. *This* † *Mark shews that the Subscriber, before whose Name it is placed, died while this Work has been carrying on.*

A.

THE Right Honourable the Lord Aston
The Hon. Edward Aston, *Esq*;
The Hon. Mrs. Catherine Aston.
Sir Francis Andrews, *Bart.*
Sir John Astley *of* Patshull *in* Stafford-shire *Bart.*
William Andrews *Esq*;
† Mrs. Eleanor Andrews.
Mr. A. Labbé, *Dancing-Master to their Royal Highnesses the young Princesses.*
Mr. Jonath. Ayleworth *Dancing-Master.*

B.

Sir Edward Blount, *of* Soddington *in the County of* Worcester, *Bart.*
The Lady Blount.
† Sir William Blacket, *of* Newcastle, *Bart.*
John Basker, *Esq; three Setts.*
B. Bagshaw *of* Wigwell *in* Derby Shire *Esq*;
Edward Brett: Bainbrigg *of* Derby *Esq*;

Subscribers NAMES.

Ed. Bigland *of* Long W--n *near* Loughborough *Esq*;
† William Bourke, *Gent.*
Miss Bullar.
Mrs. Grace Brown, *of* Bentley *in* Darbyshire.
Mrs. Deborah Bowdler *of* Queen's-square.
Mrs. Catharine Bird.
Richard Bostock, *M. D.*
Capt. William Brooks, *of* Derby *Esq*;
Mrs. Margaret Butler, *of* Maryland.
Mrs. Booth *the celebrated Dancer.*
Mrs. M. Bostock, *Paintress.*
Mr. John Brograve, *of* Rudgley, *Dancing-Master.*
Mrs. Bullock, *Dancer, at the Theatre in* Goodman's-Fields.
Samuel Buck, *Engraver, for two Setts.*
Mr. Geo. Bickham *junior, Engraver.*

C

The Right Honourable James, *Earl of* Castlehaven.
The right Honourable Elizabeth, *Countess of* Castlehaven.
† *The Right Honourable* Ann, *Countess Dowager of* Clanrickard.
† *The right Honourable the Lady* Frances Clifton.
Sir Richard Corbet, *Bart.*
The Lady Curzon *of* Kedleston *in* Derbyshire.
Mrs. Anna-Maria Calmady, *of* Devon.
† Francis Cottington, *of* Founthill-Giffard, *Esq*;
W—— C——, *Esq*;
Mrs. Elizabeth Cannon *Daughter to the late* Dean *of* Lincoln.
Richard Cresswell, *of* Bridgnorth *in* Shropshire *Esq*;
Rowland Cotton *of* Etwall *in the County of* Derby *Esq*;
Mr. Thomas Caverley, *of* Queen-Square *Dancing-Master.*

John Clark *Engraver.*
Mr. Henry Carey *Master of Music.*
Mr. Ben. Cole, *Engraver.*
Mr. Thomas Cobb.

D

Her Excellency the Marquess D'aix, *Lady of Honour to the late* Queen *of* Sardinia.
F. D——ll *Esq*;
Kenelm Digby, *of* North-Luffingham *in the County of* Rutland, *Esq*;
Mrs. Ann Darnall, *of* Maryland.
John Dalton, *Gent.*
Mr. J. Dupree, *Dancing-Master at the Theatre Royal in* Covent Garden.
Mr. Lewis Duplessy *Dancing-Master.*

E

The Right Hon. Hannah-Sophia, *Countess of* Exeter.
The Right Hon. the Lady Mary E——.
Henry Every *of* Egginton *in the County of* Derby *Esq*;
Charles Edmonds *Esq*;
Mr. John Essex *Dancing-Master.*
Miss Everet.

F

The Right Hon. Thomas, *Viscount* Fauconberg.
The Right Hon. Catherine, *Viscountess* Fauconberg.
† *The Lady* Fust *of* Hill *near* Gloucester.
C. Fleetwood, *of* Gerards-Bromley *in* Staffordshire, *Esq*;
Mrs. Mary Fairbrother.

G

Mrs. Giffard, *of* Chillington.
H. Gaylor, *M. D.*
Mr. Leech Glover, *Dancing-Master.*
† *The*

Subscribers NAMES.

H.

† *The Right Honourable the Lady* Mary Howard, *of* Workſop
The Hon. Mrs. Winifrede Howard, *of* Norfolk.
The Lady Elizabeth Heathcote, *Daughter to the late Earl of* Macclesfield.
The Lady Hanmer.
Sir Arthur Haſelrigge, *of* Noſely *in* Leiceſterſhire, *Bart.*
Thomas Heneage, *of* Cadeby *in the County of* Lincoln, *Eſq;*
George Heneage, *of* Hainton, *in the ſame County, Eſq;*
M. Hare *Eſq;*
† Richard Holland, *Eſq;*
William Herbert, *Gent.*
George Hills, *Gent.*
Mr. Henry Hargrave, *of* Newark, *Dancing-Maſter.*

J.

The Right Hon. Sir P. J——k, *B.*
The Lady Iſham.
Mrs. Dorothy Jackſon.
Mrs. Elizabeth Jennens *of* Gopſhall *in* Leiceſterſhire.
Mr. Joſeph Jackſon, *Dancing-Maſter.*

K.

The Right Hon. the Lord Kingſale.
† *The Right Hon. the Lady* Frances Keightley.
Mr. Aſcough Kirk, *of* Stamford, *Dancing-Maſter.*
Meſſieurs Knapton *Bookſellers.*

L.

Sir William Lemon, *of* North-hall, Hertfordſhire, *Bart.*
Richard Langley, *of* Grimſton *in the County of* York, *Eſq;*
George Legh, *of the* Temple *Eſq;*
The Lady Lambard *of* Sevenoak *in* Kent.
Coke Littleton, *Eſq;*
Miſs Mary Lewis *of* Tarracoed *in* Carmarthenſhire *South Wales.*
Mr. Tim. La Buſiere *Dancing-Maſter.*
Mr. Daniel Lewis *of* Briſtoll *Dancing-Maſter.*
Mr. Henry Lintot *Bookſeller, three Sets.*
Mr. Edward Langton *Dancing Maſter of* Leiceſter.

M.

Sir Richard Moor *Bart.*
L. Maſters, *of* Red-Lion-Square, *Eſq;*
William Moore, *of* Fetcham *in* Surrey, *Eſq;*
Mr. James Mechel *Printer.*
Mr. A. Moreau *Dancing-Maſter at the Theatre in* Dublin.

N.

† *His Grace* Thomas *late Duke of* Norfolk.
His Grace Edward *Duke of* Norfolk.
The Right Hon. Francis *Lord* North *and* Guilford.
Mrs. Jane Needler, *of* Hollyland *in* Surrey.
John Newton *of* Gray's-Inn, *Gent.*
Mr. William Newton *of* Burton *upon* Trent, Staffordſhire.

O.

Joſeph Offley, *of* Norton-hall, Derby, *Eſq;*
† Thomas O'Brien, *Eſq;*

Subscribers NAMES.

P.

His Grace William *Duke of* Powis.
Her Grace Margaret *Duchess of* Portland.
† J. Pearson, *M. D.*
Mr. P. P. *of* Litchfield.
Mrs. Parkhurst.
Mrs. Mary Peacock.
Mrs. Charlotte Pigott.
† Mr. Edmond Pemberton *Dancing-Master.*

R.

Aymor Rich, *of* Bullhouse, Yorkshire *Esq;*
Mrs. Catherine Rolf, *of* Lynn.
John Rich, *Esq; Master of the Theatres Royal in* Lincoln's-Inn-Fields, *and* Covent-Garden.
Mrs. Mary Ricardy.
Richard Russel *Gent.*

S.

† The right Hon. William *Earl of* Stafford
† The right Hon. Ann *Countess of* Stafford.
The Right Hon. Mary, *Countess of* Shrewsbury.
The Right Hon. the Lady Frances Shirley.
The Right Hon the Lady Ann Shirley.
The Hon John Stafford, *Esq;*
Sir Thomas Samwell, *of* Upton *in* Northamptonshire, *Bart.*
Robert Sutton, *Esq;*
Samuel Sanders *of* Caldwell *in the County of* Derby *Esq;*
Miss Elizabeth Stanley *Daughter to* Sir Edward Stanley, *Bart.*
† Mrs. Elizabeth Smith *of* Great James Street.
Thomas Southcote, *Esq;*
John Southcote, *of* Blyborough *in* Lincolnshire, *Esq;*
J. Strickland, *Gent.*
† William Somerset, *Gent.*
Richard Stanley, *Gent.*
William Stukeley, *M. D.*
Mr. P. Siris, *Dancing-Master.*
Mr. William Sawyer, *of* Rudgley *in* Staffordshire, *Dancing-Master.*
Mr. Robert Smith, *Dancing-Master.*

T.

The Hon. Mrs. Talbot, *of* Longford.
The Hon. Mrs Ann Thompson.
Wilbraham Tufton, *Esq;*
† John Tufton, *Esq;*
Mr. James Tully, *Dancing-Master.*
Mr. John Topham, *Dancing-Master.*
John Tayleur *of* Roddington *in the County of* Salop *Esq;*
Mr. W. H. Toms *Engraver.*

W.

The Hon. Lady Webb, *of* Canford.
Mrs. Webb, *of* Hadthorp.
Mrs. Mary Wingfield
William Woolfe, *of* Queen's-square, *Esq;*
Edward Walpole, *of* Dunston *in the County of* Lincoln, *Esq;*
Mrs. Alethea Walpole.
† Mrs. Mary Walpole.
Ernle Washbourne, *of* Washbourne, *in* Worcestershire, *Esq;*
Thomas Wollescot, *of* Gray's-Inn, *Gent.*
John Walkinshaw, *Gent.*
Ayliffe White, *Gent.*
Edward Wright, *Gent.*
Mrs. Jane Williams.
John Woolley *of* Darley *in the County of* Derby *Esq;*
Mr. John Weaver *Dancing-master.*

Y.

Charles Young *of the* Friers *in* Shrewsbury *Gent.*

THE
PREFACE.

I Now at last have the Pleasure of presenting to the World a Work, which has been long promised; but which, through the Difficulty of the Undertaking itself, and the many Obstacles to the Execution of it, I was not able to finish before.

This Undertaking must needs have been attended with great Difficulty, because it was really the first of the Kind. For tho' Monsieur Beauchamp lay'd the first Foundation, upon which Monsieur Feuillet built, (as some more ingenious Person may perhaps improve upon mine); yet the Works of both relate only to the Characters of Dancing; which, like the Notes of Music, can be only useful to Masters, and cannot be understood by any other without their particular Instructions. But the Piece which I here offer to the World will be of general Use to all, who either have learned, or are learning to dance: the Words describing the Manner in which the Steps are to be taken; and the Figures representing Persons as actually taking them; both which together will make the Learning more pleasant to the one, and serve as a continual Remembrancer to the other.

As most other Arts and Sciences, reduced to certain Rules, have been now long since taught in Books, I have often wondered no one should have hitherto paid the same Regard to the Art of Dancing. This is what I have endeavoured to do in the following Work. wherein I have not pretended to advance any new Laws for Dancing unknown before; but only to collect and submit to view those Principles and Rules, which I had seen taught with the greatest Success

by

THE PREFACE.

by the most eminent Masters in the genteel Way. As the Notes of the Music are placed on the Top of every Plate, the Characters of the Steps marked below, and the Figures represent two Persons in the very Action of Dancing; whoever has made any Progress in the Knowledge of musical Notes and of the Characters of Dancing, will be able by intently viewing one of these Plates, at one and the same Time, to call to Mind the Tune, to know the Order of the Steps, and to put the Body into the proper Attitude to take them. And tho' this Book, like all others which treat of any Art or Science, cannot be perfectly understood without some Study and Application; yet by a little Assistance from the Author, or others of the Profession properly qualified, all the Difficulties will be soon surmounted. The Figures in each Plate are designed only to shew the Postures proper in Dancing, but not to bear the least Resemblance to any Person to whom the Plate is inscribed; which it had been ridiculous to have attempted: The sole Intent of the Inscription being to do Honour to my self, by this small Testimony of my Gratitude to some honourable Persons. The continual Change of the Fashion will afford, I presume, a sufficient Excuse for the Drapery of the Figures: and Gloves were designedly omitted, on Purpose to shew the beautiful Shape of the Hands. The Faults, which may have happened in the Execution, either of the Printing, or Ingraving, will, I hope, be the more easily excused, if the Nicety of the Subject be considered, together with the Difficulty of the Performance, and the many Hands through which it has passed: especially if it be remembered, that this is not only my first Attempt, but likewise the first that has been made of the Kind.

It may seem a little strange, that I should claim the Honour of having first treated of the Art of Dancing; *when a Book upon the same Subject was published in* France *as long ago as in* 1725. *But the following Account will, I hope, clear up all Doubt in Relation to the Justice of my Pretensions.*

In Mist's Journal Sat. Jan. 13 1728, *appeared this Advertisement,* " Next Week will be published The Dancing-Master *or* The Art of " Dancing explain'd *by Monsieur* Rameau'. *This gave me no small Surprize, having never before heard of either any such Book, or Author.*

THE PREFACE.

thor. Had it been my Fortune to have known, either before, or after I undertook to write on this Art, that such a Book was extant, my Curiosity would certainly have led me to have consulted it; and had I approved it, 'tis highly probable, I should have given the World a Translation of it, with some additional Observations of my own. This had been a much easier Task, than to compose a Work entirely new upon the same Subject: which I had actually finished in 1724 ready for the Press, as it is now published, without any material Alteration, a full Year before the Publication of Monsieur Rameau's Book, and near four Years before this Advertisement appeared; the Truth whereof several credible Witnesses have testified under their own Hands.

I advertised this Work of mine the first Time, as ready for the Press, and that it only waited for a sufficient Number of Subscribers to defray the Expence, in Berington's Evening Post, Oct. 15, 1726, and again in the same Paper Oct. 22. This Advertisement was repeated in The White-Hall Evening Post, Nov. 12. and in The London Journal, Dec. 3. In Mist's Journal of March 4. 1727, I gave Notice of the Publication of my Proposals, together with some Plates done by Way of Specimen; and renewed that Notice on 18th, in Berington's Evening Post, and again on Oct. 28. in the same Paper. From this particular Account it appears, that I had published seven Advertisements concerning my Work; the first of which was two Years and three Months, before ever the Translation of Monsieur Rameau's Book was advertised in Mist's Journal Jan. 13. 1728.

To secure my self in some Measure from the Damage I might receive by this Advertisement; I thought it necessary to publish one my self a few Days after, in Mist's Journal Jan. 27. To which I prefixed this Motto from VIRGIL, ———Tulit alter Honores; intimating, that another Person had attempted to bear away the Honour of my Invention; and I may justly add, the Profit of it too. That this was his Intention is very plain from two Circumstances: the Addition to the Title; and the Alteration of the Form of Monsieur Rameau's Book. The Title of his in the original is onely The Dancing Master; to which the ingenious Translator, or perhaps Bookseller, thought

proper

THE PREFACE.

proper to add that of mine, The Art of Dancing explain'd: *The French Original was published in* Octavo; *but the Translation was magnified to a* Quarto, *almost the Size of mine, and yet proposed to be sold at half the Price. The assuming thus the very Title and Form of the Book proposed to the Publick by me, seems to have been done with no better View, than to raise an Advantage by anticipating my Design; and to obstruct the Success of it, by making it seem to be only a servile Imitation of the original Invention of Monsieur* Rameau. *This Contrivance was the more likely to have the desired Effect, from the unfavourable Situation in which the* Proposals *for the Subscription to my Book might at that Time appear. It was above two Years since it had been advertised as ready for the Press: and this delay in the Publication, the not fixing any certain Time for it, and the Difficulty in procuring Subscriptions, upon the Number of which the Publication must depend, might probably induce many Persons to suspect that it would never be published at all. And this Difficulty would be much increased, by offering to the Public a Book on the same Subject, with the same Title, and of almost the same Size, which yet should cost no more than half the Price of mine. To make which Book appear still more perfect and complete, and mine less necessary, or useful, the Gentleman who published it was not satisfied to present it to the World merely as a Translation of Monsieur* Rameau's *Work, approved by Monsieur* Pecour, *the greatest Master in* France; *but was prompted by his Ingenuity and Generosity to make such surprizing Improvements in the Figures, as will be a lasting Monument of his great Abilities in the Art of Dancing.*

Before I conclude this Preface, *it seems necessary to say something more particularly of my self, for the Satisfaction of those to whom I may not have the Honour to be known; who will naturally expect, before they encourage a Piece of such an extraordinary Nature, to receive some Evidence, that the Person who undertakes it is in some measure qualified for the Performance.*

In April 1707. *I was placed as an Apprentice with Mr.* Thomas Caverley, *now living in* Queen's-Square, *St.* George *the Martyr, with whom I continued till the Year* 1714. *During which Time, I*

had

THE PREFACE.

had likewise the good Fortune to be further instructed in the Theatrical Way, by that great Performer Mr. Cherreir, *once contemporary with the inimitable Mr.* L'Abbe, *with whom also I have had the Happiness of a personal Acquaintance. Mr.* Cherreir's *great Merit, after he quitted the Stage, was supported a long Time by the late Mr.* John Shaw, *who was justly esteemed not only one of the finest Theatrical Dancers, but one of the most beautiful Performers in the Gentleman-like Way: the Acquisition of both which Excellencies in Practice, must be chiefly owing to those admirable Instructions in the Theory, which he received from Mr.* Caverley, *when He and I were fellow Apprentices to that great Master.*

I beg Leave to mention in the next Place two of my Scholars, who have appeared upon the Stage with no small Applause. The one was Mr. John Topham, *who danced upon both Theatres under the Name of Mr.* Kellom's *Scholar, when he had been with me no longer than betwixt two and three Years. The other was Miss* Frances, *who, on the Theatre Royal in* Little Lincoln's-Inn-Fields, *performed the* Passacaille de Scilla, *consisting of above a thousand Measures or Steps, without making the least Mistake; but she left me in the midst of her Improvement.*

To this I hope it will not be thought improper to subjoin a short Account of some of my Compositions, which have been well received by the World. The Passepied Round O *in* 1715 *dedicated to Mr.* Caverley; *the* Shepherdess *in* 1716; *the* Submission *in* 1717, *which, by the Name of Mr.* Kellom's *New Dance, was performed by Monsieur and Mademoiselle* Salle, *the two French Children, on the Theatre in* Lincoln's-Inn-Fields, *to very considerable Audiences, every Night, for a whole Week together. To which I beg Leave to add the* Prince Eugene *in* 1728; *the* Address *the next Year; the* Gavot *in* 1730; *and the* Passacaille Diana *the Year following, dedicated to Mr.* L'Abbe. *All which I composed, wrote in Characters, and published, for the Improvement of the* Art of Dancing.

I might here add a long Account of the Honour done me by many of the Nobility and Gentry in employing me to teach their Children; and in permitting me to publish it to the World by the Dedication of

THE PREFACE.

my Plates. *But I have perhaps dwelt too long upon this Subject already, which I hope the candid Reader will excuse; and not impute this Account of my self to Vanity or Conceit, but to an earnest Desire in me to give the utmost Satisfaction to my Subscribers, and to remove all Suspicion of my Want of Talents proper for the Execution of this new Undertaking. And this was the more necessary to be done, because of the Disadvantage to which I have been exposed by going accidentally under two different Names,* Kellom *and* Tomlinson; *being known formerly by the first, but of late only by the last; the Occasion of which it may not be thought improper to relate.*

During the Time of my Apprenticeship I went generally by the Name of Kellom, *a Corruption of* Kenelm *my true Christian Name; as it is very common for young Persons to be called Mr.* John, *Mr.* William, *and the like, without the Addition of their Sur-name. At the Expiration of my Apprenticeship, several of my Friends out of Respect called me by my Sur-name of* Tomlinson; *but, being unwilling to decline the Advantage I might probably receive from the Reputation of having learned the Art of Dancing under so great a Master as Mr.* Caverley, *I chose rather to retain the Name of* Kellom, *by which I had been so universally known to have been under his Instruction. This Duplicity of Appellation turned afterwards to my great Disadvantage: many of the Nobility and Gentry, who would have had their Children taught by Mr.* Kellom, *refusing to employ Mr.* Tomlinson *tho' recommended to them; and many, who would have employed Mr.* Tomlinson, *rejecting Mr.* Kellom. *To prevent which Confusion for the future, I shall acknowledge my self obliged to those, who, instead of either singly, shall be pleased to call me by both conjunctly,* Kellom Tomlinson.

THE CONTENTS.

BOOK I.

Chap. I. OF Standing. page 3
II. Of Walking. 5
III. Of Bowing, or the different Sorts of Honours. 7
IV. Of the Dancing-Room. 18
V. Of the Coupee of one Step or Half Coupee. 25
VI. Of the Coupee. 26
VII. Of the Coupee with two Movements. 27
VIII. Of the Bouree-Step or Fleuret. 29
IX. Of the Bouree with two Movements. 32
X. Of the Pasgrave or March. 33
XI. Of the Point and March. 34
XII. Of the Spring or Bound. 36
XIII. Of the Close or Jump. 37
XIV. Of the Spring or Leap. 39
XV. Of the Rigadoon-Step of one Spring, open in the same Place and Close. 41
XVI. Of the Rigadoon-Step of two Springs or Siffonne. 44
XVII. Of the Galliard and Falling Step. 48
XVIII. Of the Bouree with a Bound. 52
XIX. Of the Slip before and then behind, or Slip behind and afterwards before, and Half Coupee sideways. 54
XX. Of the Hop or Contretemp. 58
XXI. Of the Chaffee or Driving Step. 64
XXII. Of the Chaffee or Driving Step of two Movements or Bounding Coupees. 71
XXIII. Of the Beaten Coupee or Hop. 74
XXIV. Of the Chaffee or Driving Step, of three Springs in the same Place, from the third Position. 77
XXV. Of the Flying Chaffee or Driving Step backwards, with a Close and Coupee to a Measure. 79
XXVI. Of the Hop of two Movements, from the fifth Position round in two half Turns. 81
XXVII. Of the Chaconne or Paffacaille Step. 83
XXVIII. Of the Hop and two Chaffees or Drives round in the same Place. 84
XXIX.

The CONTENTS.

Chap. XXIX. *Of the* Fall, Spring *with both Feet at the same Time, and* Coupee *to a Measure.* page 86
XXX. *Of the* Close *beating before and falling behind in the third Position,* upright Spring *changing to the same before, and* Coupee *to a Measure.* 88
XXXI. *Of the* Pirouette. 90
XXXII. *Of the* Pirouette *introduced by a* Coupee. 96
XXXIII. *Of the* Bouree *before and behind, and behind and before, advancing in a whole Turn.* 98

BOOK. II.

Chap. I. OF *the* Minuet Step. 130
II. *Of the* Hop *in the* Minuet. 113
III. *Of the* Double Bouree *upon the same Place.* 115
IV. *Of the* Balance. 118
V. *Of the two* Coulees *or* Marches. 119
VI. *Of the* Slip *behind and* Half Coupee *forwards to the right and left Hands, each, to a* Minuet Step 120
And of Dancing *the* Minuet *in general.* 124
VII. *Of the Figure of* S *reversed or second Division.* 126
VIII. *Of* Presenting *the* right Arm *or third Part.* 128
IX. *Of the fourth Division or* Presenting *of the* left Arm. 131
X. *Of the fifth Division or second* S. 133
XI. *Of the sixth Division or* Presenting *of* both Arms *and Conclusion.* 135
XII. *Of the* Mistakes *in Dancing of a* Minuet, *with their* Ocasions *and* Rules *to prevent them.* 137
XIII. *Of* Time, *or some Account what* Time *is; with Rules to be observed in Keeping it.* 141
XIV. *Of the Movement of the* Arms *in* Dancing. 152
XV. *Of* Country Dancing. 156

An Ex-

An Explanation of the *Characters* or *Steps* contained in the Tables of Plate E, in the exact Order they are treated of in this Work, shewing the different Ways in which the said Steps are performed whether forwards, backwards, sideways, or round, &c. in which you will see the Steps treated of in *Words* written down in *Characters* and *Figures*, which will not only convey a stronger Idea of the Steps, but also be very entertaining to the curious Reader.

The Steps treated of in BOOK I.

TABLE I. The *HALF COUPEE*.
FIG. 1. Forwards with either Foot.
FIG. 2. Backwards with either Foot.
FIG. 3. Sideways to the right, and sideways to the left.

TABLE II. The *COUPEE*.
FIG. 1. The Coupee forwards with either Foot.
FIG. 2. The same backwards with either Foot in two Movements, or plain, as Fig. 1.
FIG. 3. Sideways before in two Movements with either Foot, or plain, as Fig. 4.
FIG. 4. Sideways behind with either Foot.

TABLE III. The *BOUREE*.
FIG. 1. Forwards with either Foot.
FIG. 2. Backwards with either Foot.
FIG. 3. Sideways before with either Foot.
FIG. 4. Sideways behind with either Foot.
FIG. 5. Sideways before and behind with either Foot.
FIG. 6. Sideways behind and before with either Foot.
FIG. 7. Twice behind and the third Step forwards with either Foot.
FIG. 8. Bouree and Bound with either Foot forwards.

TABLE IV. The *MARCH and POINT and MARCH*.
FIG. 1. Forwards with either Foot.

FIG. 2. Point sideways with either Foot.
FIG. 3. Forwards with either Foot.

TABLE V. The *BOUND*.
FIG. 1. Forwards with either Foot.
FIG. 2. Backwards with either Foot.
FIG. 3. Sideways before with either Foot.
FIG. 4. Sideways behind with either Foot.
FIG. 5. Twice to a Measure.
FIG. 6. Thrice to a Measure.

TABLE VI. The *CLOSE*.
FIG. 1. With either Foot into the first Position forwards.
FIG. 2. With either Foot backwards into the first Position.
FIG. 3. Forwards with either Foot into the third Position inclos'd before.
FIG. 4. The same backwards with either Foot inclosed behind, and a Walk forwards to a Measure.

TABLE VII. The *LEAP or JUMP*.
FIG. 1. Forwards.
FIG. 2. Backwards.
FIG. 3. Sideways to the right Hand.
FIG. 4. Sideways to the left Hand.
FIG. 5. The upright Spring.
FIG. 6. Round in an upright Spring.
FIG. 7. Two Springs and a plain straight Step forwards to a Measure.
FIG. 8. Three Springs to a Measure forwards.

FIG. 9.

FIG. 9. *The upright Spring and plain Step forwards to a Measure.*
FIG. 10. *Two Springs to a Measure forwards.*
TABLE VIII. The *RIGADOON STEP of one Spring open in the same Place.*
FIG. 1. *Upon the same Place with either Foot in the first Position.*
FIG. 2. *Upon the same Place with either Foot inclosing into the third Position forwards.*
FIG. 3. *The same inclosing into the third Position backwards.*
FIG. 4. *Upon the same Place inclosing into the third Position, first before and then behind, upright Spring, and Change of the hind Feet first with either Foot.*
FIG. 5. *The same with either Foot, first behind and then before, upright Spring into the first Position, and plain Step forwards to a Measure.*

FIG. 6. *The same in the first Position.*
TABLE IX. The *RIGADOON STEP of two Springs.*
FIG. 1. *Forwards with either Foot.*
FIG. 2. *Backwards with either Foot.*
FIG. 3. *Sideways crossing before with either Foot.*
FIG. 4. *Sideways crossing behind with either Foot.*
TABLE X. The *GALLIARD and FALLING STEP.*
FIG. 1. *Forwards with either Foot.*
FIG. 2. *Backwards with either Foot.*
FIG. 3. *Sideways to the Presence with either Foot.*
FIG. 4. *Sideways with either Foot in a quarter Turn facing the Sides of the Room.*
FIG. 5. *Sideways with either Foot in a half Turn to the Bottom of the Room.*

An Explanation of the *Characters* or *Steps* contain'd in the Tables of the Plate marked I. as first *Slipping before,* and then *slipping behind, &c.*

TABLE XI. The *SLIP BEFORE, SLIP BEHIND, and HALF COUPEE.*
FIG. 1. *Sideways with either Foot before and behind to the Presence.*
FIG. 2. *The same with a Bound behind and before with either Foot.*
FIG. 3. *Sideways with either Foot before and behind in a quarter Turn to each other.*
FIG. 4. *The same behind and before in a half Turn to the Bottom.*
FIG. 5. *Sideways with either Foot twice slipping behind.*
FIG. 6. *The same slipping twice before.*
TABLE XII. The *HOP or CONTRETEMP.*
FIG. 1. *Forwards with either Foot from the third Position.*
FIG. 2. *The same backwards with either Foot.*
FIG. 3. *With either Foot advancing to the Sides of the Room in a quarter Turn.*
FIG. 4. *The same with either Foot to the Bottom in a half Turn.*
FIG. 5. *Sideways crossing before with either Foot to the Presence.*
FIG. 6. *The same with either Foot in a quarter Turn facing the Sides.*
FIG. 7 *The same in a half Turn with either Foot to the Bottom.*
FIG. 8. *With either Foot stepping sideways and a Draw behind.*
FIG. 9. *The same in a quarter Turn to the Sides.*
FIG. 10.

FIG. 10. *Sideways crossing before with either Foot from the fourth Position.*
FIG. 11. *The same with a Bound.*
FIG. 12. *From the fourth Position advancing up the Room with either Foot.*
FIG. 13. *The same with a Bound.*
FIG. 14. *Backwards from the fourth Position with either Foot.*
FIG. 15. *The same with a Bound.*
TABLE XIII. The *CHASSEE or DRIVING STEP.*
FIG. 1. *Of three with either Foot from the fourth Position to the Presence.*
FIG. 2. *The same sideways.*
FIG. 3. *Of four to the Presence with either Foot from the fourth Position.*
FIG. 4. *The same sideways crossing the third of the four Steps before.*
FIG. 5. *The same in a quarter Turn to the Sides with either Foot.*
FIG 6. *The same in a quarter Turn more to the Bottom.*
FIG. 7. *The same advancing, turning to each other upon the Half Coupee, or last Step of the four.*
TABLE XIV. The *BEATEN COUPEE, or HOP and DRIVING STEP of two Movements.*
FIG. 1. *The Beaten Coupee forwards with either Foot.*
FIG. 2. *Driving Step of two Springs backwards with either Foot.*
FIG. 3. *Beaten Hop forwards with either Foot.*
FIG. 4. *Driving Step of two Springs with either Foot sideways.*
FIG. 5. *The same of three Springs.*
FIG. 6. *The same of two Springs and a Close or Join.*
FIG. 7. *The same of one Spring and a Close.*
TABLE XV. The *CHASSEE or DRIVING STEP of three Springs upon the same Place.*
FIG. 1. *Of three Springs to the Presence with either Foot.*
FIG. 2. *The same to the Sides of the Room.*
FIG. 3. *The same of two Springs to the Presence.*
TABLE XVI. FIG. 1. The *FLYING CHASSEE or DRIVING STEP retiring backwards, CLOSE and COUPEE to a Measure with either Foot, and HALF COUPEE.*
TABLE XVII. FIG. 1. The *HOP of two Movements with either Foot from the fifth Position upon the same Place.*
TABLE XVIII. FIG. 1. The *PASSACAILLE STEP with either Foot to the Presence.*
TABLE XIX. FIG. 1. The *HOP and two CHASSEES or DRIVES round upon the same Place with either Foot.*
TABLE XX. FIG. 1. The *FALL and SPRING with both Feet at the same Time,* &c. *with either Foot.*
TABLE XXI. FIG. 1. The *CLOSE beating before and falling behind, upright SPRING, and COUPEE* &c. *with either Foot.*
TABLE XXII. FIG. 1. *The same beating before and falling behind in a whole Turn,* &c. *with either Foot.*
TABLE XXIII. FIG. 1. The *BALONNE with either Foot.*
TABLE XXIV. *The TURN upon a whole Position, a quarter, half, three quarter,* &c.
FIG 1. *A quarter Turn with either Foot to the Sides of the Room.*
FIG. 2. *A half Turn to the Bottom with either Foot.*
FIG. 3. *A three quarter Turn to the Sides with either Foot.*
FIG. 4. *The same with either Foot and a whole Turn.*

TABLE XXV. The *PIROUETTE crossing behind.*
FIG. 1. *A quarter Turn with either Foot to the Sides.*
FIG. 2. *A half Turn to the lower End with either Foot.*
FIG 3. *A three quarter Turn with either Foot to the Sides.*
FIG. 4. *The same with either Foot quite round.*
The *PIROUETTE crossing before.*
FIG. 1. *A quarter Turn with either Foot to the Sides.*
FIG. 2. *A half Turn with either Foot to the Bottom.*
FIG. 3. *A Three quarter Turn with either Foot to the Sides.*
FIG. 4. *The same with either Foot quite round.*
TABLE XXVI. *The PIROUETTE introduced by a COUPEE.*
FIG. 1. *The* Coupee *with either Foot*

FIG. 2. *The* Pirouette *with either Foot.*
TABLE XXVII. *The BOUREE before and behind, and behind and before, advancing in a whole Turn.*
FIG. 1. *Before and behind with either Foot in a half Turn.*
FIG. 2. *Behind and before with either Foot in a half Turn more to the Presence.*
TABLE XXVIII. *The same before and behind, and the COUPEE introducing a HOP or CHASSEE.*
FIG 1. *Before and behind in a half Turn with either Foot.*
FIG. 2. *The* Coupee *in a quarter Turn to the Sides with either Foot.*
FIG. 3. *The same before and behind in a half Turn with either Foot.*
FIG. 4. *The* Half Coupee *opening the disengaged Foot in the Air setting down inclos'd behind the Foot on which the Weight is, with either Foot.*

An Explanation of the *Characters* or *Steps* contained in Plate O, in the regular Order treated on in BOOK II.

TABLE II. FIG. 1. *The MINUET STEP of two Movements or ONE and a FLEURET.*
FIG. 2. *The same open off sideways to the right Hand.*
FIG. 3. *The same crossing behind to the left sideways.*
FIG. 4 *The same of three Movements crossing behind to the left.*
FIG. 5. *The same of three Movements before and behind to the left.*

TABLE III. *Steps by Way of GRACE.*
FIG 1. *The* Hop *or* Contretemp *in the* Minuet *forwards.*
FIG. 2. *The same backwards.*
FIG. 3. *The* Double Bouree *upon the same Place, the first,* Fig. 1. *the se-*

cond, Fig. 2. *forwards.*
FIG. 4. *The* Double Bouree *forwards the first* Fig. 1. *and the second* Fig. 2.
FIG. 5. *The* Balance, *the first* Fig. 1. *and the second* Fig 2.
FIG. 6. *The two* Marches, *the first* Fig. 1. *and the second* Fig. 2.
FIG. 7. *The* Slip *behind and* Step *forwards to either Hand.*
The Slip *behind to the right,* Fig. 1.
The Step *forwards,* Fig. 2. *Slip behind to the left,* Fig. 3.
The Step forwards, Fig. 4.
FIG. 8. *The same in two Measures.*

Plate U. contains the whole Form of the *Minuet* in the exact Order treated on in BOOK II.

THE

THE
ART of DANCING
EXPLAIN'D.

BOOK THE FIRST.

CHAP. I.
Of STANDING.

efore I proceed to treat on *Motion*, I apprehend it to be necessary to consider that Grace and Air so highly requisite in our Position, when we *stand* in Company; for, having formed a true Notion of this, there remains nothing farther to be observed, when we enter upon the Stage of Life, either in Walking or Dancing, than to preserve the same.

And, for the better understanding of this important Point, let us imagine ourselves, as so many living Pictures drawn by the most excellent Masters, exquisitely designed to afford the utmost Pleasure to the Beholders: And, indeed, we ought to set our

A 2   Bodies

4 The Art of Dancing explain'd.

Bodies in such a Disposition, when we stand in Conversation, that, were our Actions or Postures delineated, they might bear the strictest Examination of the most critical Judges.

Let us, therefore, to draw nearer to the Subject in hand, inquire into the Nature of those Positions that must be observed, in order to attain this fine and becoming Presence: And that our Readers may be furnished with proper Directions to arrive at the same, tho' perhaps, our Rules may not be so perfect as could have been wished, we flatter ourselves they will be of no small Use and Advantage; wherefore, without farther Apology, I shall enter upon the Description of *Position* in general.

Position, then, is the different Placing or Setting our Feet on the Floor, whether in Conversation or Dancing; and those for Conversation, or when we *stand* in Company, are when the Weight rests as much on one Foot, as the other, the Feet being considerably separated or open, the Knees streight, the Hands placed by the Side in a genteel Fall or natural Bend of the Wrists, and being in an agreeable Fashion or Shape about the Joint or Bend of the Hip, with the Head gracefully turning to the Right or Left, which compleats a most Heroic Posture; and, tho' it may be improper, in the Presence of Superiors, among Familiars, it is a bold and graceful Attitude, called the Second Position†: Or, when the Heel of the right or left Foot is inclosed or placed, without Weight, before the Ancle of that Foot by which the Poise is supported, the Hands being put between the Folds or Flaps of the Coat, or Waiste-coat, if the Coat is unbuttoned, with a natural and easy Fall of the Arms from the Shoulders, this produces a very modest and agreeable Posture, named the Third Position inclosed ‖: Or, if the inclosed Foot be moved open from the other, sideways, to the Right or Left, about the Distance of half a Foot, or as far as, in setting it down to the Floor, the Weight of the Body resting on the contrary Foot is not disordered by it, with the Toes handsomely turning out, the Hat under one Arm, and the

---
† See Plate III. ‖ See the Feet in Plate IV.

other

The ART *of* DANCING *explain'd.*

other in some agreeable Action, the Head also turning a little from the Foot on which the Poise rests, this we stile the Fourth Position open, and it may be very justly esteemed a most genteel and becoming Posture *.

The Positions, from which *Dancing* dates its Original, consist of five Principles: As, first, when the Toes turning outwards, the two Heels are equally placed together (a). Secondly, when both Heels are considerably separated or open (b). Thirdly, when the Poise rests upon one Foot, the other being inclosed or placed before the Ancle of that Foot by which the Weight is supported (c). Fourthly, when the inclosed Foot is advanced upon a right Line, about the Length of a Step in Walking (d). And, Fifthly, when the Heel of the advanced Foot is so crossed and placed before the Toe of that Foot on which the Body rests, as that the Turning may be made, and yet one Foot not, in the least, interrupt the other (e). Having briefly described the most agreeable Postures of *Standing* in Conversation, and laid down the Rudiments of the whole ART of DANCING, I shall now proceed to treat on *Motion*, the Result of Position, and first begin with *Walking*.

CHAP. II.
Of WALKING.

WALKING consists of Motion and a Change of Place, by transferring the Weight or Poise of the Body from one Foot to the other, by stepping or advancing the disengaged Foot (whichsoever it be) from the first Position † to the fourth advanced ‖, and so alternately, concluding as at first †, but always on the contrary Foot. In order to *walk* gracefully, it is to be observed, that, during the Step or Motion made by the disengaged Foot, as above ‖, the

---

* See Plate VIII. (a) See Plate II. (b) See Plate III. (c) See Plate IV. (d) See Plate IX. (e) See Plate XI. † See Plate I. ‖ See Plate IX.

B 2　　　　　　　　　　　　　　　　　whole

whole Weight of the Body muſt reſt on the ſame Foot as at commencing it †, until the ſtepping Foot is advanced its due Length of Step ‖; and, on its receiving the Poiſe or Weight on the Ball or full Part of the Heel, upon ſetting it to the Ground or Floor, the now diſengaged Foot, which at firſt ſupported the Weight, becoming by this means releaſed, attends the Poiſe in a gentle and eaſy Motion, until it arrive in its former Poſition †; but on the contrary Foot for the Step next enſuing, which is made in like Manner, and ſo on; for if, inſtead of the Body's waiting or attending the Motion of the ſtepping Foot, as above deſcribed ‖, it ſhould either go before or along with it, the Grace that ought to accompany our Steps, in *Walking*, is loſt, becauſe the Foot muſt conſtantly go before the Body ‖, to receive it, otherwiſe it will always repreſent the Body in a falling Poſture.

And it is farther to be noted, that, in *Walking* with a good Grace, Time and Harmony muſt be obſerved, as well as in *Dancing*: For Example, the ſetting down or receiving the Poiſe, at the End of the Step, is upon *One*; the taking up the diſengaged Foot, by a gentle and eaſy raiſing the Heel and pointing the Toe, in one intire Motion, which is the Manner of taking up the Foot to ſtep, is upon *Three* †; and *Two* is in the coming up of the diſengaged Foot, after the Step has been made †, which may be continued faſter or ſlower, but muſt always be in one certain Time, counting *One*, *Two*, and *Three*, as in Muſic. And, by this Method, the Body with a good Grace reſting or ſtanding, 'till two Thirds of the Three we count, muſt neceſſarily add great Beauty to our *Walking*, which is the Caſe under Conſideration; for the Step is made upon *One* ‖, the Preparation or Taking up the Foot, to make the Step, *Three* †, and *Two* is in the coming up of the releaſed Foot, to continue our *Walking*.

And, as to the Motion of the Arms in *Walking*, they will naturally have their due Courſe or Swing, in a continual Contraſt or Oppoſition to the Feet; for, when the right Foot ſteps for-

---

† See Plate I. ‖ See Plate IX.

wards,

The ART *of* DANCING *explain'd.* 7

wards (f), the left Arm advances, in Contradiction, as the right Arm does, when the left Foot steps forwards (g), and so alternately; and the like in *Walking* backwards, in Relation to the Contrast, but not with Respect to the Arms, because, in *Walking* backwards, the Contradiction is between the same Arm and Foot; for, when the right Foot steps back (h), the right Arm advances in Opposition, as, when the left Foot steps backwards (i), the left Arm advances, as aforesaid, and so on, if continued. Having, I hope, offered what will prove satisfactory, on this Head, I shall next inquire into the different Sorts of *Bows* and *Courtesies* in Conversation.

CHAP. III.
Of BOWING, *or the different Sorts of* HONOURS.

BOWS or *Courtesies* are the outward Marks of Respect we pay to others, which, in one Sex, are shewed by bowing the Body, but, in the other, by bending the Knees; and, if made in a regular Manner, they are, indeed, very grand, noble, and highly ornamental. They accompany our Conversation, as well in *Standing* as *Walking*; in the former, on breaking off a Conversation, as in taking Leave, or by way of Acknowledgment for some Favour or obliging thing spoken in our Praise; and in the latter, when we enter a Room, or meet a Person passing either on the Right or Left. These are the two different Classes or Sorts of *Bows* and *Courtesies*, which are, as it were, founded on the two preceding Chapters of *Standing* and *Walking*; and, to begin with leaving a Room, which relates to the first of the said Orders, I shall ob-

(f) See the second Figure or Woman's Side in Plate IX. (g) See the first Figure in Plate IX. (h) See the first Figure in Plate IX. (i) See also the second Figure in Plate IX.

serve,

8 *The* ART *of* DANCING *explain'd.*

serve, that Taking Leave in Conversation consists in stepping aside, bowing, and leaving the disengaged Foot pointed, sideways, in one intire Motion to the first Division of the Bow or counting of *One*†, during which it remains the Respect or counting of *Two*†; and, in the graceful Raising of the Body upon *Three*, it is drawn pointed, with the Knees streight 'till it crosses behind the Foot on which the Poise rests, and stands erect on the Foot that it crosses behind‖, to be repeated as often as Occasion requires; and it is to be noted, that the Respect, if repeated, is always made to the same Hand; if the Leave be taken to the Right, the Stepping aside is always with the right Foot§, as it is always to the Left, if taken the contrary Way (k).

In Conversation with a Gentleman or Lady standing, the very same *Bow* is made, as in leaving a Room, the receiving the Poise on the Foot drawn behind excepted‖; but, instead thereof, it remains, on Conclusion of the Bow, in the Third Position, upon the Point, without Weight, behind the foremost Foot which here supports the Poise, in readiness to repeat the Respect, if necessary (l), because, in this Bow of Repetition, it always steps first to one Hand†, and then to the other†, in order to preserve the same Ground; otherwise, if made as leaving a Room (m), it would have the contrary Effect and cause the Persons to retire, instead of resting in the same Place; and it is a very genteel and becoming Bow, if the Stepping aside, Bow, and Point of the disengaged Foot, be made, at once†, and a Pause or Counting of *Two* is observed between the Stepping aside and Bowing†, and the graceful Rising up again from thence, in drawing of the pointed Foot up, at the same Time, into the abovementioned Position*, be also in one intire Motion. As to the Reverence or Courtesy of a Lady, on the present Occasion, with Regard to the Feet, it is much the same, but not so, in Relation to the Body; because, as I have already said, the Respect the former

---

† See the 2d and 4th Plates in the 2d Book. ‖ See the 3d Plate in Book the 2d. § See the 2d Plate in Book the 2d. (k) See Plate 4 in Book the 2d. (l) See the Feet in Plate 5. (m) See Plate 3, Book the 2d. * See the Feet in Plate 5.

shews

The ART of DANCING explain'd.   9

shews to any is by bending the Body, but the Courtesy or Respect, which a Lady pays to those of either Sex, is by a graceful Bending of the Knees†, accompanied with a becoming and suitable Disposition of the different Parts of the Body: As, having the Hands before them, in some agreeable Posture supporting, as it were, the slanting or falling Shoulders, which, at the same Time, lengthen and more gracefully expose a fine Neck, as well as a beautiful Face composed of so many delicate and charming Features, with which they are usually adorned by the Bounty of Nature; and, tho' it may be, in some Measure, presumptuous to attempt any Addition to the natural Charms of the Fair Sex, I flatter myself they will forgive me, if I acquaint them, that a modest Look or Direction of the Eye, an agreeable Smile or a lively and pleasant Aspect, with a Chin neither poked out nor curbed in, but the whole Countenance erect and graceful, will add a Lustre to the whole, where any of these are wanting, whether in one Sex or the other; and, together with the easy Situation or Posture of the whole Head, Neck, and Arms, with the handsome Turn of the Feet, they compleat the intire Fashion or agreeable Disposition of a fine accomplished Lady, as well in Conversation in general, as the *Courtesy*†, or *Walking*, from its being thus disposed, from Top to Toe, is only to preserve the graceful Position of the Body, as above described.

It only now remains to inquire, whether a Lady steps aside and makes her Honour, in the Manner we have shewn a Gentleman leaves a Room, after stepping aside §, by drawing the disengaged or pointed Foot † into the first Position, equal to the Foot, which stepped aside ‖, instead of drawing it crossing behind, as aforesaid (n); or that Courtesying, without stepping aside at all ‖, as some do, is only to let the Weight or graceful Fashion of the Body, as just described, fall, or rather seat itself, as on a

---

† See Plates 2d and 4th in Book the 2d. § See Plate t e 2d in Book the 2d. ‖ See Plate the 2d. (n) See the 4th and 11th Plates.

10   *The* ART *of* DANCING *explain'd*,

Chair or Stool, without Disorder, upon that Foot which is drawn or crossed behind (n), as in leaving Company, or on both Legs equally alike ‖, if the pointed Foot be drawn into the first Position ‖; and the like, if made on both Legs, without moving from the same Place ‖, only with this Difference, in Relation to the Weight's coming upon the pointed Foot † or that which is crossed behind (n), after touching the Heel of the Foot on which the Poise rests *, in like Manner as when the Gentleman takes Leave †, and retires back, as it were a Seat for the Weight to rest upon (n), whilst the *Court sy* or Lady's Respect is paid, upon the Beginning or first Division; whereas, in a *Bow* for the Man, it does not receive the Weight, 'till the third Division †, resting the Counting of *Two* for the Respect, as we have observed, in the contrary Sex; and, upon counting of *Three* or compleating the Courtesy, it rises in the same slow, graceful, and deliberate Manner, 'till it stands upright on the crossing behind Foot **, as at first it seated itself thereon, in the Courtesy or Bending of the Knees †, compleating the Respect or Courtesy, on a Lady's leaving a Room, in the disengaged or foremost Foot's being at Liberty to renew the Respect, as Occasion requires **.

As to which Foot the Stepping aside begins with, in Relation to taking of Leave, it is altogether the same, as was described for the other Sex; but, as this Courtesy or Respect has the like Effect, as I observed, in treating of the *Bow* in Conversation with another; viz. Retiring from each other, it is to be evaded in rising, by transferring the Poise from the hindmost Foot to the foremost, which, being then at Liberty, is ready to repeat the Complaisance on the contrary Side, and so to preserve the same Ground. And the like may be said, in Relation to concluding the Courtesy on the stepping aside Foot,

---

(n) See the 4th and 11th Plates.   ‖ See Plate the 2d.   † See Plates the 2d and 4th in Book the 2d.   * See the Feet in Plate 5.   ** See Plate the 3d in Book the 2d.

The ART *of* DANCING *explain'd.* 11

when the pointed Foot is drawn into the first Position *; or the like, without stepping at all, by swaying or waving the principal Part of the Body, as Occasion offers, either upon the right (o) or left Foot (p), as will be most to Advantage, in the graceful bending or sinking down upon the Knees ‖ ; which Wave or Sway of the Body not a little contributes to the Beauty of the Courtesy, as does also the handsome Position of the Waiste, neither too much forwards nor backwards, the whole Poise of the Body being beautiful and upright, as before described, directly perpendicular or right down over the Heel or Heels, on which the Poise rests (q); and this, I think, concludes all that is necessary to be said, concerning the *Reverence* or *Courtesy* made by Persons of either Sex, according to the first Class, relating to *Position* or *Standing*, at leaving a Room, or in Conversation with others.

I now proceed to the *Second* Sort of HONOURS, viz. those which are introduced by *Motion*, as in *Walking*, &c. and I shall, first, finish what concerns the Ladies, before I return to the Gentlemen, who are to observe, that, at the End of the last Step, after their Entrance into a Room, before they pay their Respect or *Honour*, they are to make a graceful Pause or *Stand* upon the Foot that made the last Step, which, as has been already said, in *Walking*, is compleated upon counting of *One*; so that the whole Person rests the counting of *Two*, in the coming up of the disengaged Foot into the first *Position*, equal to the Foot which made the last Step preparatory for the *Courtesy* (r); and *Three* is the Rest it makes, when thus joined in the graceful Disposition of the whole Fashion, or upon taking it up, if afterwards stepping aside (s), and thus erect from Head to Foot, it is duly prepared to make the Courtesy in that smooth Manner of bending the Knees we have described, directing the Eye, as Occa-

---

* See Plate the 2d. (o) See the 2d Figure or Woman's Side in Plate 1. (p) See the 1st Figure in Plate 1. ‖ See the 2d and 4th Plates in the 2d Book. (q) See Plate 2d in the 2d Book. (r) See the 1st and 2d Plates. (s) See Plate 1.

12 *The* ART *of* DANCING *explain'd.*

sion requires; or the like, if the *Courtesy* be made in stepping aside, as in taking Leave†, for there is no other Difference between the *Honour* or Respect, on leaving Company and coming up to them, than that, as I have observed, the former proceeds from *Position* or *Standing* ‖, and the latter is introduced by *Motion* or *Walking* §; but, having shewn, what that *Preparation* is, there is no Occasion for any farther Enlargement.

If a *Lady* makes an *Honour Passing*, either on the Right or Left, or in meeting any One, in *Conversation*, *Walking*, or the like, at the End of the Step preceding the Complaisance or Respect, she turns about half way towards the Person, upon Conclusion of the said preparatory Step or Counting of *One*; and, upon Counting of *Two*, she lets the disengaged or coming up Foot touch the Heel of that Foot which stepped, crossways, before the said coming up Foot††, which now attends the Poise, in order to make the *Honour*; and, upon *Three*, she sets it down, somewhat obliquely or slanting off from the Person to whom the Respect is paid, without Weight**, and thus becomes duly prepared to make the *Courtesy* *; I mean, when the Head is beautifully turned to the Right or Left, according to the Side on which the Respect is made, in a graceful Contrast of the whole Fashion; and, being so disposed, she makes the *Honour* by a smooth and easy Bending of the Knees. The whole Poise of the Body, during the Counting of *One* or Bending, as aforesaid, rests the Counting of *Two**, or, as we have already said, the Respect in a fine Contrast; and, upon the *third Division* or compleating the *Courtesy*, it rises gracefully from the Foot on which it rested, all the while, in this becoming Twist, passing on, 'till it stands erect upon the Foot which was placed or advanced for that Purpose **, by transferring the Poise from the Foot that made the preparatory Step for this Respect, which, being now at

---

† See Plates 2d and 4th in Book the 2d.   ‖ See the 4th, 5th and 8th Plates.
§ See Plate 1.   †† See the Feet in Plate 5.   ** See the Feet in Plate 10.   * See Plates 3d and 4th in Book the 2d.

Liberty,

The ART of DANCING explain'd. 13

Liberty, is ready to repeat the same, as often as Occasion requires?; and from hence it becomes a Kind of *Walking Courtesy*, changing the Poise from one Foot to the other. And it is to be noted, that it must always be the Foot next the Person, which makes the last Step in *Walking*, before the Respect: For Instance, if the Person be on the Right, the right Foot makes the Step; and the left, if the *Honour* be paid to the other Side, turning, as before described, towards the Person or Foot which made the Step in Preparation for the *Court.sy*, and directing the Eye, sideways, upon the Person to whom the Respect is paid, instead of right forwards, as when entering a Room, or meeting One, which is the only Difference. And it is to be farther observed, that, tho' this Complaisance may be repeated, once or more, after passing a Person, it must never be made, before we come parallel to the Person to whom we pay this Respect; and if Occasion requires its being transferred to the other Side, which often falls out, as when Company are seated or standing, on both Sides of a Room or Gallery, &c. we continue *walking* on, till we arrive at the next Occasion of paying this Respect, as when Company are scattered, at some Distance, and then make the Pause or Stand, at the End of the Step next the Person or Persons, by turning, &c. as before; or if the Change or Transferring may be soonest performed, as when Company are thick on both Sides, it must be divided by two Steps made between the preceding *Courtesies*, the second Step preparing to pay the Respect, as I have already shewn, which will be the left Foot, the foregoing *Honour* being supposed to the Right; and the right Foot, if the Complaisance be first paid to the Left. And, in these *Passing Honours*, it must be noted, that no Regard is to be observed, with Respect to the Quality of the Person, but only Conveniency, in Relation to the Right or Left, as the Company first present themselves, as we pass along; nor, indeed, can it well be otherwise,

§ See Plate 1.

because

becaufe they are all to receive it, in their Turns. As what has been faid is all that I apprehend to be material, relating to the *Ladies*, I flatter myfelf, that they will not be wanting in putting thefe Rules into Practice, fince I have been at fo great Pains in compofing them for their Service.

I fhall now proceed to the Conclufion of what I have to offer to the *Gentlemen*, on this Head, which is much to the like Effect with what was obferved to the *Ladies*; for, when a *Gentlemen* enters a Room, the graceful Stand or Reft he makes, as already defcribed, in the *Courtefy* for a *Lady* on this Occafion, muft be always made on the laft Step before *Bowing*, which may be on the left Foot; whilft the right, in coming up, as aforefaid, in its Attendance on the Poife, inftead of ending in the firft Pofition†, as in *Walking*, is placed confiderably more open, fideways, without Weight, the Heel being fomewhat raifed, the Ball or Inftep pointed or preffing lightly on the Floor, the Knee ftreight, and the whole Weight of the Body, in a Gentleman-like Manner, refting on the left Foot‖, bows, as Occafion requires, by bending the Body and fcraping the open Foot, at the fame Time, in one intire *Motion* forwards; upon the Counting of *One***, remains the Refpect or Counting of *Two*, in this refpectful Pofture, with the Knee on which the Body refts bended, to prevent its being awry, which otherwife would be the Confequence, and the Arms naturally hanging under the Shoulders; and, upon *Three*, it rifes from this humble Pofture in one intire flow *Motion*, 'till it ftands erect on the right or fcraping Foot; and the left, at the fame Time, being releafed from the Weight of the Body, falls into the firft *Pofition*, as in *Walking* *, to repeat it, if it be neceffary.

The *Bow Paffing* differs, in no Refpect, from that advancing or coming into a Room, xcept in the Situation of the Perfon: For Inftance, in entering a Room, the Perfon is before us, but only

---

† See Plate 1. ‖ See the Feet in the 2d Figure or Woman's Side of Plate 6.
** See the Feet of the 2d Figure in Plate 9. * See the 2d Figure in Plate 1.

The Art of Dancing explain'd. 15

upon one Side, on the present Occasion. From hence it appears, that, after the Step preceding the *Bow* and Pause, placing the contrary Foot or Preparative, is made †, the Respect is paid in the very same Method, as forwards, only that the Body is turned in a beautiful and agreeable Twist or Contrast, sideways, looking upon the Person to whom we pay the Respect; if the *Bow* be made upon the Right, the antecedent Step is made with the left Foot, and the right, during the Pause, is placed for the Scrape in *Bowing* †; as, if it be made on the contrary Side, the right Foot makes the preparatory Step, and the left will be placed, as aforesaid, to pay the Respect *; and, if repeated, it will always begin and end with the same Foot, 'till changed by adding a second Step, which transfers the *Bow* to the other Side, as Occasion offers. This *Bow* is also made, in *walking* with a *Gentleman* or *Lady*, upon some obliging Expression in Conversation, once or oftener, as Necessity requires, with the right Foot scraping, if the Person be on the Right, but the contrary Foot, if the Person be on the Left. It must also be noted, that the Step made, before placing the Foot for the *Bow*, is to be made with the contrary Foot to the Side the Person is on, to whom the Respect is paid, and the placed Foot is that next the Person; tho' it is the Reverse in the *Ladies*, because the Step preparatory for this Respect is made with the Foot next the Person, and the contrary is the placed Foot.

It will not be improper, before I conclude with the *Gentlemen*, to take some farther Notice of a Difficulty that may arise, in the Application of the *Bow Passing*; I mean, the Changing or Transferring it from one Side to the other, because, in passing through a Lane or Room full of Company, we cannot, as I have already observed to the *Ladies*, bow on both Sides, at once; and therefore the Rule is, to pay this Respect to those that first fall in our Way,

---

† See the Feet of the 2d Figure in Plate 6. * See the Feet of the 1st Figure in Plate 6.

and

and, if possible, conclude on that Side, and then, by walking two Steps or more, to make the like Compliments on the other; which will be, by bowing and scraping the left Foot §, if the first Respect be paid to the Right, and the contrary Foot, if it be first paid to the Left *. And if it should fall out, as in St. *James*'s *Park*, or other publick Places, where you may walk, perhaps, a considerable Way, before you find an Occasion for paying this Respect, you are to note, that these *Bows*, as we said, in Relation to the *Ladies Courtesies*, are never made, before you come equal to those you salute; and, if it be a Person of Nobility or extraordinary Fashion, an additional Bow, sideways, as when leaving a Room, may be added, with the contrary Foot to that which made the Scrape, turning full to the Person to whom you pay this uncommon Respect, in *passing*; nor must you forget, that, in entering a Room, or meeting any one, it is always to be added to the *Bow Forwards*, as being of singular Use, in paying Respect to the Company in general, as the former is to the Person we salute in particular, by a Cast of our Eye round the Company, omitting none, for an Omission may, many Times, be esteemed an Affront and ill Manners. It will be likewise expedient to observe, that some *Ladies* make the *Passing Honour* the very same, as that I have described for the *Gentlemen*; the only Difference is, that, after placing the Foot †, instead of *bowing*, in the Scrape of the Foot ‖, they *courtesy* to the Right ** or Left ††, as Occasion requires, in the graceful Contrast described for the other Sex's *Bowing*, concluding on the scraping Foot ‖; which, if on the Right, will be the right Foot §§, and left at Liberty to step and place the preparatory Foot; as, on the contrary Side, it will conclude on the left Foot ═, and the right will

---

§ See the Feet of the 1st Figure in Plate 6.   * See the Feet of the 2d Figure in Plate 6.   † See Plate 6.   ‖ See the Feet in Plate 9.   ** See the Feet of the 2d Figure in Plate 6.   †† See the Feet of the 1st Figure in the same Plate.   §§ See the 2d Figure in Plate 9, and 2d of Plate 1.   ═ See the 1st Figure in Plate 9, and 1st of Plate 1.

then

The ART of DANCING explain'd.

then be in Readiness to make the Step, and place the Foot, in order to its being repeated, according to the various Occasions before mentioned. Some also use this Method of *Courtesying*, when they enter a Room, or meet a Person, which is, in all Respects, agreeable to the *Gentleman's Bow*, as above described, except in the Scrape or Sliding of the prepared Foot forwards †, *viz.* to bend both Knees, at the same Time, and to let the Poise fall gracefully upon the hind Foot, during the first and second Divisions; and afterwards the Body rises beautifully, as aforesaid, 'till it stands on the advanced Foot †, by transferring the Weight from the hind Foot, which, being released, is ready to *walk* (t), and place the contrary Foot, in order to repeat it, in like Manner, if necessary: Or, if the *Courtesy* used, at leaving a Room, be added *, it will then, in all Respects, be answerable to the *Gentleman's Bow*, at coming into a Room. But in Fine, let the *Bow* or *Courtesy*, notwithstanding all the various Methods, and the several Occasions, here described, be made in which of those Forms we please, they cannot fail of being performed to Advantage, but must necessarily produce a good Effect, provided they be made in the Manner already shewn, upon Counting of *One* *, the Pause or Rest *Two* *, and the Rising upon *Three* (u). Having, therefore, in this Discourse upon *Honours* in general, endeavoured to take Notice of every Particular, that might prove useful or instructive, so as to omit nothing material, I flatter myself, that, if it be not, in all Respects, accomplished, according to my Intentions, the Difficulty of the Subject will plead my Excuse; and, as I have, in the preceding Chapters, regularly gone through what I apprehended necessary, upon *Standing*, *Walking*, and *Honours* in general, under the last of which Heads, as the Reader will easily perceive, it was scarce possible to avoid some Repetitions, in my treating distinctly on *Bows* and *Courtesies*, I shall now proceed to the various *Steps* of *Dancing*.

---

† See the Feet in Plate 9. (t) See Plate 1. * See Plates the 2d and 4th in Book the 2d. (u) See Plate 3d in Book the 2d.

C   CHAP.

CHAP. IV.

Of the DANCING-ROOM.

BEfore I enter upon the various *Steps* of *Dancing*, it will be neceſſary to deſcribe the Room in which the *Dancing* or *Steps* are to be performed; which indeed ſeems to claim our more immediate Notice, ſince it will greatly aſſiſt us, in forming clear and diſtinct Notions of the enſuing Work.

Firſt then, you are to obſerve, that the Shape and Figure of *Rooms* differ exceedingly; for ſome are of a direct Square, others not ſquare but oblong or longiſh, namely, when the two Sides are ſomewhat longer than the Top or Bottom, and various others that, in Reality, are of no Form at all; which renders *Dancing* extremely difficult and confuſed to thoſe, who have not a juſt and true Idea of the Room, in its different Situations; becauſe, if this be wanting, altho' they may perform very handſomely, at their own *Houſes*, or in *School* with a Maſter, yet, in *Aſſemblies* or *Rooms Abroad*, they are as much diſordered and at a Stand, as if in an *Uninhabited Iſland*. I therefore conclude, that the Crime, if it ſhould by any be eſteemed ſuch, of dwelling ſomewhat longer than I intended on this Subject, will the more eaſily be pardoned by the *Ladies* and *Gentlemen*, when I acquaint them, that it intirely proceeded from the earneſt Deſire I have of rendering them Service, by endeavouring to remove the above mentioned Cauſes of Diſorder and Confuſion; which I cannot but perſuade myſelf will meet with a favourable Reception, eſpecially from the Hands of thoſe who, by this Means, ſhall receive Improvement.

The ART *of* DANCING *explain'd.* 19

Encouraged by such a pleasing Prospect, I proceed to inform the *Gentlemen* and *Ladies*, that, when they are about to dance in a *Room* of the first Sort, *viz.* a direct Square (a), the dance may be begun, at any of the four Sides or Parts of the Square or Room; but then they are to note, that the Side or Part, on which the *Dance* begins, is always called the *Bottom* or *Lower End* (b); the Side or Part which they face, the *Presence* or *Upper End* (c); and the two remaining Parts or Sides of the *Room* receive their Names, according to the Hand they are on: For Instance, the Side, to which the right Shoulder points, is call'd the *right Side* (d), and the other the *left* (e); from whence it is to be understood, that the Back is to the Lower End of the Room, and the Face to the Upper, so that, if, instead of Beginning, as aforesaid, you was to commence, either upon the right or left Sides, they would not be then *Sides*, as before, but the *Upper* and *Lower Ends* of the Room; that is to say, if upon the right Side (f) the left would be the *Presence* or *Upper End* (g), and if upon the left (h) the right (i), and consequently the Parts or Sides, which at first were the *Lower* (k) and *Upper Ends* (l), now are the Sides; but all this is subservient to, and depends upon the Company, who must always be seated at the *Presence* or *Upper End.*

As to the *longish* or second Sort of *Rooms*, they differ from the *square*, in the Sides being longer than the Ends (m); and it of Course follows, that the *Dance* must begin, at one of the said Ends (n), which is likewise decided by the Company; or, if the Door be hung near the End of one of the Sides, as usually it is,

---

(a) See the Square or Room, marked 1, in the 1st Plate distinguish'd by the Letter A. (b) See the Letters A B in the said Square. (c) See the Letters C D. (d) See the Letters E F. (e) See the Letters G H. (f) See the Letters A B in the Square mark'd 2. (g) See the Letters C D in the said Square. (h) See the Letters A B in the Room or Square marked 3. (i) See the Letters C D in the said Square. (k) See the Letters A B in the Square marked 1. (l) See the Letters C D in the same Square. (m) See the Letters E F G H in the Rooms marked 4, 5, 6. (n) See the Letters A B in the Rooms marked 4, 5, 6.

the *Dance* commonly begins, at the End next the Door (o). However that be, the *Dancers* must have a particular Regard to the *Presence* and *Bottom of the Room*, where they begun, otherwise it is no Wonder that those, who are of a timorous and bashful Nature, with the Fears of being out together with the various Turnings and Windings of some *Dances*, should be perplex'd and nonplus'd; and this I have perceived to be the Case, when I have seen a *Minuet* begun at the *Bottom* of the Room, and ended at the *Upper End*; which could not possibly have happened, had they observed the preceding Rules.

I shall, for the more fully Clearing of this Point, add an Observation or two more that may be of Service: Supposing one Page or Leaf of the Book you now read, or any other, to be the Room or Floor in which the *Dances* or Practise of the *Steps* contain'd in the following Work are to be perform'd, lay it flat and open upon a Window or Table, at the Upper End of the Room; and if, when the Book is open, the two Pages make a Square, it will be agreeable to the *first* Room, and the one half or single Page to the *longish* or *second*; but you are to take special Notice, as to the Part or End of the Room intended for the *Presence*, that the Title or Page of the Book be so placed or laid upon the Table or Ground, as that, when you stand at the Bottom facing the Upper Part of the Room, to perform the foresaid *Steps* or *Dances*, you can read the said Book: Or, supposing the whole Floor to be the same Book, and to contain the Matter written in the Page or half Page, the Book lying fix'd and immoveable upon the Table or Ground, let the Turn be made to the Right or Left, in a Quarter, Half, or Three-quarter Turn, and you cannot possibly make the least Mistake; for tho' the Book, by which you are directed in Compliance therewith, turns along with you, yet any other you shall lay upon the Ground will remain fix'd; so that from what has been said upon

---

(o) See the following Mark † in the Rooms aforesaid.

The ART *of* DANCING *explain'd.* 21

this Head, I think it plainly appears, that the Lower End of the Page or Leaf is the Bottom of the Room, and the Title above the Presence or Upper End; the Beginning of the Lines, as you read these in *Dancing*, is the left Side, and the Breaking off of the Lines the right (p), tho' the Sides of the Book are not so term'd. The Reason of this may be understood, by placing a Person at the Upper End of the Room facing the Bottom, holding a printed Book or written Paper perpendicular in his Hands, so as that you can read it; for you will find it the Reverse to *Dancing*, in that the right Hand will hold the Part of the Paper from whence the Lines begin, and the left that where they break off. It is farther to be noted, that, supposing the *Dance* for *one* Person alone in the square Room or two Pages of the Book, as just mentioned, the *Dancer* places him or herself in the Center, or upon the Joining of the two Pages, which, when open, is directly in the Middle (q); or, to practise any Step of this Book, the Case is the same; but, if the *Dance* be of *two*, the *Lady* takes the right Side of the said Center or Line (r), and the *Gentleman* the left (s), so that the joining or presenting of Hands, if necessary, would fall upon the Line or Center upon which the single *Dancer* begun (q); in which it is to be noted, as on other Occasions, that the *Lady* takes the Right of the *Gentleman*.

And as I have now said what, I hope, will prove sufficient to remove all the Difficulties that may arise, in *Dancing*, on Account of the *Room*, or in Relation to the *Steps* I am about to explain, I shall no longer detain those who are ambitious of attaining to Perfection in a Science, of which I have the Honour of being a Professor; but, having prepared and made them thoroughly acquainted with the *Room*, in which the *Steps* of *Danc-*

(p) See the 7th Example of the Book in the Plate of the Room. (q) See the Letter S in the said 7th Example. (r) See the Letter W in the Example aforesaid. (s) See the Letter M in the before mentioned Example.

ing are to be perform'd, I shall invite them into the same; but, before I describe the various *Steps* of *Dancing*, I shall, in a few Words, endeavour to prepare their Minds to form a clearer and more distinct Idea of the following Descriptions.

As the *Human Structure* is composed of different Parts, *viz.* Head, Neck, Body, Arms, Legs, Feet, &c. so likewise is *Dancing* of Positions, Steps, Sinking, Rising, Springing, Capering, Falling, Sliding, Turning, Figures, Cadence or Time, &c. And as the *Head* consists of Eyes, Ears, Nose, Mouth, &c. the *Arms*, of the Shoulders, Elbows, Wrists, Hands, Fingers, and Joints of the Fingers, the *Body*, as it were, remaining in the Center or Middle of the Human Frame, supporting the said *Arms*, as the *Legs*, which support them both, are composed of the Hips, Knees, Ancles, Feet, Toes, and Joints † of the said Toes, on the first of which the Rising upon the Instep is always made; and as all these different Parts have their peculiar Excellencies, to adorn the Whole, so the Eyes give Life to the Face, as well as direct the Steps; the Ears mark Time to the Tune; the Nose, as it were, points out the graceful Twists or Turns the Head makes, in Opposition to the other Parts of the Body, whilst the Mouth, at the same Time, adds those becoming Smiles, which, together with the Brightness and Lustre of the Eyes, compleat a most agreeable and pleasing Countenance. The Neck too, in its graceful Compliance with the Turn of the Head; the Shoulders, in their natural Rising, Falling, or Hanging down (v); the Elbows, in their easy Bendings, according to the Occasion (w); the Wrists, in their pliable Correspondence with the Elbows and Shoulders, as the handsome Shaping or Bending of the Thumbs and Fingers produces beautiful Hands compleating the Arms (x); which, in their respective Opposing the Head, in Conjunction

---

† See the Figure in Plate III. (v) See the different Parts, as above described, in the Ladies Figures contained in the 2d Book. (w) See the Figures in Plate 10. (x) See the Parts above mentioned in the Arms and Fingers contained in Plate 13.

with

The ART of DANCING explain'd.   23

with the Body, is a farther and large Addition to the Whole (y); the Legs, in the gracefully supporting the Frame of the Body, Head, Neck, and Arms (z); and the Hips or Joints, which unite the Legs and Body, agree with the various Movements or Bendings and Risings of the Knees or Insteps †, the Positions or handsome Turn of the Feet compleating the Beauty of the Legs, on the neat Management of which the Perfection of *Dancing* so much depends *; and these together, in Confederacy with the Head, oppose the Body and Arms, rendering the whole Body compleat and capable of *Dancing*, in all its various Attitudes or Postures **.

Having, by the foregoing Simile or Comparison, given an Account of the outward Form of the *Human Structure*, so far as it relates to, or corresponds with *Dancing*, or may, in any Respect, conduce to the better Understanding of the ensuing Subject, by running over the different Parts of the *Body*, from the Head to the Feet, which compose the Positions, with a short Explanation of the said Parts, shewing how they agree in forming the most pleasing Object, to grace the ART of DANCING ††, before I proceed to treat on its various *Steps*, I shall, by the way, observe, that the foresaid Particulars, from whence the whole BODY or ART of DANCING is produced, namely, *Position, Sinking, Stepping, Rising, Springing*, &c. are of the very same Use, in *Dancing*, as the *Alphabet*, in the *Composition of Words*; for as Words vary and are produced, according to the different placing of the Letters; and different Subjects, Languages, &c. according to the different Composition of Words; or, as in *Music*, by the different placing of the Notes, that compose the Gamut upon the Scale or Spaces between the Lines, are produced dif-

---

(y) See the Turn of the Head, Body, and Arms, of the Figures in Plate 6, or in the 4th, 5th, 7th, 9th, 11th, 12th, and 14th Plates.   (z) See the Figures contained in the 3d, 6th, and 8th Plates.   † See the Figures in the 3d and 10th Plates.   * See the Feet of the Figures in general.   ** See the Figures in the 4th, 6th, 9th, 11th, 12th, and 14th Plates.   †† See the Figures in Plate 13, &c.

ferent

ferent Sounds, which, as they afcend or defcend, compofe various Bars or Meafures, that may be compared to Words, and the various Bars and Meafures compofe the various Pieces of *Mufic*, in different Keys and Movements; fo the different *Steps* of *Dancing* are produced, according to the various Placings of the *Sinks*, *Rifings*, *Bounds*, &c. upon the *Step*, whether confifting of one, two, three or more Steps to the Meafure, and the different Steps produce Variety of *Dances*, according to the Compofer's Fancy, upon all Sorts of Movements in *Mufic*, whether *grave* or *brisk*.

We are, next, to fhew, how thefe Actions or Motions of the *Body*, which, as we faid above, compofe the whole ART of DANCING, correfpond with the Pofitions and various Motions and Steppings of the Feet, in compofing the following Steps and Movements; and the Manner, in which they are made, will fully appear from the Defcription I am about to give of the faid Steps, beginning with the HALF COUPEE, the Movement that firft occurs in *Dancing*.

CHAP.

CHAP. V.

Of the COUPEE of one Step, or HALF COUPEE.

IT is, first of all, to be observed, that the *Half Coupee*, tho' a very agreeable Step in *Dancing*, as well as one of the most difficult to be performed well, by Reason of its Plainness, is originally nothing more than a single Step, made with either Foot, from one Place to another with the additional Ornament of a Movement or Bending or Rising of the Knees in Time to *Music*; and it is most amiable, when executed in that gentle and graceful Manner it ought to be, whether upon the Toe or Heel.

The *Half Coupee* may be perform'd various Ways, as by Sinking, Rising, and Stepping forwards; and the like backwards, sideways, to either Hand, or in turning a quarter or half Turn (a), &c. It usually takes up a Time or Measure of the Tune, and, being continued, transfers the Weight, as in *Walking*, from one Foot to the other; and, in Distinction from the rest, the *Dancing-Masters* have named it a *Half Coupee*, tho' I think it may rather be called a *Coupee of one Step*, as the Title above specifies: But, as I shall have Occasion to give a farther Account of this Step, when, in treating of the *Bouree* or *Ficuret*, I carry on a Comparison between that Step and the *Half Coupee*, I shall, in the mean Time, proceed to the *Coupee*, the Movement that next occurs in *Dancing*.

(a) See the Explanation and Table of this Step in the Plate mark'd E.

D   CHAP.

CHAP. VI.

Of the COUPEE.

THE COUPEE, on the other Hand, is a compound Step; that is to say, it is formed of two Steps joined together, which, however, are to be accounted but as a single Step: The first Movement of which begins in a Sink and Rise. If the Tune, to which it is perform'd, be of triple Time (as a *Saraband*, for Instance, which admits only of three Notes in a Bar) then the first Step takes up one of the three Notes, and the other two Notes are counted in the remaining Step. The Weight of the Body must always rest on the contrary Foot to that, on which you begin; so that, if you begin your *Coupee* with the right Foot, the Poise must be on the left †, and continue so to be, 'till you have compleated the first Step of the two, which, as I said, compose the *Coupee*. The first Part being finished, the right Foot immediately receives the Weight, * in the rising from the Sink which is made, at commencing the Step, and in the same Instant beats Time, as we call it, to the first of the three Notes contained in the Bar; supporting the Body ||, whilst the left Foot, to compleat this compound Step, slides with a slow and gentle Motion, filling up the remaining two Notes of the Bar or Measure **, and the whole Step is compleated, at the Instant when the left Foot a second time receives the Weight ††. This Step, like the *Half Coupee*, admits of being variously per-

---

† See the 1st Figure or Man's Side of Plate I.   * See the second Figure or Woman's Side in Plate 9. || See the 2d Figure or Woman's Side of Plate I.   ** See the 1st Figure or Man's Side in Plate 9.   †† See the 1st Figure of Plate I.

formed,

formed, as forwards, backwards, sideways, and circularly (b). It differs, indeed, from the *Half Coupee*, in the Continuance of performing it; for whereas the *Half Coupee*, as in *Walking*, transfers the Weight, every Time, from one Foot to the other, the *Coupee* does the very Reverse, in that it always begins with the same Foot: For, if you begin it with the left Foot, it will end with the right; and, if with the right, it concludes on the left (c); and so mutually, as often as ever it is repeated, and until it is changed by some other Step. It is called a *Coupee*, from its containing two Steps instead of one, which is all that the *Half Coupee* employs.

CHAP. VII.

Of the COUPEE *with two Movements.*

THE *Coupee with two Movements* is composed, as the *Coupee* I have already explain'd, of two Steps; but it differs in this, that whereas the *Coupee* treated of before consists only of one Movement, that is to say, of one Sink and Rise, which is what we call a *Movement*, and made to the first Step; so it consequently follows, that there must be another Movement added to the second, tho' different from the first; for in that the Sink is made, before the Foot moves; and the Rise, after the Foot has moved, that is to say, when you have made a Step, as I have already observed, as in *walking* either forwards, backwards, or sideways, &c. but, in this additional Movement, the Sink and Rise are together in the Midst of the Motion the

---

(b) See the Explanation and Table of the Coupee in the Plate mark'd with the Letter E. (c) See the Table and Explanation, as aforesaid, of the Plate of Tables mark'd E.

28   *The* ART *of* DANCING *explain'd.*

Leg makes, in stepping, as in the preceding; and supposing the Step is to a *Louvre,* or such like slow Air, it is performed in the Manner following, *viz.* to make the first Step which is to sink, before the Foot moves †, and rise in moving, or immediately after it has moved ‖; which said Rising and Receiving of the Weight upon the Foot, that made the first Step†, marks Time to the first Note of the three, which each Bar or Measure contains. The second Note is taken up with the Sink of the second Movement; and the Rise from it takes up the third Note of the same Measure, and compleats the Step; so that the first Movement and Step are made to the first Note of the three, and the second to the remaining two, and may be performed the different Ways aforesaid, as forwards, backwards, sideways before, or sideways behind, &c. (d) and, as to its Continuance in *Dancing,* it is the same as the *Coupee of one Movement,* that is, always beginning with the same Foot, whether right or left: It is named a *Coupee of two Movements,* from its having the Addition of a second added to the former; which second Movement is made sometimes smooth upon the Floor, and sometimes by bounding off.

---

† See Plate 1. ‖ See Plate 9. (d) See the Explanation and Table of this Step in the Plate mark'd E.

CHAP.

CHAP. VIII.
Of the BOUREE-STEP or FLEURET.

THE *Bouree* is compofed of three plain ftreight Steps or Walks, except the firft, which begins in a Movement, and is to be performed in the fame Method, as the *Half Coupee*, or *Coupee with two Movements*, that is to fay, muft always fink, at the Beginning of the Step or Walk, and rife at, or gradually before the End of it; which is the Manner in which the firft Step is ufually taken, in the Performance of all Steps, except *Springs*, *Bounds*, *Hops*, or *Chaffees*, &c. wherefore, for the Future, I need not fay any more of the Method of beginning thefe Sorts of Steps, in *Dancing*, otherwife than to make a Movement, without mentioning how the Sink and Rife are to be made, fince they have been already explained.

A *Bouree* or *Fleuret*, as I have obferved, confifts only of three plain ftreight Steps; but a Movement is added to the firft of them, the Rife of which Movement, as has been faid, always ftrikes the Cadence or Time; and, if this Step is done to a Tune of three Notes in a Meafure, the firft Step anfwers to the firft Note, the fecond Step to the fame Note, and the third Step to the laft Note of the Meafure, concluding together.

You are alfo to note, that tho' in the *Bouree* there are three diftinct Walks or Steps, yet neverthelefs, thefe three Steps are to be efteem'd but as one Step, in Regard of its being a compofed Step; as will appear by the *Half Coupee*, which, tho' no more than a fingle Step, is, however, a Step, becaufe it generally takes up a Meafure, but more efpecially in Tunes of triple Time; and it is made by a fmooth and eafy Bending of the Knees, rifing in a flow and gentle Motion from thence; which Rifing, as I have faid, is upon the firft Note of the Meafure, the Weight

of

of the Body being supported by the Foot that made the Step, during the Counting of the second and third Notes of the Bar.

The graceful Posture of the *Dancer*'s Standing adds not a little to the Beauty of this Step, who, 'till the Time be expired, is to wait or rest; by which it is evident, that the *Half Coupee*, tho' a single Step, is equal, in Value, to any compound Step whatsoever, whether of two, three, four, or more Steps in a Measure.

But to return, the *Bource*-Step may be perform'd various Ways, as forwards, backwards, sideways, crossing before, the same behind, before and behind, behind and before, &c (e), the Explanation of which, I think, may not be improper, in this Place; and therefore I shall proceed to shew the Method of their Performance, one after the other, in the Order above set down, except the *Fleurets forwards and backwards*; which being so intelligible of themselves, and having Occasion hereafter to speak of this Step, by way of Grace to the *Minuet*, instead of saying any thing farther of them here. I shall begin with the *Bource-Step crossing before, sideways*; which is to be perform'd, as follows, either with the right or left Foot: For Instance, provided you begin with the Latter, the Weight must be on the right (f); and the left Foot, which is at Liberty, commences by making a Movement and Step, to the right Side of the Room, crossing before the Foot on which the Body rests †, the Face being to the Upper Part of the Room, and it receives the Weight ‖. The second is the right Foot, which steps the same Way*; and the third and last, which is with the left, crosses before, as at first †, only without a Movement ‖. The *Bource crossing behind, sideways*, differs from the Former in this, that whereas that was before, this is behind; that is to say, the Weight being, as aforesaid (f),

---

(e) See the Explanation and Table of the Bource in the Plate mark'd E. (f) See the 2d Figure or Woman's Side of Plate I. † See the first Figure in Plate 4, and the 2d Figure or Woman's Side of Plate XI. ‖ See the first Figure or Man's Side of Plate 5. * See the 2d Figure in Plate 6.

the

the left Foot, instead of making the Movement and first Step crossing before the right, it now is made crossing behind it; and the next Step, which is with the right Foot, moves the same Way, after which the third and last Step with the left Foot is drawn behind the right, and concludes. The *Bouree before and behind* is, when the first Movement and Step are made crossing before the Foot on which the Weight is, whether right or left, the second Step moving sideways, the same Way, and the third drawn behind it, facing upwards as before. The *Bouree behind and before* is done in the like Manner, only the first Step is not cross'd before but behind, the second stepping sideways, and the third drawn crossing before. The *Bouree*, which I call *twice behind*, is made as follows: Suppose, for Example, you make a Movement, stepping backwards with the right Foot (g), into the third Position inclos'd behind the left on which the Weight is, and releasing it (h); upon which it makes the second Step of the *Bouree*, in a plain Step backwards, receiving the Weight inclos'd in the third Position behind the right (i), which then performs the third Step of the *Bouree*, in a plain Step forwards†.

There are many other Ways of performing this Step, which would be too tedious to be mention'd here; and, as they are not to my present Purpose, omitting them, I shall only observe, that this Step, continued several Measures, changes the Foot, every Step, as has been taken Notice of in the *Half Coupee*; but with this Difference, that whereas the *Half Coupee* changes the Weight, every single Step, as in *Walking*, the *Bouree* or *Fleuret* only changes it, at the End of every third Step.

(g) See the 1st Figure of the 1st Plate. (h) See the 1st Figure of the 4th Plate. (i) See the 2d Figure of the 4th Plate. † See the 2d Figure in Plate 9.

CHAP.

CHAP. IX.

Of the BOUREE *with two Movements.*

THE *Bouree with two Movements* consists of the same Number of Steps, as the former; but as that was of *one Movement,* this is of *two;* which second Movement is added to the last of the three Steps of which the *Bouree* is compos'd. This Step, in Effect, contains in itself two distinct Steps, namely, the *Whole* and *Half Coupee;* only it is not the same, in the Manner of its Performance; for they, as was already observed, in treating of them, are both equal to a Measure of themselves, but, in this Step, they are both to be performed to a Time or Measure, and must be accounted only as one Step: For Example, to a Tune of three Notes in a Bar, admitting it begins with the right Foot (k), it is to be likewise granted, that the Weight must be on the left (k), which supports the Body, 'till the first Step and Movement are made*; the Rise of which Step is to the first of the three Notes belonging to the Measure, on which the Weight rests, until the second Step is performed, that answers the same Note † and ends the *Coupee;* whereas the second Step of the *Coupee* to a Measure takes up the second and third Notes, and consequently is as slow again, in its Performance, as this; which third Note of the *Coupee* to a Measure is taken up in this Step with the Rise from the *Half Coupee,* and is the third and last Step on which the second Movement falls*, from whence this Step derives its Name.

(k) See the 1st Figure of Plate the first.   * See the 2d Figure in Plate 9.
† See the 1st Figure in Plate 9.

The ART of DANCING explain'd. 33

From what has been obferved we may fee, in what this Step differs from the two faid Steps before defcribed. In the Continuance of this Step the Weight changes (l), as in the *Bouree with one Movement*, and may be perform'd forwards, backwards, fideways, circularly, &c. Note, this Step may be done with a *Bound*, that is to fay, on the laft Step upon which the fecond Movement is made, with a Spring from the Ground, which is what we call a *Bound*; and of this I fhall take Occafion to fay fomething in its proper Place, and give it the Name of *Bouree with a Bound*, as not being made on the Floor, as the *Bouree with two Movements*.

CHAP. X.
Of the PASGRAVE *or* MARCH.

THE *March* is originally a fingle or plain Step, as the *Half Coupee*, but different in the Manner of its Performance, in that the *Half Coupee* bends or finks, before the Step is performed, and rifes, after it has been made; whereas, on the contrary, in this Step, the Movement or bending and rifing are made together, as in the fecond Movement of the *Coupee with two Movements*, after which commences a Slide; and the Sink, Rife, and Slide compofe this Step, which, in its Performance, is as follows: For Example, if forwards, the Foot, you defign to begin with, is to be intirely difengaged from the Weight behind the Foot on which the Body refts in the third Pofition, that is to fay, the Ancle of the beginning Foot muft touch the Heel of the Foot that fupports the Weight (m); from which Pofition this Step always begins and is performed by making a Sink and Rife; but inftead of ftepping forwards, as in the *Half Coupee*, you rife and point the right or left Toe, fideways, according to the Foot you commence with, about

---
(l) See the 2d. Figure in Plate I.   (m) See the 1ft and 2d Figures in Plate V.

the Diſtance from the Foot the Body is upon, as half the Step you take in *Walking* (n).

After this the Foot moves ſlowly forwards †, preſſing the Floor, as it paſſes along, about the Length of a Step in *Walking* †; which Preſſing of the Toe or Inſtep to the Ground, as it moves †, is what we call a *Slide* in *Dancing*. And as to its Agreement with the Notes of triple Time, as mentioned before, you are to obſerve, that the Riſe or Point ‖ marks Time to the firſt Note; the March or ſliding forwards of the Foot † takes up the ſecond and third Notes, on the Expiration of which it receives the Weight, concluding in the third Poſition, as at firſt, but on the contrary Foot *. This is one of the moſt agreeable Steps in *Dancing*; and it may be performed either forwards, backwards, or ſideways, &c. and in Performance, when continued, it transfers the Weight from one Foot to another, as in the *Half Coupee*.

CHAP. XI.
Of the POINT and MARCH.

THE *Point* and *March* is ſo call'd from having a *Point* more added to the *March*, which *Point* is equal, as to its Time, with a *March*, and in its Performance the ſame, except that, inſtead of the ſecond and third Notes being taken up in the marching or ſliding of the Foot forwards or backwards † &c. they are counted, during the Time you ſtand or reſt, in the graceful Manner before obſerved in the *Half Coupee*; only with this Difference, that the diſengaged Foot, inſtead of being in the firſt Poſition, as in *that*, is upon the Point *here*, as may be ſeen by the Beginning or firſt Movement of the foreſaid *March* ‖. The *Point* is made with either

---

(n) See the firſt and ſecond Figures in Plate VI. † See Plate IX. ‖ See Plate VI.
* See Plate V.

Foot,

The Art of Dancing explain'd. 35

Foot, as has been observed in the *March* (o), which *Point* is performed with a soft easy rising from the foregoing Sink†, made to the first Note (o); in which Posture it remains the counting of the second and third Notes of the Measure, concluding what we call the *Point* (o), the Body all the while resting upon the same Foot as at commencing; after which follows the *March* ‖; as it has been before described, and the *Point* (o) and *March* ‖, generally fill up two Measures of the Tune, tho' sometimes they are both performed to a Measure.

It will not, I think, be here improper to take some Notice, how the *Point* (o) and *March* ‖ agree with the Notes of the Measure: For Instance, if you make a Movement and Point, sideways, the Rise of the Point answers to the first Note (o); the Rise of the second Point or Movement, which immediately ensues upon the same Place, on which the first Point was made, marks the second Note(o), and the third is counted in the March or Progress of the Foot, either forwards or backwards from thence ‖; which are the two Methods, in which this Step is usually perform'd. But when this Step is perform'd to two Measures of the Tune, the Point (o) and Time you rest upon it, that is to say, the counting of the second and third Notes, whilst you are beautifully standing (o), takes up the first Measure. The second is in the March or Slide ‖, and, if continued, transfers the Weight every other Step, as in the *Half Coupee*; and in fine, as to the Manner of performing this Step, it is fully shewn in the *March*, since it is no more than the first Movement, or Sink and Rise thereof, on which Rising and Pointing of the Toe or Instep (o), you pause or rest, until the Measure is expired *.

(o) See the Figures in Plate VI.   † See Plate V.   ‖ See Plate IX.
* See the Explanation and Table of this Step in the Plate marked E.

CHAP. XII.
Of the SPRING or BOUND.

THE *Spring* or *Bound* is produced from a plain and single Step, as the *Half Coupee*, or *March*, but it very much differs from them in Performance; for, as they are both made on the Ground, the *Bound* springs off from thence. For Example, suppose you was about to perform a *March*, then, instead of sinking and rising on the Floor, you are to sink, and, in the Spring or Rise from the said Sink, throw the Body into the Air, off from the Foot on which the Weight was, when you begun, and light upon the contrary Foot; that is to say, if the *Bound* is on the right, the Weight is to come from the left (p), where it was upon commencing this Step. And in like Manner, if performed with the left Foot †. One *Bound* alone rarely, if ever, answers to a Measure; but, in Tunes of common Time, or of four in a Measure, as in *Rigadoons*, *Marches*, &c. two *Bounds* answer a Time; and, in *Sarabands* or slow Tunes of triple Time, three of them may be done in one Bar.

This Step may be performed various Ways, as forwards, backwards, sideways before, or sideways behind, as also in turning either to the right or left, &c. (q). And it is farther to be noted, that the Foot, on which the *Bound* is to be made, commences from the third Position behind the Foot upon which the Weight rests, as in the *March*, and advances, much in the same Manner, from the third to the third Position; only that it bounds off from the Ground, and if continued to a Tune of common Time, as above, changes the Weight twice, in every Measure, and in triple thrice.

(p) See the first and second Figures in Plate V. † See the second and first Figures of the foresaid Plate. (q) See the Explanation and Table of this Step in the Plate marked E.

The ART of DANCING explain'd.

CHAP. XIII.
Of the CLOSE or JUMP.

WHAT we call a *Close* in *Dancing* is, when, the Weight being upon one Foot, we sink, and in the Rise *jump* or *close* both Feet equal one to the other, in the first Position (r), or the Feet are inclosed either before or behind, in the third Position †; and this Step generally concludes in the said Positions or Postures. It may be performed two different Ways, *viz.* on the Ground, and off from the Ground, as in the *Bound*; but it differs in its Method of Performance, for as *that* advances forwards or backwards, about the Length of the *Half Coupee*, or *March*, this never proceeds farther than from behind the Foot which supports the Body, either to the first Position even, or to the third inclosed before or behind, as aforesaid.

I shall, in the first Place, begin with the Description of the *Close* in the first Position, which is as follows: For Instance, the Foot that is free from Weight begins whether it be the right or left, in making a Movement, or Sink and Rise from the third Position behind (s), as when you begin the *March*; that is to say, so far as the *Point* ‖; but, instead of pointing the Toe to the Ground as in that here, in rising from the Sink aforesaid, preparing for the *Close* ensuing, you give a Kind of a Spring upon the Toe or Instep of the Foot the Weight is on, and the same Time or Instant both Heels come to the Floor together, and receive the Weight equal alike (t); but you are to observe, that the Body is thus thrown into the Air by the Spring of the Instep, I mean no higher than you can rise

---

(r) See the Figures in the first and second Plates.   † See the Figures of Plate IV.
(s) See the Figures of Plate V.   ‖ See Plate VI.   (t) See Plate the second.

without

The ART *of* DANCING *explain'd.*

without quitting the Ground with your Inftep or Toe, and from hence it is call'd a *Clofe on the Ground.*

To *clofe* in the third Pofition is perform'd intirely in the fame Manner, except that, in lighting on both Feet in the firft Pofition as before (t), the Fall or coming down is in the third; that is to fay, the Feet are inclofed one before the other, the Heel of the foremoft Foot touching the Ancle of the hind Foot (u). In the Performance of this Step backwards it is the very fame, only, inftead of beginning from behind the Foot on which the Weight is, it commences from before the fame, or fourth Pofition open in the Air †; fo that what we have defcrib'd forwards is to be accomplifhed backwards in the fame Method: For Example to *clofe* backwards in the firft Pofition ‖, or *inclofe* backwards into the third (u), when this Step is performed off from the Ground, the Difference is only in this, that you fink, in order to fpring, as before; but, inftead of rifing to the Extremity or Point of the Toe, you only fpring quite off from the Floor, lighting on both Feet in any of the before mentioned Pofitions, whether forwards or backwards, and it is called a *Clofe* or *Jump.*

You are alfo to obferve, that this Step never advances either forwards, backwards, or fideways, as is ufual in others, but is always perform'd upon the fame Place; for, altho' the difengaged Foot moves from behind or before that on which you ftand, the Weight always comes down in the fame Place: For Inftance, fuppofe you was to be in the third Pofition on the left Foot (v) and to perform this Step to the firft Pofition even from behind, the right Foot is brought equal to that on which the Weight is, the very Inftant the *Clofe* or *Jump* is made (w); and, if the Fall or coming down be inclofed in the third Pofition before the Foot (x), inftead of joining even to the Foot on which the Weight is (w), the Heel of the right

---

(u) See the Figures in Plate IV. † See the Figures of Plates the IVth, IXth, XIth, XIVth, or XVth. ‖ See the Figures in the firft and fecond Plates. (v) See the firft Figure or Man's Side of Plate V. (w) See the firft Figure or left Side of Plate I. (x) See the fecond Figure or Woman's Side of Plate IV.

Foot

The ART *of* DANCING *explain'd.* 39

Foot is inclosed or joined before the Ancle of the left (x), and the same backwards from before.

This Step in *Dancing* much resembles a *Period* or full Stop in *Letters*; for, as that closes or shuts up a Sentence, the *Close* in *Dancing* does the very same in *Music*, since nothing is more frequent than, at the End of a Strain in the Tune, to find the Strain or Couplet of the *Dance* to conclude in this Step, as also at other remarkable Places of the *Music*. Besides, this *Close* gives great Life and Variety in the Composition of *Dances*; for whereas most other Steps lead the *Dancers* a regular Figure, and consequently render a Change thereof more difficult, in this Step, the Body being as much upon one Foot as the other, the Change is more familiar, since it is as easy to take up one Foot as the other. This Step generally takes up a Measure, that is to say, with the Time you rest or stand still: For Instance, to a Tune of triple Time the *Close* is performed to the first of the three Notes, and the second and third are counted, during the Time you rest; but to Tunes of common Time, as *Marches*, *Gavots*, *Rigadoons*, &c. this Step and Time it is to rest sometimes are a Measure, and at others not, as having a plain Step or Walk added thereto, which said Close and Step together fill up the Time.

CHAP. XIV.
Of the SPRING or LEAP.

THE *Spring* or *Leap* is the same as the latter End of the foregoing *Close* or Spring from one Foot upon both, except that the Close or Jump always begins from one Foot †, the Weight constantly coming down in the same Place *, whereas this Step be-

---

† See the Figures of Plate V.   * See the Figures in Plate I.

gins

gins and ends upon both Feet ‡, whether in the first or third Position †* and may be performed several Ways, viz. forwards, backwards, sideways, to the right or left, upright and circularly ‡*; but, when it is performed either of the two latter Ways, the Weight comes down in the Place from whence the *Spring* was made, as in the Close aforesaid, tho' in any of the former, as forwards, backwards, &c. they *spring* or *leap*, about the Length of the *Half Coupee* or *March*, and light on both Feet, as in *Leaping*.

As to the Agreement of this Step with the Notes of the Tune, it is uncertain; for to a Tune of three it sometimes takes up a Measure, and at others not: For Example, if you *spring upright* in this Step, the Fall marks what we call the *Time* or *Cadence* upon the first Note, whilst the other two are counted during the Time you rest; and in the like Manner, when it is performed *circularly* upon the same Place. *Upright* and *circularly* are the two Ways in which this Step is performed, when it singly answers to a Bar, as it frequently happens on the ending of a Strain or other remarkable Part of the Tune; and when it does not, as it rarely, if ever, does in the other Ways of performing it, we often meet, instead thereof, two Leaps and a plain straight Step in a Measure, which together with the two Springs agree with the Notes of the *Music*; and many Times we find a third Spring added, instead of the plain straight Step; which three Springs agree with the Notes, as before, tho' they are seldom used except in *Comic Dancing* and Tunes of common Time, that is to say, of four in the Bar, as in *Gavots, Marches, Rigadoons*, &c. in which this *Spring* or *Leap* on both Feet is the same, in its answering with the Notes of the Tune, except that, instead of two Springs and the plain straight Step to a Measure, or the three Springs, as in triple Time, in these of common there is but one Close and the straight Step; and also, instead of three Springs or Leaps, here are but two, which Steps agree with the Notes, as follows: The Fall or

‡ See the Figure in Plate II. †* See the Figures of Plate IV. ‡* See the Steps in the second Plate and the Explanation and Table of this Step in the Plate of Tables marked E.

The ART *of* DANCING *explain'd.* 41

Coming down of the Weight from the first Spring beats Time to the first Note of the Bar; and the second and third Notes are counted, during the Performing of the plain Step. The fourth Note is always taken up with the Sink which prepares for the succeeding Step; and consequently it is very necessary to take Notice, that the two Leaps are performed in the same Method. The Coming down of the first Spring, as I said before, marks the Time or first Note; the Sinking or Bending of the Knees, in order for the second Rise or Spring, answers the same Note; and the third is in the Coming down of the Weight in the Sink, &c. as was just observed, which Step, if continued, is a sort of an harmonious Leaping to *Music* either forwards or backwards, &c. (y). It is to be likewise noted, that the *upright Spring* or *Close* affords the *Dancer* the like Opportunity of changing the Foot, during the Time of resting as in the foregoing *Close*, the Difference being only in its beginning and ending on both Feet; and, if performed on the Ground, it is intirely in the same Manner, as we have already described it in the *Jump* or *Close* from one Foot.

CHAP. XV.
Of the RIGADOON STEP of one Spring open in the same Place and Close.

THE *Rigadoon Step* of one Spring open upon the same Place is composed of two plain Steps or Motions of the Feet, except that the first commences with a *Spring* or *Hop*; which said Spring and plain Step is to a Measure, and introduces the *upright Spring* or *Close* on both Feet, before treated of, to another Measure in its Attendance on the former, from which it is almost inseparable; info-

---
(y) See the Table of the Leap or Jump, in the Plate marked E or second Plate.

much that the said *Rigadoon Step* is seldom, if ever, without this *Close* following it, as adding the greatest Grace and Beauty thereto, and being from thence so strictly united that, altho' in themselves they are two distinct Steps, the first never appears but concludes in the latter which in its Performance is as follows, *viz.* commencing from the first Position, or the Feet join'd even one with the other, from whence the Sink or Preparative for the *Hop* is taken, and may be done with either Foot. However, for the better Understanding thereof I shall describe it, with the right Foot: Therefore, as has been already observed, the Weight being on both Feet in the first Position (z), you sink and give a Rise or Spring, either off from the Ground, or upon it, as you shall think most agreeable, since it may be perform'd both Ways; which said Spring is made upon the left Foot, in rising from the aforesaid Sink, by taking the right Foot up from the Floor, the very same Instant the Spring or *Hop* is made, and moves open off to the right Side of the Room, if to the upper End, or otherwise according to what Part of the Room the Body is directed in the Air, about the Length of a Step in *Dancing* (a); and then it returns to the first Position from whence it came receiving the Weight; upon which the left Foot, being now disengaged, moves open sideways in the like Manner (b), and, in returning, receives one half of the Weight in the same Position as at first (z); after which comes the Close on both Feet (c) which sometimes is to a Measure, and at others not, in that there often follows in *Rigadoon* Movements, a plain Step or Walk in the Time or Measure, as for Example, you'll find in this Movement of the *Bretagne*; that is to say, the Beginning of the second Part is the very same Step I have here described.

As to the Agreement of this Step with the Notes of the Tune, which is of four in the Measure, the Spring or Hop, that is made

---

(z) See the Figure in Plate II, only instead of facing down the Room you may suppose it looking to the Presence. (a) See in some Measure the Feet in the second Figure of Plate XV. (b) See the Feet in the first Figure of Plate XV. (c) See Plate II.

The Art of Dancing explain'd. 43

upon the left Foot, on the taking up of the right, marks the Time or firft Note; the fetting of it down the fecond; the third is in the fetting down of the left Foot; and the fourth and laft Note, in the Sink for the enfuing Clofe that attends this Step, which together compofe one of the moft agreeable Steps in *Dancing*.

There are, befides thefe already defcribed, many other Ways of performing this Step, as in the third Pofition forwards, and the fame backwards; but, for the better Underftanding of this, fuppofe you are ftanding in the firft Pofition, or the Feet are joined even to each other (d, you perform this Step into the third Pofition, that is, you make the firft Step which is with a Spring, and inclofe it before the Foot on which the Weight refts (e), and the fecond before that (f) in the like Manner.

To perform this Step backwards differs in this, that as the foregoing was inclofed before, after the Spring, this is inclofed behind the Foot that fupports the Weight (g), and the fecond Step behind that (h); or elfe the firft of the faid two Steps, namely, the *Spring*, may be done in the third Pofition before (i), and the fecond behind (j); or the firft with a Spring behind (k), and the fecond Step before (l), and are to be performed from either of the faid Pofitions, whether the firft or third, as is alfo the *Spring* or *Clofe* that follows them, whether upright or changing of the Pofition; that is, inftead of coming down in the firft, or in the third, as at Beginning, the Feet are changed, for Inftance, the firft laft, and the laft firft (m).

(d) See the Figure in Plate II, fuppofed to be looking up the Room. (e) See the fecond Figure of Plate IV. (f) See the firft Figure of Plate IV. (g) See the firft Figure of the faid Plate IV. (h) See the fecond Figure of Plate IV. (i) See the two firft or inclofed Feet of Plate IV. (i) See the two hind Feet of Plate IV. (k) See the hindmoft Feet in Plate IV. (l) See the inclofed Feet in Plate IV. (m) See the Table and Explanation of this Step in the Plate of Tables marked E.

F 2 CHAP.

CHAP. XVI.

Of the RIGADOON Step of two Springs or SISSONNE.

THE *Rigadoon* Step with two Springs differs from the former of one in this, that whereas the aforesaid is performed in the same Place, and only with one Spring, this is of two; the first of which advances or retires, about the Length of a *March*, whilst the second Spring is in the same Place upon one Foot.

This Step may also be perform'd sideways crossing before, or sideways crossing behind, either to the right or left, or turning †, &c. the Difference of which, in the Manner of Performance, I shall describe in their Order. For Example, first *forwards*, which may be done with one Foot as well as the other; yet, for the more easy comprehending thereof, I intend to explain it, beginning with the right Foot, which is as follows, viz. the Weight is on the left in the third Position, and the right behind; that is to say, the Ancle of the right Foot rests against the Heel of the left, but is intirely free from any Weight of the Body (n); from whence you make the first Spring which is upon the left Foot, whilst the right, at the same Instant, moves directly the same Way, as in the *March*, except that the *March* is performed on the Ground from a Bend and Rise only, but this off from thence, by an upright Spring into the Air from the Sink you make upon your left Foot, on which the Weight falls in the same Place, the right advancing, as has been already observed, about the Length of a *March*; but it does not receive the whole Weight of the Body, as in that, by Reason of its continuing principally on the same Foot on which it was, at com-

---

† See the Explanation and Table of this Step in the Plate of Tables marked E. (n) See the first Figure of Plate V.

mencing;

The Art *of* Dancing *explain'd.* 45

mencing; so that, altho' the right Foot is advanced before the other, it receives no more than its own Weight, the whole being to follow on making the second Spring (o). Having thus far only concluded the first Spring or Movement, the second is made from the aforesaid Position divided; that is to say, the right Foot is, near the Length of a Step in *Dancing,* before the left; in which Position or Posture both Knees bend, the right to receive the Body, and the left to be disengaged from it, as it intirely is on giving the Hop or Spring; for, at the Instant the Foot on which the Weight was, is taken from the Floor, the other receives it, ending the Step in the third Position upon the right Foot, the left being behind but free from any Weight; the Ancle of which rests against the Heel of the Foot that supports the Body, in the same Position in which it begun, only with the contrary Foot (p), and may be continued from one Foot to the other, as in the *March, &c.*

This Step *backwards* is performed in the like Manner as *forwards* except that *forwards* it is taken from the third Position behind, but in this begins from the same Position before; that is, the Heel of the right Foot touches the Ancle of the left on which the Body rests (q), from whence you make the Spring in the same Method already described in this Step *forwards, viz.* the right and foremost Foot, at the same Moment the Spring is given upon the left, moves backwards, as in the *March,* much about the like Distance, and receives half the Weight, at the same Time the other half comes down upon the left, leaving the Weight divided to the first Spring or Hop (r); and the second is made on the right Foot, in the taking up of the left, which falls inclosed in the third Position as at beginning except that the contrary Foot is foremost (s), and the left is ready to commence, as before. This Step *Sideways crossing before* is so called, from its being crossed before the Foot on which the Weight of the Body rests, and it chiefly differs from the two Ways already described namely, *forwards* and *back-*

(o) See the second Figure in Plate IX.
(q) See the second Figure of Plate IV. Plate IX, or second Figure in Plate XI.
(p) See the second Figure of Plate V.
(r) See in some Measure the first Figure in
(s) See the first Figure in Plate IV.

wards

wards, in that it begins from the third Position behind, as aforesaid (t), but instead of the right Foot's moving, as in them, you in this give the Spring and Fall in the fifth Position, the right or beginning Foot crossing before the left, the Weight being divided, as before; that is, the Heel of the right Foot is equal to the Toe of the left (u), which Manner of placing the Feet we call the *fifth Position*. The second Spring or Hop is made upon the right Foot on the taking up the left, which is then brought into the third Position behind, and the right Foot into the same Position as the beginning but contrary Foot (v); which said Foot is ready to perform the same Thing either *sideways crossing before* the right on which the Body is, or *sideways crossing behind*, the latter of which I shall explain, in the next Place, and it is as follows.

Sideways crossing behind varies from the former only in this, that, instead of commencing from the third Position behind, it begins from before: For Example, the Weight being upon the left Foot (w) you sink and make the first Spring with the right, falling in the fifth Position crossing behind; that is, the Toe of the right Foot is equal to the Heel of the left, the Weight being divided, as has been already explained (x). The second Spring is performed upon the right, on the left's being taken up from the Ground, as aforesaid, which falls inclosed in the third Position before; that is, the Heel of the left Foot is joined to the Ancle of the right, and, being disengaged from Weight, is at Liberty to perform the same with the left Foot, as we have described with the right (y).

Having now shewn, how this Step is performed *sideways crossing before*, as also the same *behind*, it is unnecessary here to take any farther Notice of this Step *sideways to the right*, than that it differs in Nothing from what we have described *to the left* but in the contrary Foot; nor likewise of the Manner of its Performance in *turn-*

(t) See the first Figure of Plate V.   (u) See the Feet of the first Figure in Plate XI.
(v) See the second Figure of Plate V.   (w) See the second Figure in Plate IV.
(x) See the Feet in the second Figure of Plate XI.   (y) See first Figure of Plate IV.

ing, otherwise than that it may be performed several Ways, as to the right or left, in a quarter Turn, half Turn, or three quarter Turn, &c. since I shall take Occasion hereafter, in the ensuing Steps, to treat more particularly on that Head. I shall only observe at present, that those who learn to *dance*, and are acquainted with the *Rigadoon* of the late Mr. *Isaac*, will meet with this Step, *turning* in all or most of the Ways above mentioned, in the different Parts thereof; and it is here, for Distinction sake, named of *two Springs*.

There is still another Way in which this Step is often made, and not as yet observed, which is the Reverse in the second Spring to the foregoing; for, instead of taking up, in the second Spring, the Foot on which the Body was, when you begun, the contrary Foot or that Foot which advances or retires is taken up: For Instance, admitting this Step to begin with the right Foot, of Consequence the Weight must then be upon the left, from whence you make the first Spring, as is usual, upon both Feet; but, instead of the left Foot's being taken from the Floor, as in the aforesaid, the right or beginning Foot is taken up on making the second Spring; which Choice of Feet in this Step renders it of equal Use, in the Composition of *Dances*, as the *Close*, in that the Change of Figure is to be effected in this, as well as in the aforesaid.

Having described most of the different Manners of performing this Step in *Dancing*, I shall proceed to shew its Agreement with the Notes of this Movement, which, as we have already said, is of four in the Bar, and it agrees as follows: The first Spring is made upon the Time or first Note; the Sink for the second is in the second Note, which second Spring is performed to the third Note; and the fourth is in the Sink preparing for the succeeding Step. And, when it is done to a *Saraband* or Tune of triple Time, it is in all Respects the same, except that, instead of four Notes in a Bar, in this you have only three, which are, in their Performance, much slower than the before mentioned of four to the Measure; and it is farther to be observed, that one half or the third Note is borrowed for the Sink that prepares for the ensuing

Step

Step, in which it chiefly differs from the foregoing of common Time, but that it is not so brisk.

CHAP. XVII.
Of the GALLIARD and FALLING Step.

THE *Galliard* Step is in a Manner the same, as the besor described *Close* from one Foot to both, except that in this the Weight of the Body, after making the Spring or Movement for the *Close*, remains on the same Foot upon which it was at the Beginning; from whence it follows, that the Foot which, in the foregoing *Close*, received one half of the Weight, is here to be disengaged, and at Liberty to perform the succeeding one which is a plain straight Step or Walk; which Step could not have been performed with the commencing Foot, had it received one half of the Weight, as in the *Close* from one Foot. And you are to note, that this Step always ends with the same Foot it begins, whether it be the right or left, and is various, as to its Performance in *Dancing*. I shall describe the most usual of these Ways, which are as follow *viz.* forwards, backwards, sideways to the right or left, and also in turning a quarter Turn, half Turn, &c. (z) and, in all the aforesaid Methods of performing the *Galliard* Step, the *Falling* Step rarely, if ever, fails to accompany it, in that they are inseparable, in their Performance, as the RIGADOON Step open in the same Place of one Spring and upright *Close* upon both Feet we have before described, tho' they are two distinct Steps in themselves. However, sometimes, instead of the *Galliard* Step, we find the *Coupee* crossing before sideways introducing the *Falling* Step; which it does very naturally, their Endings being directly alike.

(z) See the Explanation and Table of this Step in the Plate of Tables marked E. and Plate VII.

Now

The ART of DANCING explain'd.

Now, as to the Method of performing the *Galliard* Step which, as I have faid in the Defcription thereof, is compounded of a *Clofe* and plain ftraight Step or Walk, I fhall begin with the right Foot advancing forwards, in the following Manner, *viz.* the Weight of the Body is upon the left Foot in the third Pofition, and the right difengaged behind (a); from whence you fink and give an upright Spring upon the left Foot, clofing the right or hindmoft Foot equal to it directly the fame Way as has been defcribed in the *Clofe* from one Foot to both, except with this Difference that, as I have faid, the before mentioned lights on both Feet, but this comes down only upon one, namely the left; and it varies from the aforefaid, the right Foot being in the firft Pofition, joined even with the left, and at Liberty to perform the following plain ftraight Step (b), which together with the foregoing *Clofe* compleats the *Galliard Step*; that is to fay, after the plain ftraight Step has been made forwards with the right Foot, about the Length of a Step in *Walking*, it does not bring up the left equal to it, as in that, but leaves it in the fame Place, whilft the Weight of the Body advances forwards with the ftepping of the right Foot, the End or fetting to the Floor of which receives the Weight; fo that, as I have juft obferved, the left Foot is upon the Point behind, the like Diftance, and the right advanced from it, in which Pofture the *Galliard Step* concludes (c). Upon this commences the *Falling Step*, which is performed in the following Manner, *viz.* the Weight of the Body ending in the *Galliard Step* upon the right, the left Foot is pointed behind; at the fame Time the Body bends or bows forwards, in order to the enfuing *Fall* which is backwards, but is prevented in it by the left Foot, which was planted for that Purpofe upon the Point behind; and, at the very Inftant the Weight of the Body inclines forwards preparing for the *Fall*, the left is advancing up to prevent it; which it does by receiving the falling Weight in a Sink or Bend of the Knee, in the third Pofition inclofed behind, releafing the

---

(a) See the firft Figure of Plate V.   (b) See the firft Figure of Plate I.   (c) See the
fecond Figure in Plate VII.

right Foot (d), which is then ready to receive the Weight, on the Spring that is given from the left, immediately after its receiving the aforesaid falling Weight, and comes down upon the right Foot again, in the Nature of a latter Part of the *Balonne*, of which more hereafter; concluding in the same Position from whence the foregoing *Galliard* Step was taken, with the contrary Foot (e) and, in continuance together with the *Galliard* Step, it changes the Foot, as in the *Half Coupee*, or *March*, &c.

In performing this Step *sideways*, either to the right or left, it only differs from the former in the plain Step, which, instead of being made, as in the aforesaid *forwards*, is here performed *sideways*; and it may easily be understood by comparing it with the foregoing described, advancing to the upper Part of the Room: for Instance, supposing the Close to be made in the first Position, as before, the right Foot, instead of making the plain straight Step as in that, here makes it *sideways* to the right Hand, in like Manner as *forwards*. That is, the End or Setting down of the plain straight Step receives the Body; leaving the left Toe upon the Point sideways the like Distance from the right on which the Weight is, as has been shewn in this Step *forwards*, when the said Toe was left pointed behind, as it now is *sideways*; from whence commences the *Falling* Step, which, instead of forwards, as before, is made as follows, *viz.* the Weight being on the right Foot, and the left Toe upon the Point (f), as was already observed, the Weight of the Body falls to the right Hand, but, as I have said, is prevented; for, at the same Time the Weight falls, the left Foot which was upon the Point is brought with a swift Motion to its Relief, crossing behind the right on which the falling Weight is in the fifth Position, receiving the Body (g) which must otherwise have fallen, and releases the right Foot (h) which immediately receives the Weight again, in a *Bound* or *Balonne* sideways to the Hand the

---

(d) See the second Figure in Plates IV and XIV. (e) See the second Figure in Plate V. (f) See the first Figure in Plate VI. or Plate XV. (g) See the first Figure in Plate XI. (h) See the second Figure in Plate XIV.

Fall

Fall was on, in that the left no sooner receives the falling Weight in a Sink or bended Knee, than it gives a Spring, in rising, and throws the Body, as in bounding back, upon the right Foot, concluding the *Falling* Step in the third Position, with the left upon the Point behind, instead of the right, as at first (i); from whence the said *Galliard* and *Falling* Step may be performed to the left Hand, in like Manner as the foregoing to the right, the Difference being only in the contrary Foot, Examples of which with both Feet begin the second Strain of the *Rigadoon* Part of a *Dance*, named the *Bretagne*, the first Time of its playing over, for they are the very same Steps here treated of.

These Steps may also be made with a quarter Turn, or a half Turn, *&c.* which, to give a more perfect Idea thereof, I shall explain with the left Foot, as follows, *viz.* the Weight being upon the right in the third Position, the left upon the Point behind (i) begins, in making the Spring or Close in the first Position as aforesaid only, instead of the Presence looking up the Room after the Close, it now faces to the right Side, which is a quarter of a Turn, and in this it differs from the two Ways last described; but the remaining Part of the Step is intirely the same, stepping the beginning Foot sideways to the left Hand, and facing to the right Side of the Room, as before to the upper. The *Falling* Step is also the same as before except, as I have said, in not facing to the same Part of the Room; and turning a half Turn only differs in this, that the first Spring or Close, instead of ending in a quarter of a Turn to the right, as before, continues a quarter Turn more, facing to the Bottom of the Room, the left Foot stepping sideways to the same Hand, as aforesaid, *&c.*

As to the Agreement of these Steps with the Notes of the *Music*, it is much the same as in the others: For Example, in the following Tunes, as *Forlanes*, *Jigs*, *&c.* the Close is made to the first Note; the second and third are counted in the straight Step of the *Galliard*, that is to say, the second Note, at the Beginning of

---

(i) See the second Figure in Plate V.

said Step, and the third, at its ending or receiving the Weight of the Body. And, suppose instead of performing this Step with a plain straight Step, as in *Walking*, you add thereto a Sink and a Rise, the Sink then answers the second Note, and the Rise the third; and in the succeeding Step the Fall of the Body marks the first Note, the Pause or Rest the Weight makes upon the Knees bent the second, and the third is in the contrary Foot's receiving the Body upon the Spring or Bound given from the Foot which preserved the Weight from falling, where ends the second Measure or Time. When these Steps are performed to Tunes of common Time, as they for the most Part are in *Galliards*, *Bourees*, *Rigadoons*, &c. they are intirely the same as in triple, only, instead of borrowing half the third Note for the Sink in common Time, the Sink or Preparative for beating the Time is upon the fourth Note, as has been shewn in the *Rigadoon* Step of two Springs; and the most usual Manner of performing this Step is in a soft and gentle Movement upon the Floor, tho' it may be done to Advantage either Way, *viz.* off from the Ground, or upon it.

CHAP. XVIII.
Of the BOUREE with a BOUND.

THE *Bouree with a Bound*, so called from its having a *Bound* added to the *Bouree*, is a compound Step consisting of four plain Steps and two Movements, the first whereof is made upon the Ground, but the other not: For Instance, you make a Movement or Sink and Rise to the first of the four Steps, the second and third compleating the *Bouree* or *Fleuret*; and the fourth and last is a *Bound* which is always performed off from the Floor, as we have already shewn, in treating of that Step.

I shall now proceed to shew, how these four Steps are to be reduced to agree with the Notes of triple Time or of three in the

Measure,

The Art of Dancing explain'd. 53

Measure, which may be accomplished, as follows, viz. the left Foot, with which we shall for Example begin, and the right are to be performed in a Motion as swift again, as the remaining two Steps, by reason they are both to be accounted but as one Note, and are made to the first of the Measure. The third Step, which is with the left Foot, is to the second Note, upon which the *Bouree* concludes; and the fourth Step is a *Bound* with the right Foot to the third Note, and compleats the *Bouree with a Bound*. This Step continued in *Dancing*, whether it be the right or the left, always begins with the same Foot, as has been already observed in the *Coupee*, and may be performed forwards, backwards, sideways to either Hand, crossing before, crossing behind, or crossing before and behind in the same Measure, or twice behind; and they are all of them directly the same, in their Manner of Performance, as was shewn in the *Bouree of one Movement*, only, as that was but of three Steps and one Movement to a Bar, this is of four and two Movements; and consequently, instead of performing the first two Steps equally slow, as in them, they must be quick here, in that they are both to be accounted as no more than one Step, as I have said; and as the *Bouree* or *Fleuret* breaks off, at the End of the third Step which is upon the left Foot, the Bound must be added thereto with the right, which is the only Difference from the *Bouree* aforesaid. It is unnecessary to say any thing farther of these Steps, in this Place, since they will be understood by what has been said in the *Bouree* or *Fleuret of one Movement*, having in that described all the different Ways mentioned here; but only to observe, that the first two Steps, as above, and the Bounds must be added.

CHAP.

CHAP. XIX.

Of the SLIP before and then behind, or SLIP behind and afterwards before, and HALF COUPEE sideways.

THE *Slip before and then behind* is a Step composed of four plain Steps, in a Measure, and two Movements; which said Movements may be done upon the Ground, or off from thence; but it differs from the *Bouree* with a Bound in this, that, whereas, in the *Bouree* aforesaid, the first Movement is always to be made on the Floor, and the second off, in this Step both are performed alike, either springing from the Ground, or upon it; and it is also to be noted, that these Steps seldom, if ever, are performed any otherwise than sideways to the right or left Hand, or with a quarter Turn, half Turn, &c.

These are the Ways this Step is usually made, as either *slipping before and afterwards behind*, or *slipping behind and then before*; the first of which I shall describe, beginning with the right Foot. For Example, the Weight of the Body is upon the left Foot in the third Position, the right being intirely disengaged from the Weight, so that it may be at Liberty to begin (k); which it does by making the first Movement or Bend and Rise from behind the left Foot to the first of the four Steps, stepping open off sideways to the right Hand (l), and the second Step, which is with the left Foot, is drawn crossing before it, (m) after which the right Foot makes

---

(k) See the first Figure in Plate V. (l) See the Point or second Figure of Plate VI.   (m) See the Point or first Figure in Plate VI. and second Figure of Plate XI.

the second Movement the same Way, which is the third Step; but, instead of the left and last Foot's being drawn before, as in the first *Slip* (n), it must now be drawn behind where it concludes receiving the Weight in the fifth Position (o).

To *Slip behind and then before* is, when the right Foot has made the first Movement and Step sideways in the Manner just described; and the second Step, which is with the left Foot, (p) instead of being drawn crossing before, as in the former, is drawn behind (q). The second Movement is also with the right Foot, stepping to the same Side (r), which is the third Step; and the fourth and last, which is with the left Foot (s), is drawn crossing before the right into the Position aforesaid (t).

To perform this Step with a quarter of a Turn, either to the right or left Hand, is only turning a quarter Turn to one of the said Hands, as it shall fall out; in Dancing however, as an Example, I shall explain it sideways to the right Hand, facing to the left Side of the Room, viz. *before and behind*, and *behind and before*, which are both to be performed, as follows: For Instance, these *Slips*, as before described, were sideways, facing the upper End of the Room to the right Hand; whereas, in a quarter Turn to the left Side of the Room, in the Sink of the first Movement, you prepare for the Rise or Beating Time; but, instead of performing it, facing to the upper End of the Room, as in the foregoing, in the rising, it makes a quarter of a Turn to the left Hand, which then will face to the left Side of the Room; yet in the Performance of the rest of the Step to the right, it is intirely in the same Manner as I have explained it, to the upper Part of the Room, there being no Difference except in the Turn.

A half Turn is the same as the quarter; only that, in the Rise of the first Movement, which is made with the right Foot, instead of

---

(n) See the second Figure in Plate XI. (o) See the first Figure in Plate XI. (p) See the first Figure in Plate VI. (q) See the first Figure of Plate XI. (r) See the second Figure in Plate VI. (s) See the first Figure in Plate VI. (t) See the second Figure in Plate XI.

turning a quarter Turn as before, that is, facing the left Side of the Room, in this you make a half Turn, which then faces the Bottom of the Room, performing the rest of the Step to the right Hand, in the same Manner we have described it to the upper End.

These Steps may likewise be done, both *slipping behind*, or both *slipping before*; the former is, when, in making the Movement to the right or left Side, the second Step, which is the *Slip*, is drawn crossing behind the first or beginning Foot; and the second Movement and *Slip* are performed in the like Manner.

Both *slipping before* is, when, in performing the said Movements, the Foot, which makes the *Slips*, is both Times drawn crossing before the Foot which begun, that is, the second and fourth Steps; and the first of these Steps, namely, *twice slipping behind*, is in the *Rigadoon* of the late Mr *Isaac*, where, in the Beginning of the Tune, the second Time of playing over, it forms a perfect Square, which is no small Addition to the Beauty of the said *Dance*; and this Step *slipping before* is no less remarkable, in that it is frequently met with in *Dancing*.

This Step, in all the different Ways of performing it, as above described, is seldom, if ever, without the *Half Coupee* sideways following it, on the same Hand to which the *Slips* were made, which seem not to have received their utmost Perfection, without this Step attending them; and as the Slips, before explained, were to the right Hand, this must be so likewise, and consists of one plain Step, as has been observed, in treating of the *Half Coupee*; to which is added a Movement or Sink and Rise, made with the right Foot stepping open off, sideways, from the Position in which the foregoing Slips ended, receiving the Weight on the setting of the Toe or Heel to the Floor (u); after which the left Foot makes a Motion in the Air, in the Form of a half Circle, before the An-

---

(u) See the second Figure in Plate VI.

cle of the right Foot, opening to the left Hand, and accomplishes the Time or Meafure (v).

It ftill remains to fhew, how thefe Steps agree with the Notes of common or triple Time; for they are very different in their Manner of Performance, which we fhall proceed to explain, and chiefly in this, that in Tunes of triple Time either the firft or fecond Slip, inftead of being made quick as in Tunes of common Time, are as flow again; yet, for the farther Illuftration of this Point, I fhall obferve, how thefe Steps agree with the Notes both of common and triple Time; which is as follows: To common Time or of four in the Bar, as in *Rigadoons, Bourees, &c.* But having already defcribed the Motion or Stepping of the Feet, I fhall wave the faying any Thing farther of it here, and only fhew, that the firft *Slip* or firft and fecond Steps are to be performed in the fame fwift Manner we have fhewn, in the Beginning or two firft Steps of the *Bouree and a Bound*, and are both to be made upon the firft of the four Notes. The fecond Note is counted in the Sink which prepares for the fecond *Slip*, which is the third and fourth Steps; the Rife which is made on the fetting down of the third Step, or Beginning of the laft *Slip*, beats Time to the third Note, which faid *Slip* is compleated in the Sound of the third Note, in the fame Manner as the firft Movement to the firft Note; and the fourth and laft Note is counted in the Sink which prepares for the enfuing Step

When this Step is performed to a Tune of triple Time or of three Notes in the Meafure, as in *Sarabands, Louvres, Paffacailles, &c.* fometimes the firft *Slip* is quick, as in the aforefaid, and the fecond not; and at other Times the firft is flow, and the fecond fwift. When the Movement is made quick, it is performed, as above, to the firft of the three Notes; the fecond, which is flow, takes up the fecond and third Notes. For Inftance, as was already faid, the firft *Slip* or *Coupee* being made with the firft and fecond Steps to the firft Note, the fecond *Slip*, which begins with the third Step, is to the fecond Note; and the third is taken up in the gentle fliding or drawing of the fourth and laft Step, whether before or behind.

(v) See the firft Figure in Plates XIV. and XV.

Half the third Note is borrowed, to mark the Sink which is for the next Step, as has been observed before; and, if the first *Slip* is slow, the beginning Step is to the first Note, the *Slip* or easy drawing of the second Step behind or before to the second Note, and the remaining *Slip* is swift to the third Note.

As to the *Half Coupee*, the first Movement or stepping sideways marks Time to the first Note; the second and third are counted in the half Circle the Foot makes in the Air; and the fourth in the Sink, provided it be common Time; but, if triple, half the third Note is borrowed, as I have said.

CHAP. XX.
Of the HOP or CONTRETEMP.

THE *Hop* or *Contretemp* is a compound Step consisting of two Walks or Steppings of the Feet, as the *Coupee*; and it may be performed various Ways, as advancing, retiring, sideways to the right or left, turning, &c. There are also two different Positions from whence this Step is taken and performed, namely, the third and fourth; the first of which we shall explain forwards, beginning with the left Foot, which is behind the right in the third Position(w), but so disengaged from the Weight of the Body as to be ready to act; which it does in the Sink that prepares for the *Spring* or *Hop* which is made upon the right Foot, lighting in the same Place; and at the Instant the *Hop* or Rise from the Ground is given, it leaves the aforesaid Position where it rested, during the Sink, and straightens the Knee, pointing the Toe directly sideways, as in the *March* (x); but it does not press upon the Floor, as in that, by Reason the *March* is performed upon the Ground, and this off from thence which is the principal Difference; for, instead of the Progress made by the disengaged Foot, as in the *March*, in this it

---
(w) See the second Figure in Plate V. Figure of Plate XV.   (x) See the first Figure in Plate VI, or first

must

The ART *of* DANCING *explain'd.* 59

must be performed in like Manner off from thence in the Air, the Weight all the while continuing on the same Foot upon which it was at commencing, 'till the left has advanced the Length of a *March* or Step in Walking (y); after which it receives the Body, and releases the right Foot that supported it, during its Procession, as aforesaid, which then makes a plain Step or Walk forwards †, which is the second Step of the *Contretemp*, and is compleated on the setting down or receiving of the Weight upon the said Foot in the Position as at first (z), being a Sort of *Hopping Coupee*.

To perform this Step *backwards* is intirely the same as *forwards*, only, instead of the left Foot's being in the third Position behind, the right is now inclosed before in the same or fourth Position (a), from whence it makes the *Spring* or *Hop backwards*, in the same Manner as was described *forwards* (b); after which the right Foot, instead of stepping forwards, as before, in this makes the second Step backwards (c).

When this Step is done with a quarter or half Turn, &c. the Weight of the Body, as has been observed, being on the right Foot, the *Hop* or *Contretemp* is performed, as we have already explained, but not to the upper End of the Room, instead of which it turns a Quarter of a Turn to the right Hand; but the rest is the same, as in the foregoing, only you are to observe, that it is facing to the right Side of the Room to which it advances.

The half Turn in no Respect differs from the former, except in its not stopping at the right Side of the Room; but, instead of that, it adds a Quarter more facing to the lower End of the Room, to which it is performed in like Manner, as above, to the upper; and if, instead of the right Hand, it be performed to the left, as it equally is in turning, as aforesaid, it is much the same, except that the quarter or half Turn, instead of being made to the right

---

(y) See the first Figure in Plate IX. † See the second Figure in Plate IX. (z) See the second Figure in Plate V, as aforesaid. (a) See the first Figure in Plate IV, or first Figure in Plate IX. (b) See the first Figure in Plate VI, or first Figure of Plate XV aforesaid. (c) See the second Figure of Plate IX, and for the second Step of the *Contretemp* the first Figure in the same Plate concluding as at first. See the first Figure in Plate IV.

H 2 Hand,

The Art of Dancing explain'd.

Hand, as in the foregoing, are now advancing to the left Side or Bottom of the Room; of which the *Royal George* affords us an Example, in that the said *Dance* begins with this Step, both to the right and left Hands, viz. the *Gentleman* performs it to the left Hand here spoken of, whilst the *Lady* does the same to the right.

There are, besides, other Ways of performing this Step from the said third Position, as sideways crossing to the right Hand, and in a Hop, Step, and Draw behind sideways to the left; which Steps differ from the foregoing in this, that whereas they were made either forwards or backwards, facing to the upper Part of the Room, or the same turning to the Sides or lower End of it, these, on the contrary, are always sideways, tho' they are performed turning all the Ways aforesaid: For Instance, to the right Hand sideways, the Face or Presence being to the upper End of the Room, and the Weight in the Position already explained (d), the *Hop* is performed in like Manner excepting that, instead of the left Foot's advancing as in that, or retiring from the *Hop* or *Spring* which is made on the right, it is here cast crossways before the right upon which the Body rests, about the Length of a *March*, and then receives the Weight (e); after which the right Foot makes the second Step of the *Contretemp* open off sideways, in the Manner above described in *forwards* (f).

When it is performed turning with a quarter Turn, or a half Turn, &c. it only varies in its not advancing to the Sides or lower End of the Room, as in the other, but, instead of that, it is made sideways to the right Hand, facing to the right Side of the Room in a quarter Turn, in the same Manner as to the upper End; the half Turn the like, only not facing to the right Side of Room, but instead thereof to the lower Part of it, which is a quarter of a Turn more.

The second of the Ways aforesaid is the Hop, Step, and Draw behind sideways, which is as follows, viz. to the right or left Hand,

---

(d) See the second Figure of Plate V.   (e) See the second Figure of Plate XI.   (f) See in some Degree the second Figure in Plate VI.

The Art of Dancing explain'd. 61

the laſt of which begins from the ſame Poſition treated of in this Step, namely, the third, the diſengaged Foot being upon the Point behind the right (g), from whence this Step commences by making a Sink and upright Spring or Hop, falling in the ſame Place and Poſture, as at firſt, only the Knees are bent; after which the left Foot upon the Point ſteps open off ſideways to the ſame Hand, and receives the Weight of the Body from the right, either placing the Heel to the Ground or upon the Toe (h); and the right Foot, being then releaſed, after the Hop and Step are made, as aforeſaid, is drawn behind the left, the Toe preſſing the Floor (i); as it is brought behind, and receives the Weight of the Body, as at commencing in the third Poſition, except that, inſtead of the left Foot's being pointed behind, it is now incloſ'd before and concludes (j).

This Step with a quarter Turn differs from the *Hop* croſſways to the right, only in the latter's not being made to the ſame Hand; for the quarter Turn, inſtead thereof, is performed, as above deſcribed, ſtepping to the left Hand, facing full to the right Side of Room, as in the other, and the half Turn, facing the lower Part of the Room, is, in its Performance to the left Hand, the ſame as the quarter to the right.

Having explained the foregoing *Hop*'s Beginning with the left Foot from the third Poſition, I ſhall now deſcribe it ſideways with the ſame Foot, from what I call the *fourth Poſition*; that is to ſay, the Weight of the Body is upon the right, the left being directly the ſame ſideways as the Beginning or firſt Movement in a *March*, only the Toe is not pointed to the Ground, as in that, but the Heel placed without any Weight (k); from which Poſture of Standing this Step is taken and performed: For Inſtance, the Weight being upon the right Foot, and the left Heel placed, as aforeſaid, about the Length of a Step in *Walking*, you make the Sink or Preparation for the *Spring* or *Hop* (l) by transferring the Weight from the

---

(g) See the ſecond Figure in Plate V. (h) See the firſt Figure in Plate VI. (i) See the ſecond Figure in Plate VI. (j) See the firſt Figure in Plate IV, or ſecond of Plate XI. (k) See the firſt Figure in Plate VI. (l) See the firſt Figure in Plate X.

right

right to the left Foot, the very Moment before the *Spring* is made, in taking up the right Foot from the Ground, the left at the same Instant receiving the Body, upon which the Hop is begun and compleated, as follows: The right Foot, being then at Liberty (m), makes a plain Step or Walk sideways crossing before the left, that supports the Weight, to the same Hand (n); after which the left Foot steps out the same Way and places the Heel, being ready to make the *Spring*, as before (o), by Reason you are now in the same Position, as at commencing, and concludes the Step.

This *Hop*, as just described, is to be found in the second Strain of the *Rigadoon* of the late Mr. *Isaac*, the first Time of playing over, at the End of the third *Bouree* of the *Woman*'s Side; where the *Lady* stands upon the second Step of the said *Bouree, viz.* the right Foot, whilst the left, instead of receiving the Body as it would otherwise have done, only sets down the Heel to the Ground. From this Posture proceeds the *Hop* or *Contretemp* we are now treating of, which takes up the fourth Bar or Measure; and, as I have referred to this Place for an Example, I think it will not be improper to say something here of the *Hop* that follows the foregoing: Which differs in this, that whereas in the former the Heel is to be placed to the Ground upon the last Step, in this a *Bound* is made instead thereof, which is the only Difference, and the Reason of its being called a *Hop, Step,* and *Bound*; and it also remarkably varies from the aforesaid, in that it again conducts the *Dancer* into the *Bourees, Coupees,* and *Half Coupees, &c.* as the other leads him out of these Steps. To perform this *Contretemp* or *Hop* from the *fourth Position forwards*, the left or beginning Foot instead of being open sideways, as before, must be advanced, about the like Distance before the right, as the other was upon one Side of it; which Manner of Standing is what we call the *fourth Position*, from whence the *Hop* is to be made, being, in all Respects, the same as *sideways*

(m) See the second Figure in Plates VI and XV.   (n) See the first Figure in Plate XI.
(o) See the first Figure in Plate X.

The A R T *of* D A N C I N G *explain'd.* 63

to the left Hand only, as I have said, the left Foot must be advanced up the Room, which is done as follows: The Weight of the Body being upon the right Foot, and the Heel of the left to the Ground, as aforesaid (p), the *Contretemp* is made forwards upon the left Foot, the right being taken up from the Floor; which said right Foot then makes a plain Walk or Step forwards (q), that in the foregoing was made sideways crossing before the left; after which the left Foot is advanced, the Length of a Step, and the Heel placed in the fourth Position, as at commencing this Step, in Readiness to repeat the same (r). But, instead of that, I shall proceed to shew, how this Step is performed from the said Position *backwards, viz.* by the Weight's not advancing *forwards* to the left Foot, as before, but on the contrary the *Hop* is made on the right Foot *backwards* by taking up the left Foot, in like Manner as the other *forwards* in taking up of the right, except that the Weight is not transferred, as in the former, and then it makes the Step or or Walk *backwards* the same as before *forwards* (s); after which the right Foot makes the second and last Step *backwards* also and receives the Body, leaving the left Heel to the Floor, as at first, either to advance or retire (t); and these are the most usual Ways of performing this Step from the fourth Position.

The Method of performing the *Hop* or *Contretemp,* both from the third and fourth Position, being now explained, I shall take some Notice, how they agree with the Notes of Music, either of common or triple Time, *&c.* as for Example, from the third Position *forwards,* beginning with the left or advancing Foot to a Tune of common Time; which being accomplished will shew the Manner of the rest, whether *backwards, sideways,* or *round,* in that the same Method of counting will bear in them all, since the *Hop* certainly marks the first Note or what we call *Time,* tho' it be upon the right Foot, as in the third Position, or on the left in the

---

(p) See the first Figure in Plate IX. (q) See the second Figure in Plate IX. (r) See the first Figure in Plate IX. (s) See the second Figure in Plate IX. (t) See the first Figure in Plate IX.

fourth as follows, viz. the *Spring* or *Hop*, that is made upon the right Foot, beats Time to the firſt of the four Notes; the ſecond Note is counted in the ſetting down or receiving the Weight of the Body upon the eft Foot, after its having advanced the Length of a Step forwards; and the third Note is counted, when the right Foot receives the Body, as before, and finiſhes. The remaining fourth Note, as has been ſaid, is in the Sink which prepares for the ſucceeding Step; and, to triple Time or of the Notes in three Bar or Meaſure, it is the very ſame, except that, as there are only three Notes, half the third muſt be borrowed for the Sink that prepares to mark the Cadence of the ſucceeding Step.

CHAP. XXI.
Of the CHASSEE or DRIVING STEP

THE *Hop* or *Contretemp* laſt explained having introduced us to the Poſition from whence the *Chaſſee* or *Driving Step* is performed, namely, the *fourth*, ſince in that we took no farther Notice than of its being *ſideways*, or *forwards*, in the ſaid Poſition, without explaining the particular Manner in which the laſt Step, whether of a *Bouree*, *Coupee*, *Half Coupee*, or *March* is to be performed, when introducing any of the aforeſaid *Hops* or *Driving Steps*; and as this Step conſiderably varies, in its Method of Performance, from the Way in which it would otherwiſe have been done, had a *Bouree*, or *Coupee*, &c. followed, I ſhall obſerve, that it is much the ſame as when, in *Fencing*, we put ourſelves in a Poſture of Defence; but, this Poſture being probably unknown to the *Ladies*, I ſhall endeavour to give an Explanation of it, which take as follows: The Poſture of Defence moſt uſually is to the right Hand, the whole Weight of the Body being upon the left Foot, and the right ſtepped out ſideways to the ſame Side of the Room, about

The ART *of* DANCING *explain'd.* 65

the Length of a Step, as in *Walking*; the full Part of the Heel firſt comes to the Ground, but afterwards the Foot is flat, only free from Weight, both the Knees being bent (u); from which Poſition or Poſture the *Hop* before treated of is taken, as well as the *Chaſſee* we are now about to deſcribe, or from whence the *Longe* or *Paſs* is made in *Fencing*.

However it ſtill remains to ſhew the Method, how the above-mentioned Step is to be performed, when we put ourſelves in the ſaid Poſition or Poſture, in which conſiſts the Perfection of it; and, for the greater Variety, in deſcribing the ſame we ſhall begin to the right Hand, having already obſerved it to the left, in the *Hop* aforeſaid. But, for the better underſtanding of this, we muſt take Notice, that in a *Bouree* we are to make a Stop or Reſt upon the ſecond Step, when any of this Sort of Steps follow; in the *Coupee* upon the firſt, and in a *Half Coupee* or *March*, *&c.* we ſtand in one of the Poſitions from whence it is to be taken, which differ according to the foregoing Step's being performed forwards, backwards, or ſideways; but, in all of them, it is generally taken from the firſt or third Poſition either before or behind (v). We ſhall begin with the laſt: For Example, the Weight of the Body being upon the left Foot, the right at Liberty behind it prepares for the *Kick* or ſoft *Stamp* ſideways, for ſo I muſt name it, as not knowing what more properly to call it, by raiſing the Heel of the hindmoſt Foot, whether right or left, with a gentle and eaſy Motion, the Toe or Ball of the Inſtep pointing down to the Ground, but not ſo as to bear upon it, by Reaſon it will not be ready to perform the Step aforeſaid; which is exceeding ſwift, becauſe, as I have ſaid, the *Dancer* makes a Pauſe or Reſt, until the fourth Note in common Time is almoſt ſpent, and in triple the third; but, *before either of them* expire, the eaſy *Stamp* or *Kick* is given, and inſtead of the Foot's being flat to the Ground, as in *Fencing*, in *Dancing* the Heel muſt firſt be placed thereto in order to receive the *Chaſſee*

(u) See the ſecond Figure in Plate X. (v) See the firſt Figure in Plate I. ſecond Figure in Plate IV. or firſt Figure in Plate V.

or *Hop* that succeeds (w). How the latter of them is to be executed, we have shewn in the *Hops*; and, having just before observed the raising of the Heel and pointing of the Toe, I shall also take Notice, that, just as the *Kick* or *Stamp* is about to be made, the Toe, instead of pointing to the Floor, as at commencing, rises from thence; and the Heel comes down, but does not receive the Weight, 'till the *Hop* or *Chaffee* is made, which, in *Dancing*, is always immediately after this Step, it being a Preparation to that Purpose; for, as I have said, the Knees being bent, at the Instant the right Heel is struck against the Floor, it only remains to perform the Steps treated on; and whether *forwards*, or *backwards*, the Method is the same, as *sideways* above explained to the right Hand.

Having now given some Hints, as to the Manner how the Step, that introduces a *Hop* or *Chaffee*, is to be performed, I shall proceed to the Explanation of the latter, which is a Step composed sometimes of three, and at other Times of four Steps to the Measure or Bar; and the most usual Way of their Performance is *forwards* and *sideways*. I shall begin with the former of these, namely, the *Chaffee* or *Driving-Step* of three Steps in a Measure, advancing to the upper Part of the Room, which is as follows, viz. the Weight of the Body being upon the left Foot, and the right stepped forwards, as just explained, into the fourth Position (x) with the Knees bent, in order to the Performance of the *Chaffee*, it begins by transferring the Weight; that is to say, before the rising from the said Sink, the Body, that was on the left Foot, is conveyed upon the right and foremost Foot, which then supports it, whilst the left, disengaged from the Weight, advances the Length of a Step, in rising from the aforesaid Sink into the third Position inclosed behind the right, and again receives the Body. The said Rising beats Time to the first Note of the Measure (y), upon which the right, being at

---

(w) See the second Figure in Plate X.   (x) See the second Figure in Plate IX.
(y) See the second Figure in Plate IV. or first of Plate XI.

Liberty,

The Art *of* Dancing *explain'd.* 67

Liberty, makes the second of the three Steps (z); but it differs somewhat from that of the *Bouree*, in its being stepped more open off to the right Hand, whereas the *Bouree* is directly advancing forwards upon which is counted the second Note; and the last is reckoned in the *Kick* or light *Stamp* that prepares for the *Chassee* following, which is the last of the three Steps, and made with the left Foot; for, as I have said, the Body, being on the right, rests thereon, whilst the left moves slowly forwards, the Toe pressing to the Floor, as in the *March*; but not much above half its Length, in that the remaining Part is allowed to the light *Stamp* the left Foot gives forwards, on the Expiration of the last Note; upon which it is then in readiness to perform the same thing over again, as in the *Bouree* (a); for this Step, in Continuance, changes the Foot, every three Steps, the same as a *Bouree*. This Step with the contrary Foot differs only in the Weight's being upon the right Foot, instead of the left, as in the former; and the left, at the End of the second Step of the foregoing *Chassee*, being advanced into the fourth Position, in the Manner we have just observed, begins by transferring the Weight, and taking up the right Foot, as the other did by the left (b), and so on if continued.

This Step *sideways* is the same as above explain'd, except that, instead of forwards, it is made sideways, which is the principal Difference; however, for the more easy comprehending of the same, I shall observe, that it begins from the fourth Position sideways to the right Side of the Room, the Face or Presence of the Body being to the upper End of the Room, the Weight upon the left Foot as before, with the right placed, as described by the Posture of Defence, or Step which introduces this Sort of Steps (c). The Weight is transferred, as before; and, in rising, the left Foot is taken from the Ground, but, instead of advancing up the Room, is now brought

---

(z) See the second Figure in Plate IX. only the right or advanced Foot is more open.
(a) See the first Figure in Plate IX. (b) See the first Figure in Plate IV. or second of Plate XI. For the second Step only more open, as has been said, see the first Figure in Plate IX. and for the last Step, see the second Figure in the same Plate. (c) See the second Figure in Plate X.

sideways

sideways into the third Position inclosed behind the right, and receives the Weight in Time to the Music (d). The second Step, with the right Foot, is sideways, the same Way, and receives the Body (e), which it supports, 'till the third or fourth Note is expired (f), according to the Time in which it is done, that is, whether it be of triple or common; upon which the last Step or *light Stamp* is made, the same Way crossing before the right (g), with the Knees bent in readiness to proceed to the *Chassee* following, which is performed in like Manner, but on the contrary Foot.

As we are now come to the *Chassee* of four Steps in a Measure, the foregoing of three having been described commencing with the left Foot, both *forwards sideways* and *to the right Hand*, I shall, on the contrary, explain this beginning with the right Foot, *to the left Hand*; but, in the first Place, I shall describe it, *advancing* up the Room, which is as follows: The Weight being upon the right Foot, the left advanced into the fourth Position (h), in the Method already explain'd, begins, as before, by transferring the Weight, but, as I have said, with the other Foot; for, as the *Chassee* of three in the Bar transferred the Weight from the left to the right, this does it from the right to the left, the right and hindmost Foot advancing into the third Position inclosed behind the left (i), directly the same Way as in that of three, except with this Difference, that as the first Note in that was counted in the rising and bringing of the Foot into the third Position, in this the two first Steps of the four must be performed swift to the first Note, as has been noted in the *Bouree* and *Bound*; and the second Note is in the stepping forwards of the third Step (j), only, as I have observed, a little open; upon which the Weight rests, 'till the third Note

---

(d) See the second Figure in Plate IV. or first Figure in Plate XI. (e) first upon the Toe and afterwards upon the Heel. See in some Measure the second Figure in Plate VI. and second Figure in Plate X. (f) See the Point or first Figure in Plate VI. (g) See the second Figure in Plate XI. (h) See the first Figure in Plate IX. (i) See the first Figure in Plate IV. or second of Plate XI. and, for the second Step which is made quick at the same Time, see the first Figure in Plate IX. (j) See the second Figure in Plate IX.

The Art of Dancing explain'd. 69

in triple Time is spent, or in common the fourth, in like Manner as, in the *Driving-Step* of three, it rested on the second, waiting for the Expiration of the third or fourth last Notes, at which Instant the Step or Preparative for the next ensuing is made, and concludes (k).

In performing the *Chaffee* of four Steps in a Measure, above explained *forwards*, *to the left Hand sideways*, the left Foot, instead of being advanced, is open sideways in the fourth Position, the like Distance to the left Hand, as in the *Point* or Beginning of a *March*, only the Heel and Foot are flat, as has been shewn, in the *Hop* or *Contretemp*, to this Side of the Room (l) and it commences by changing, as above, forwards, only the right Foot, instead of advancing as in that, moves sideways and is brought, in the rising behind the left, into the third Position (m), at which Instant the left Foot, which is the second of the four Steps, is stepp'd with a swift Motion, the same Way, and marks Time to the first Note (n). Note The second is in the stepping and crossing of the right Foot before the left (o), which is the third Step; and the third is in the setting of the left Heel down, in order to perform it again, as was illustrated by the Posture in *Fencing*, or in common Time upon the fourth as has been said (p).

This Step may also be performed with a quarter Turn, which only differs in this, that, after the Rise or Movement is made to the first two Steps that mark Time to the first Note, the third Step, which is with the right Foot, instead of crossing before the left, as before, in the stepping of it, turns a quarter Turn, which then faces full to the left Side of the Room to the Music as above; the fourth and last Step, which is with the left Foot, steps sideways to the left Hand, the same Way as the foregoing to the Presence, and, if continued one Step farther, the first two Steps face to the left Side

---

(k) See the first Figure in Plate IX. (l) See the first Figure in Plate X. (m) See the first Figure in Plate IV. or second Figure of Plate XI. (n) See in some Measure the first Figure in Plate VI. (o) See the second Figure in the same Plate, and first Figure in Plate XI. (p) See the first Figure in Plate X.

of the Room, as the foregoing did to the upper Part; and the third Step, in which you turn the quarter, instead of stepping to the left Side of the Room, now faces to the lower End of it; the fourth Step, with the left Foot, steps sideways to the same Hand, and so on, if you please, 'till arrived to the Presence as at first. It is to be noted, that this Step does not, in Continuance, change the Foot, as the *Chaffee* of three in the Measure, or *Bouree*, but always begins with the same Foot, as in the *Bouree with a Bound*.

There is another Way of performing this Step, of which I shall take some Notice, *viz.* two Movements and Steps to the Measure, that is to say, the *Chaffee* of three Steps in a Bar already explain'd, to which is added a Sort of a *Half Coupee*, in the Nature of a *Driving-Step*; which said Step is the fourth of the last described *Chaffee*, except that it is made plain here with a Movement or Rise from the fourth Position from whence it begun, and the released Foot opens in the Air, forming a quarter of a Circle, or a half Circle, &c.

As to the Performance of this *Chaffee* or *Driving Step* of two Movements, the most usual Way is forwards, turning a quarter, half, three quarter, or a whole Turn, the first of which is as follows, *viz.* beginning, as we will suppose, with the right Foot, upon which the Weight stands in the fourth Position, and the left advanced, but without any Weight (q), as has been said, except its own, commences by transferring the Weight in the same Manner as described in the *Chaffee* of four Steps with one Movement forwards to the upper Part of the Room; that is, the first two Steps, namely, with the right Foot and the left (r); but not the third Step with the right, for, altho' it steps a little open, as in the aforesaid, it does not receive any Weight, by reason it prepares for the *Half Coupee*, which is to be made in the Manner of the *Chaffee* before mentioned. This Step is made upon the second Note of the three, as was explained by the Posture in *Fencing*, only instead of *sideways*

(q) See the first Figure in Plate IX. (r) See the first Figure in Plate IV. For the second Step which is made quick at the same Time, see the first in Plate IX.

The A**RT** *of* D**ANCING** *explain'd.* 71

it is forwards (s); and, as was already shewn, the Knees being bent and Weight upon the left Foot, the *Half Coupee*, the second Movement of the *Chassee*, begins by conveying or transferring the Body from the left to the right and foremost Foot, immediately before rising, on which the left or hindmost Foot advances, sliding the Ball or Instep flat to the Ground into the third Position behind the right (t), which it releases; and, in its being taken up from the Floor, it makes a quarter of a Circle in the Air, opening to the right Side (u), facing the upper Part of the Room, or a quarter Turn to the right Side; or a half Turn to the Bottom, a three quarter Turn to the left Side, or a whole Turn; which said *Coupee* is performed to the third Note, if to triple Time; and in common to the fourth.

CHAP. XXII.
Of the CHASSEE, *or* DRIVING STEP *of two Movements or Bounding* COUPEES.

THIS Step is performed two different Ways, *viz. advancing* and *retiring*; the former of which begins by transferring the Weight resting on the right or left Leg in the fourth Position, and the latter by a Sway or Wave of the Poise of the Body, either on the right or left Leg from the second Position, which is the most usual Method of performing this Step; for, being in the second Position, and the Weight as much on one Foot as the other, it is only waving or swaying the Body, whether upon the right or left Foot, during the Sink, preparing for the *Chassee* or *Driving Step*, that is made by the disengaged and pointed Foot, whichsoever it be, al-

---
(s) See the second Figure in Plate IX. (t) See the second Figure in Plate IV.
(u) See the second Figure in Plates XIV and XV.

ways *retiring* to the right or left, or backwards. But, if it begin from the Weight resting on the right or left Foot, as *advancing* to make the *Contretemp*, *Chaffees*, or the like, it begins by changing, otherwise directly, without changing, being duly prepared; tho' in its Performance *advancing*, it much resembles the *Chaffee* to the left Hand, of oneMovement to four Steps, except that, instead of oneMovement made upon the Ground, here are two Movements or *Coupees* off from thence; and it is a Step frequently found in Tunes of common Time, not much unlike what we often see *Boys* perform in Play, when they run along, and, in rising from a Sink, knock or beat on eHeel against the other, lighting in the fourth Position, with the Knees bent, continuing the same, perhaps, the Length of a Stret or Field.

The *Driving Step* or *Chaffee* of two Movements or *Bounding Coupees* is usually perform'd sideways, tho' sometimes to one Part of the Room, and sometimes to another, as it falls out, which is according as the foregoing Step ended *to the right or left Sides*, *or upper or lower Ends* of the Room; for the better understanding whereof I shall give an Example of it to the left Hand, facing up the Room as follows, *viz.* the Weight of the Body being upon the right Foot, the left in the fourth Position sideways, as in the foregoing *Chaffee* or *Driving Step* of four Steps, to the same Side of the Room, the Knees bent (v), *&c.* it begins by transferring the Weight to the left Foot, as in that, only in the rising, instead of the right Foot's being brought behind the left in the third Position as in that upon the Ground, it is here made off from thence, in a sort of Springing or Bounding sideways, in which the right and commencing Foot, in a Manner, *drives* the left and second Step of the *Coupee* before it; for the Spring or Bound no sooner is given and the right Foot brought into the first Position even, or the third Position behind the left (w), than the left being at Liberty is *driven* the Length of a Step sideways (x) and then set down in the fourth

---

(v) See the first Figure in Plate X. (w) See the second Figure in Plate I. or first Figure in Plate IV. (x) See in some Measure the first Figure in Plate VI.

Posi-

Position, the Knees being bent, as in the Posture of *Defence*. This second Step concludes the first of the two Movements or *Coupees* (y), the Bound or Beginning of which is made upon the first of the four Notes, in that they are both counted as no more than one Step, as has been already shewn, not only in the *Bouree* and *Bound* but also in the *Chaffee* of four Steps; the second of the four Notes is reckoned in the Rest or Pause the Weight makes upon the Sink that prepares for the second Movement, *viz.* the third and fourth Steps, perform'd in the same Method as the first, by transferring the Weight, as aforesaid, and being made upon the third Note concludes the Step; and the fourth, as I have said, is in the Sink or Preparation for the succeeding Step, whether it be of the same, or any other Sort.

To perform this Step *to the right Hand* is only to transfer the Weight: For Example, instead of the Body's resting upon the right Foot, as before, it must be placed on the left, with the right disengaged from any Weight, except its own, as has been shewn by the foregoing (z); the rest intirely, in the like Manner, advancing sideways to the right Side of the Room, as the other to the left.

Having explained this Step *advancing*, I will proceed to its Method of *retiring*; and the Difference between this and the former principally consists in the Weight of the Body's not being changed on its beginning now, as in the foregoing; but instead thereof it directly commences from the fourth Position in which we stand: For Instance, suppose you would perform it *retiring*, the same Way we have described it *advancing*, *viz.* sideways to the left, then, instead of the Body's resting upon the right Foot, as in the aforesaid, it must now rest on the left, the right being in the fourth Position sideways flat to the Ground, without any other Weight than its own, except the Toe a little pointed or pressing to the Floor, from whence it begins.

However, before I proceed in that, I shall explain it *retiring* down the Room; which is from the same Position, only the right

---

(y) See the first Figure in Plate X. (z) See the second Figure in Plate XI.

Foot is advanced, and not sideways, as here; and because a *Beaten Coupee* or *Hop*, either forwards or sideways, generally introduces this Step, it may likewise not be improper to take some Notice of it, which I shall do, in the Explanation of the said Step's *advancing* up the Room, since that will be sufficient for the comprehending of it both Ways, in that the same Manner of Performance is to be observed in the one as in the other, only in the former the *Beat* is made sideways, instead of backwards, as in the present.

CHAP. XXIII.
Of the BEATEN COUPEE or HOP.

THE *Beaten Coupee* or *Hop* forwards, beginning from the first Position, the Weight of the Body being upon the left Foot (a), makes a Movement or Sink and Rise, as was shewn in the *Half Coupee* up the Room (b) and receives the Weight, as in that, upon the first Note, supporting the Body, whilst the left Foot *strikes* or *beats* against the Heel of the right (c), which *Beat* is upon the second Note; and then it steps back to the Place from whence it came, in order to receive the Weight again, which after the *Beat* retires off from the Foot upon which it was, in a slow Motion, waiting for the Expiration of the third Note; upon which it comes down on the left Foot, in the fourth Position, much in the swift Manner described in the Preparation for a *Hop* or *Chaffee* (d).

If you would perform this Step with a *Hop* you only need, instead of the Movement as above, make a *Spring* or *Hop* upon the left Foot, whilst the right advances, as was explained in the first Spring of the *Rigadoon Step* of two; but tho' the Weight there does

---

(a) See the first Figure in Plate I. (b) See in some Measure the second Figure in Plate IX. (c) See the second Figure in Plate V. (d) See the second Figure in Plate IX.

not come upon the advancing Foot, by Reason a second Spring is to be given first, here it must, as in the ending of a *March*, after which receiving of the Body the *Beat* is given, as above.

Having explained the *Beaten Coupee* or *Hop*, which conducts us to the Step we are treating of, and being in the Position from whence it is taken, that is to say, in the fourth, with the Weight upon the left Foot, and the right advanced, or more properly speaking, where it was left, in finishing of the *Beaten Hop* or *Coupee*; being I say in the fourth Position, with the Knees bent, the *Flying Chassee* or *Driving Step* of two Movements commences backwards, by bringing the right and foremost pointed Foot, in the Nature of a Spring or low Bound in rising from the Sink or Bending aforesaid into the third Position inclos'd before the left (e); which Bound or coming down of the right Foot marks Time to the first Note and relieves the left, which it drives backwards, the Length of a Step, receiving the Weight in the fourth Position (f), with the Knees bent as at commencing, upon which the first Movement is ended. The Bound and Step are both reckoned, on account of their Swiftness, but as one; and the second Movement is made to the third and fourth Steps, which are, in their Performance, intirely the same as the first. The second Note is in the Bending of the Knees, after finishing of the first Spring or *Coupee*; the third in the Bound upon the right Foot, which begins the second Movement; and the fourth is in the Bending of the Knees, as aforesaid.

As the Method, in which this Step is perform'd *retiring*, is now shewn, I shall return to the Place where I left off, and proceed in explaining it, as retiring sideways to the left Side of the Room and conclude what I shall farther say, on that Head; and first of all it must be noted, that it is the Reverse to the foregoing *advancing*, for as in that the Foot, on which the Body rests at beginning, *pursues* or *drives* before it the Foot without Weight, in this the disengaged Foot *drives* or *pursues* the *retiring* Foot that supports the Body, much like *retiring* in *Fencing*, as the first explain'd is a Sort

---

(e) See the second Figure of Plate IV. (f) See the second Figure of Plate IX.

76   *The* ART *of* DANCING *explain'd.*

of *advancing*, which I think plainly appears from what has been said in the Description of them.

The latter of the said Steps being now fully described, it only remains to add that, instead of backwards, it must be made *retiring* directly sideways, crossing the Room to the left Hand, in the same Manner as *retiring* down it, which is all the Difference; and consequently it is unnecessary to make a farther Repetition, except that, as where I left off (g), it commences from the fourth Position; and if perform'd *retiring* cross the Room to the right Side, it is taken from the same Position as when *advancing* to the left, only as I have observed, it begins without transferring the Weight; but, when taken from the second Position, it is only swaying or waving the Body to the Side you would perform it, whether right or left.

It is to be noted, that the foregoing *Chaffee* or *Driving Step* of two springing Movements, when perform'd in triple Time, must have a *Springing Coupee* more added to fill up the Bar or Measure; or instead thereof a *Close*, which is nothing more than that instead of finishing the additional *Coupee*, or in the Bound's lighting upon one Foot, as in that I described, it comes down upon both Feet, at the same Time, to the third Note in triple Time, compleating the Measure, as if the *Coupee* had been finished. Examples of the latter are to be found in the *Chaconne de Phaeton* of Monsieur *Pecour*, twenty Bars before the End; and the foregoing of two *Springs* and a *Close* is to be met with in the *Paffacaille de Scilla* by the same Master, twenty seven Measures before the End, and in Tunes of common Time, as *Allemaignes*, *Rigadoons*, *Bourees*, &c. but, instead of the *Chaffee* or *Driving Step* of two *Springs*, we frequently meet with one of them put with the aforesaid *Close* to a Measure (h).

(g) See in some Measure the second Figure in Plate VI.   (h) See the Table of this Step in the Plate of Tables mark'd I.

CHAP.

CHAP. XXIV.
Of the CHASSEE or DRIVING STEP, of three Springs in the same Place, from the third Position.

THIS *Chassee* or *Driving Step* differs from the aforesaid, in its not being taken from the fourth Position, but from the third, in which Position as an Example we shall describe it, beginning with the right Foot, as follows, viz. the Weight is upon the left Foot, and the right in the third Position behind, being at Liberty (i), commences by bending both Knees, and at the same Time preparing for the *Close* or *Drive*, which is accomplished in the Straightening of the right Knee directly sideways (j), in the Rise or Spring from the Sinking aforesaid; in which it is brought into the third Position before the left on which the Body rests (k), and *drives* the left off sideways, or rather obliquely, in the Air (l), the Length of a Step. The said *Spring* or *Drive* with the right Foot marks Time to the first Note of the three in a Measure or triple Time; and the second is in the *Spring* or *Drive* with the left Foot now in the Air, which together with the right Knee that supports the Body bends, in order for the second Spring, which is made in a Rise from the same by a Spring or Bound into the third Position behind; then it releases the right by receiving the Weight (m) and *drives* the right Foot sideways into the Air, the Length of a Step (n), from whence the third *Drive* or *Close* is made to the same Note,

---

(i) See the first Figure in Plate V. (j) See the second Figure in Plate XV, or second Figure in Plate VI, only the Toe does not touch the Floor. (k) See the second Figure in Plate IV. (l) See the first Figure in Plate VI, only the Foot is in the Air. (m) See the second Figure in Plate IV. (n) See the second Figure in Plate XV.

by bending both Knees, as before; and, in the Spring or Rising from thence, the right Foot in the Air *bounds* into the third Position before the left † which it releases, tho' it is not *driven*, as in the others, but instead thereof remains in the third Position behind the right on which the whole Weight rests, concluding the Step on the contrary Foot (o), in Readiness to perform the same Step over again, and commencing with the left Foot.

The second Strain of the *Louvre* begins with this Step, the last Time of its playing over, with the same Foot as here, that is to say, on the *Man's* Side, but with the contrary on the *Woman's*; and in the *Dance* it is performed facing to the right Side of the Room or *Lady*, and not to the upper End of it, as here described.

In triple Time this Step transfers the Weight and Foot, every Measure as in the *Half Coupee, March,* or *Bouree*; but, when done to Tunes of common Time, instead of three *Drives* or *Springs* in a Measure, as in triple aforesaid, there must be only two; and consequently, if continued, they will always commence with the same Foot as the *Bouree* and a *Bound*, or *Coupee, &c.* unless Steps of a contrary Nature, as the *Bouree, Half Coupee,* or *March* be made between them.

The *Driving Step* of two Springs agrees with the Notes of common Time, in the same Manner as was described in the *Flying* or *Driving Step* of two Movements; and it makes no small Figure, either in common or triple Time, since in the latter it is rare to meet with a *Paffacaille*, or *Chaconne*, without it; but, on the contrary it is sometimes found in three or four Places of one *Dance*, which demonstrates, how greatly it is valued and esteemed by *Masters* (p).

---

† See the second Figure in Plate IV.   (o) See the second Figure in Plate V.
(p) See the Table of this Step in the Plate of Tables mark'd I.

CHAP. XXV.

Of the FLYING CHASSEE or DRIVING STEP backwards, with a CLOSE and COUPEE to a Measure

THE Step, which I am now about to explain, begins from the fourth Position, as well as the *Hop* or *Chassee*; but, before I proceed, it must be observed, that it is composed of three different Steps, and commences with the first Movement of the *Flying Chassee* or *Driving Step* retiring down the Room exactly in the same Manner as was explained, in treating of that Step †, ending in the fourth Position to the first Note, the Weight being upon the left Foot, and the right advanced, or rather, as I have said, left without Weight, in Readiness to begin the second Movement of the said Step (q); which Movement is made upon the second Note of the *Saraband* or *Passacaille*, to which it is done by making a *Close* from the Position above mentioned, in rising from the Sink or Bending of the Knees in which the *Chassee* to the first Note ended; which *Spring* or *Close* is made, in turning a quarter Turn to the right Side of the Room, from the upper Part thereof, into the third Position, by taking up the right or advanced Foot, at the Instant the *Close* is made upon the left, before which the right is inclosed (r). The third Note is in the *Coupee*, which is the third Movement and concludes the Step; and the said *Coupee*, which must be performed swift to the last Note, commences, by the right

---

† See Page 75. (q) See the second Figure in Plate IX. (r) See the second Figure in Plate IV, only it must be supposed facing to the right Side of the Room.

or inclosed Foot's making a Movement or Sink and Rise, stepping open off sideways to the right Hand (s), facing, as aforesaid, to the right Side of the Room, rather inclining backwards than directly sideways, by Reason of its making Way for the left or hind Foot's more easy and natural crossing before the right sideways into the fifth Position, in the Method shewn in treating of the *Slip before and then behind*, ending, as I have said, upon the third Note, with the Knees bent preparing for the following Step, which most usually is a *Half Coupee* (t); and it begins by taking of the right or hind Foot up, in rising from the aforesaid Bending of the Knees, which is brought behind the left into the third Position (u), turning a quarter Turn back again, from the right Side of the Room to the upper End, upon the first Note of the Measure. The second and third Notes are in the half Circle or Motion the left Foot makes in the Air, in its being taken from the Floor, (v) which, as I have said, is upon the right Foot's receiving the Weight in the Rise from the first Step; and the left Foot, being in the Air, is ready to perform a *Pirouette*, or any such like Step.

If, instead of the right Side of the Room, you would perform it to the other Hand, the left Foot must be in the fourth Position advanced before the right on which the Body rests, in like Manner as the right was before, without any Weight except its own (w), from whence it commences to the left Side of the Room, directly as the foregoing to the right; and the Step here treated on is to be found in the *Passacaille Darmid* for a *Woman*, composed by Monsieur *L'Abbee*, in the sixth Measure, beginning with the right Foot, as above explained (x).

(s) See in some Respects the second Figure in Plate VI, only it must be supposed to be facing as aforesaid on the right Side of the Room. (t) See the second Figure in Plate XI. and it also must be facing as aforesaid. (u) See the first Figure in Plate IV. (v) See the first Figure in Plate XV. (w) See the first Figure in Plate IX. (x) See the Table of this Step in the Plate of Tables marked I.

CHAP.

The ART *of* DANCING *explain'd.* 81

CHAP. XXVI.

Of the HOP *of two Movements, from the fifth Position round in two half Turns.*

THIS Step is much used in *Stage Dancing*, to which, indeed it properly belongs, as well as the foregoing; but as there are *Ladies*, who frequently arrive at such a Perfection as to be capable of performing this Sort of Steps, it may not be improper here to give an Explanation of some of the most remarkable of them, of which Number that under Consideration is one; which is often found in Tunes of triple Time, and sometimes in those of common, consisting of two Movements, *viz.* a *Hop* and a *Bound* both made in turning, the first commencing either from the fourth or fifth Position; from which last we shall explain it, beginning with the right Foot that supports the Body, as in the *Chaffee* or *Driving Step*, only the left, instead of being either open sideways or advanced in the fourth Position, from whence the aforesaid Steps are taken, must be a little more crossed, that is to say, the left Heel towards the Toe of the right Foot, without the least Weight bearing upon it, by Reason the Step begins by transferring the Weight (y), which is accomplished in this Manner: The Body, as has been observed, being on the right Foot, immediately before the *Hop* or first Movement is made, is conveyed upon the left and foremost Foot, by transferring the Weight, upon which the *Hop* is given on the left Foot, in the right's being taken up from the Ground turning a half Turn from the upper Part of the Room to the lower End thereof, to the right Hand, making a half Circle in the Air the same Way behind the left Foot where it arrives. At the same

---

(y.) See the second Figure in Plate XI.

L Instant,

Inftant, the Hop is made upon the firft Note of the Meafure; the fecond is in fetting down the faid right Foot in the fourth Pofition advanced before the left, on which the Weight refts, in its being brought from behind the left Foot, where it mark'd the firft Note (z). The third Note is in the coming down of the *Bound*, which is made, as aforefaid, in transferring the Weight from the left to the right, the very Moment before the *Spring* or *Bound* is made, by rifing from the Sink or Bending of the Knees, which was on the fetting down of the right Foot to the fecond Note, and bringing the left Foot on which the Body refted in a low *Bound* or *Spring* into the third Pofition behind the right; which being then releafed makes the remaining half Circle in the Air, by turning a half Turn more to the fame Hand, as in the *Hop* or firft Movement from the lower End of the Room to the upper Part, and finifhes the Step with the right Foot in the Air fideways (a). To perform the fame Step with the other Foot, we are only to fet down the right Foot into the fifth Pofition before the left, on which the whole Weight refts, which begins, as aforefaid, by transferring the Weight (b); and the *Hop* turns a half Turn to the left, exactly as the foregoing was defcribed to the right (c), &c. This Step is to the third Meafure of the *Paffacaille Diana*, beginning with the fame Foot, as above defcribed (d).

(z) See the firft Figure in Plate XII. (a) See the fecond Figure in Plate XV.
(b) See the firft Figure in Plate XI. (c) See the fecond Figure in Plate XII.
concluding &c. as in the firft Figure of Plate XV.   (d) See the Tables of this Step in
the Plate of Tables mark'd I.

The Art *of* Dancing *explain'd.* 83

CHAP. XXVII.
Of the *CHACONNE* or *PASSACAILLE STEP.*

THE *Chaconne* or *Passacaille Step* is composed of three Movements, *viz.* first a *Bound,* secondly a *Hop,* and lastly a *Bound,* or *Balone,* and it is most usually taken from the third Position. I shall, as an Example, describe it commencing with the left Foot which in its Performance is as follows; that is to say, the left Foot disengaged and at Liberty behind the right, in the Position aforesaid (e), begins the first Movement by making a *Bound,* in the Manner already shewn in treating of that Step, which, as I have there said, is accomplished by a Sink or Bending of the Knees; from whence the Body is thrown into the Air, in the Spring from the Sink or Bending aforesaid, only turning a half Turn to the right Hand, and comes down upon the Toe of the left Foot to the first Note; at which Instant the right, on which the Weight rested before the Change was made, follows or rather attends the left Foot, in the same swift Manner as explained in the *Bouree* and a *Bound,* remaining behind the left up in the Air, in order to perform the Movement that next succeeds, facing to the lower End of the Room (f); from which Posture the *Hop* or second Movement is taken, and marks the second Note, by sinking and making a *Spring* or *Hop* upon the left Foot which supports the Body, turning half a Turn to the right Hand, from the Bottom to the upper Part of the Room. The right Foot, which at the End of the *Bound* was behind the left, about the Length of a Step in the Air, is now the like Distance before it (g), ready to make the *Bound*

(e) See the second Figure in Plate V. (f) See the second Figure in Plate XIII.
(g) See the second Figure in Plate XIV.

or

or *Balone*, as the *French* call it, to the third Note of the Measure, which is in bending both Knees; and, in springing from thence, the Weight is transferred from the left Foot, and lights upon the Instep or Toe of the right which was in the Air, concluding in the third Position, as at commencing (h).

This Step, if continued, always begins with the same Foot, as the *Coupee* or *Bouree with a Bound*; and to perform it with the contrary Foot only differs in this, that, instead of being in the third Position just described, the Weight must be upon the left Foot, with the right at Liberty behind (i); and, instead of turning to the right Hand, it now turns to the left, beginning with the right Foot, &c. (j) as the foregoing with the left.

This Step, as above explained, is to the fifth Measure of the *Passacaille Diana* aforesaid, and also in the same Measure of the *Passacaille de Scilla* mentioned before, commencing with the right Foot; and it is a most agreeable Step in *Dancing*, rarely missing to be found more than once in one of these Sorts of *Dances* (k).

CHAP. XXVIII.
Of the HOP and two CHASSEES or DRIVES round in the same Place.

THE *Hop* and two *Drives* or *Chassees* is likewise a Step composed of three Movements, as the Title above specifies, and is performed from the fourth Position, in the Manner described in the foregoing *Hop* of two Movements from the fifth Position; which

---

(h) See the second Figure in Plate V.   (i) See the first Figure in Plate V.
(j) See the first Figure in Plate XIII. the first in Plate XIV. and the first in Plate V.
(k) See the Table of this Step in the Plate of Tables mark'd I, and also the List or Explanation.

The Art of Dancing explain'd. 85

said Step begins by transferring the Weight in the like Method as the present. Having explained the former, beginning with the right Foot, I shall explain this with the contrary, and it is performed as follows, viz. the Weight being upon the left Foot, the right in the fourth Position advanced and at Liberty is prepared to receive the Body (l); which it does, the very Instant before the *Hop* or first Movement is made to the first Note, and from thence, I say, begins by sinking or bending of the Knees, in order for the following *Spring* or *Hop*, which is made upon the right Foot, in the left's being taken up from the Floor, and marks Time to the first Note, as was before observed, turning a half Turn from the upper End of the Room to the left Hand and leaving the left Foot without Weight, in the third Position behind the right, facing the lower End (m); from whence the first of the two *Drives* begins in bending of the Knees, as already shewn in the *Chaffee* or *Driving Step* of three Movements, upon the same Place, in Preparation for the *Spring* or *Bound* made in straightening of the Knees, turning a quarter Turn farther to the left Hand, facing full to the right Side of the Room, and lighting upon the left Foot, on its being brought into the third Position before the right, which is *drove* by it backwards, the Length of a Step in the Air; which said coming down of the left Foot is to the second Note, and the third is in the *Spring* or *Bound* made upon the right; and, in the Rise or Spring from the sinking or bending of the Knees, as aforesaid, the right Foot advances into the third Position behind the left, which being then released is *drove*, the Length of a Step in the Air, turning a quarter Turn more, opening to the left from the right Side of the Room to the upper End, and concluding in the Air (n).

To perform this Step with the other Foot only differs in this, that, instead of the right Foot, the left Foot must be advanced (o)

(l). See the second Figure in Plate IX. (m) See the first Figure in Plate XIII, only the left Foot, instead of being in the Air, must be supposed to rest against the Heel of the right. (n) See the first Figure in Plate XV. (o) See the first Figure in Plate IX.

and,

and, instead of turning the half Turn to the left Hand, as before described, it turns to the right, directly in the same Manner as the aforesaid (p); Examples of both which are to be found in the *Chaconne de Phaeton* of Monsieur *Pecours*, in the eighty seventh Measure beginning with the right Foot, and in the ninety first of the same *Dance* with the left, as above described (q).

CHAP. XXIX.

Of the FALL, SPRING *with both Feet at the same Time, and* COUPEE *to a Measure.*

THE foregoing Step, ending in the Air with the left Foot, naturally introduces us to the present, which is of three Movements, and taken from thence in *falling, springing* with both Feet at the same Time, and a *Coupee*; all which Steps are to be performed to a Measure, and consequently accounted but as one Step, which, in its Performance, is as follows, *viz.* the Face or Presence of the Body being, as in the foregoing, supposed with the Weight upon the right Foot (r), the Step begins by falling much in the same Manner, as explained in treating of this Step, when introduced by the *Galliard* sideways to the right Hand, only this is backwards in a slow and easy Motion, the very same as if you intended to fall quite to the Floor; but, as I said before, it is prevented from that by the left Foot which is in the Air, with the Toe pointed towards the Ground, attending and watching the falling Body so narrowly that, the very Instant it is in a manner past Recovery,

---

(p) See the second Figure as aforesaid in Plate XIII, and the second Figure of Plate XV. (q) See the Table of this Step in the Plate of Tables marked I. and also the List or Explanation. (r) See the first Figure in Plate XV, or first Figure of Plate XIV.

it

The ART *of* DANCING *explain'd.* 87

it flies swift to its Relief, to save it from falling, by receiving half the Weight in the fourth Position behind the right Foot (s), with the Knees bent upon the first Note; from whence the Spring is immediately made with both Feet, acting at the same Juncture upon the second Note, that is, by changing the right Foot backwards and the left forwards (t), the Knees being bent, as aforesaid, in Readiness to make the succeeding *Coupee;* which is done by taking up the left or foremost Foot from the Floor and from the Bending aforesaid rising upon the Toe or Instep, making an open Step to the left Side of the Room to the third Note, neither directly sideways nor forwards, but between both. The second Step of the *Coupee,* which is with the right Foot, follows it, stepping the same Way in the like swift Manner, as the Beginning of the *Bouree with a Bound,* into the fourth Position before the left (u), with the Knees bent as above.

In order to make the *Half Coupee,* that usually follows this Step, which is very slow in that, of itself, it answers to a Bar, like the foregoing of three Movements, upon the Weight's being changed, the left Foot, which before supported the Body, being at Liberty, advances, in rising from the Sink or Bending aforesaid into the third Position behind the right (v), which then is released, and makes a Circle in the Air to the second and third Notes, the first being upon the left's receiving of the Weight as aforesaid; and the *Half Coupee,* concluding thus with the right Foot in the Air, is ready to perform either a *Pirouette,* or the same Step over again with the contrary Foot (w); which only differs from the foregoing, in its beginning with the right Foot, and is found in the *Passacaille de Scilla,* twelve Bars before the End, beginning with the last mentioned Foot, and in other Places of the same *Dance* (x).

(s) See the second Figure in Plate IX, only the Weight must be equally upon one Foot as the other.   (t) See the first Figure in Plate IX.   (u) See the second Figure in Plate IX.   (v) See the second Figure in Plate IV.   (w) See the second Figure in Plate XV.   (x) See the Table of this Step in the Plate of Tables marked I, and also the List or Explanation.

CHAP

CHAP XXX.

Of the CLOSE beating before and falling behind in the third Position, upright Spring changing to the same before, and COUPEE to a Measure.

THE *Close beating before &c.* which we are now about to explain, differs from the before described Step of this Name, in its being done to the first Note of the Measure, and, instead of resting the remaining two Notes, as in the aforesaid to the second, there are the *upright Spring* and *Coupee* to the third; and, instead of the *Close*'s ending either in the first or third Position with the Knees straight, as in the former, it here comes down behind with the Knees bent, after its beating before. This Step is to be performed as follows, *viz.* commencing either with the right or left Foot from the third Position (y), by sinking or bending not only the foremost Foot on which the Body rests, but likewise the hind Foot without Weight; or from thence it begins, by making the *Close* in the like Manner, as aforesaid, in treating of this Step in the Rise or Spring from the above named Sink; but, instead of the *Close*'s lighting in the first or third Position, as in the foregoing, the beginning Leg beats before against that on which the Body rested at first (z), and comes down in the third Position, as at commencing, only the Weight is equally upon both Feet (a), and the Knees are bent, marking the first Note. The second, as I have observed,

---

(y) See the first and second Figures in Plate V. Feet of the first and second Figures in Plate IV. said Figures in Plate IV.
(z) See the first or inclosed (a) See the hind Feet of the two

The ART of DANCING *explain'd.* 89

is in coming down after the Rife or *upright Spring* from thence into the Air, in which the Feet are changed, *viz.* the firſt laſt and the laſt firſt (b), the Knees being bent, as aforeſaid, upon the firſt Note in Preparation to make the following *Coupee*, which is ſwift upon the third and laſt Note of the Meaſure, whether of a *Saraband* or *Paſſacaille, &c.* by riſing in the Step the firſt Foot makes forwards, opening either to the right or left Hand and receiving the Weight (c); after which the hind Foot and ſecond Step of the *Coupee* move ſwift, the ſame Way, into the fourth Poſition before (d) it, with the Knees bent, concluding in Readineſs for the *Coupee* that uſually attends theſe Steps; which is, as I have ſaid, in the laſt deſcribed Step, as exceeding ſlow as the foregoing or its Introducer was quick, and made in riſing from the aforeſaid after transferring the Weight, and bringing the hind Foot into the third Poſition behind the foremoſt (e), which being releaſed makes a Circle in the Air, as aforeſaid, either to the right or left Hand, according to which Foot the Step begun with (f), and is ready to perform the Step over again with the contrary Foot to that with which you commence.

You are to take Notice, that theſe two Steps are in a Manner inſeparable, as I have already obſerved of ſome others in the Beginning of this Diſcourſe, and are to the laſt Meaſure excepting two and a half of the *Spaniſh Entree* for *two Men*, compoſed by Monſieur *Pecour*, belonging to the *Opera de l' Europ Galante*; and alſo in the *Entree Eſpagnole* for a *Man* and a *Woman*, in the aforeſaid *Opera*, compoſed by the ſame Maſter (g).

The above deſcribed Step is ſometimes performed, turning a whole Turn round, that is to ſay, half a Turn upon the *Cloſe* beating before and coming down behind in the third Poſition, the o-

---

(b) See the Change in the firſt and ſecond and ſecond and firſt Figures in Plate IV.
(c) See the two firſt or advanced Feet in the Figures of Plate IX. (d) See the right or advanced Foot in the ſecond Figure of Plate IX, and the left or advanced Foot of the firſt Figure in the ſame Plate. (e) See the ſecond and firſt Figures in Plate IV.
(f) See the Figures in Plate XV. (g) See the twenty firſt Table in the Plate of Tables marked I, and the Liſt or Explanation of the ſaid Table.

ther half being in the *upright Spring*; and instead of the *Beat*'s being made against the Foot on which the Weight rested, when facing the upper End of the Room, it is here made to the lower Part in a half Turn, either to the right or left Hand, lighting in the third Position behind; from whence the *upright Spring* is taken, in rising or springing from the Floor, as aforesaid, only, instead of the Feet being changed facing the Bottom of the Room, the remaining half Turn is made to the same Hand up it: For Example, suppose it commences with the right Foot from behind (h), then the Turn must be to the left, the *Close* ending to the lower End in the third Position, with the right Foot behind (i); but, in the half Turn belonging to the *upright Spring*, it is changed in the Air, and comes down in the third Position before the left, on which the Body rested at first (j).

The *Coupee* is intirely the same, as described in the foregoing, beginning from the first or inclosed Foot; and, if with the left Foot, it begins in the same Manner, by making a *Spring* or *Close*, &c. turning to the right, as above (k).

CHAP. XXXI.
Of the PIROUETTE.

THE *Pirouette* is a Step that altogether consists of Motion and Turning. There are two different Ways of performing it; either from a whole Position, the Weight resting on both Feet; or a half Position, when the Weight only rests upon one Foot, the other being in the Air, from whence it begins, as will appear: For

---

(h) See the first Figure in Plate V.   (i) See the first Figure in Plate IV. and for the Beat before see the second Figure in the same Plate, only the Feet must be supposed in the third Position down the Room.   (j) See the second Figure in Plate IV.
(k) See the twenty second Table in the Plate of Tables mark'd E and the List or Explanation of the said Table.

instead

The Art of Dancing explain'd.

instead of performing it from the fifth Position, directly as we stand, as in the former, in the latter it is made by adding a Step with the Foot in the Air backwards into the abovementioned Position behind, from whence they turn equally alike to either Hand upon the same Place, the Weight of the Body resting mostly upon that Foot which at first supported the Weight, the Difference being only in the stepping of the Foot which may as well be made forwards as backwards.

I shall now proceed to explain the Method of performing this Step, both these Ways, beginning in the first Place with the whole Position, which is as follows, *viz.* being, as was already observed, in the fifth Position, that is to say, when the Heel of either the right or left Foot, instead of being advanced right forwards, as in the fourth Position, is, as I have before shewn in the *Hop* of two Movements, round in two half Turns from the Position now treated on, and about the Length of half a Foot more cross'd before the hindmost Foot; so as that the Heel of the first in a Manner touches the Toe of the hind Foot, the Weight of the Body bearing as much upon one Foot, as the other, instead of the whole Weight's being upon the Foot which is behind, as in the *Hop* of two Movements (l).

Having shewn the Position or Posture of standing, from whence this Step is taken, I will continue its Explanation, turning to either Side of the Room; and it is no more than making a Sink or Bending of the Knees in the above explain'd Position, the Rise whereof is made upon both Insteps to the first Note, in binding or pressing them strong to the Floor and raising the Body into the Air, during the Turning or Measure to which it is made: For Instance, if to the right, the left Foot is foremost (m), if to the left the right (n) From the last of these we shall describe it, as follows: The Sink and Rise being made, as aforesaid, to the first Note, the second and third, if to triple Time, are in the slow Turning of the quarter Turn, which is to the left Side of the Room, in which

---

(l) See the first and second Figures of Plate XI. (m) See the second Figure in Plate XI. (n) See the first Figure in the same Plate.

the Feet are changed; namely, the right, which at commencing was firſt, is now laſt, and the left firſt, facing full the Side of the Room to which the Turn was made; and, if a half Turn, it is only adding a quarter Turn more, which then will be full to the Bottom of the Room; and, if a three quarter Turn, it continues on to the right Side of the Room a quarter Turn further.

It is alſo to be obſerved, that, if a quarter Turn be to a Meaſure, the ſecond and third Notes are counted, during the Turning or *Pirouette*; the ſame, if a half or three quarter Turn; or, if to common Time, the ſame as already ſhewn in many Places of this Diſcourſe. And, if it be a whole Turn, it is intirely the like in Relation to the Notes, but not in its Method of Performance; for, inſtead of the Body's bearing equally upon both Toes, as above, it now bears, in riſing from the Sink or Preparative for the whole Turn, upon the Heel of one Foot and Toe of the other: For Inſtance, in the riſing, as aforeſaid, or marking the Time, the Weight bears half upon the Heel of the right or foremoſt Foot and the Toe of the Foot that is behind, in which Manner it turns to the left, as before, as far as the Bottom or lower End of the Room; at which Time the Toe of the fore Foot and Heel of the hind come to the Floor, continuing the Turn, 'till you arrive to the upper End of the Room or Place of ſetting out, and finiſh in a Readineſs to perform the ſame to the other Hand if Occaſion requires, by Reaſon of the Feet being changed, as I have ſaid, in the middle of the Turn or ſetting down the Heel of the hind Foot and Toe of the foremoſt (o). Both the Ways of performing this Step, as above explained, turning a whole Round, are to be found in the fourth Bar of the *Saraband* belonging the *Royal Galiard*, compoſed by the late Mr. *Iſaac*, and written by Mr. *De la Gard*, the ſecond Time of its playing; the foregoing three quarter Turn, in the ſhort *Saraband* for a *Man*, compoſed by Mr. *Pecour*, in his Collection of *Dances* publiſhed at *Paris*, in the Year 1704, by

---

(o) See the contrary Figures in Plate XI; that is to ſay, for the firſt ſee the ſecond, and for the ſecond ſee the firſt Figure.

Mr.

The Art *of* Dancing *explain'd.* 93

Mr. *Feuillet*, the thirteenth and fifteenth Bars before the End of the said *Dance*; and the quarter and half Turns are to be met with in most *Dances* (p). I shall now proceed to describe the second Way in which this *Pirouette* is taken and performed, *viz.* from a half Position instead of a whole, as was, for Example, the foregoing; that is to say, when the Weight of the Body is either upon the right or left Foot, and the other open in the Air pointed sideways, as in the *March*, or about an Inch or two more forwards, only it does not touch the Floor, as in that, by Reason of its being the commencing Foot; from whence it begins, by making a Step backwards into the fourth Position, if it be a quarter or half Turn; but, if a three quarter or whole Turn, it must be made into the fifth, as aforesaid, all of which are performed directly in the same Manner, as the foregoing or whole Position, by dividing the Weight, at the End of the stepping backwards of the Foot that was in the Air, which, upon setting it to the Ground, receives so much of the Weight as only serves to direct and assist the Body in turning, as well as marking the Time, as aforesaid, in rising from the Sink made for that Purpose, on the stepping of the Foot backwards upon both Toes, and turning either to the right or left Hand, which is according to the Foot that is in the Air, for the Turn must be made to the same Side; for Example, if the right Foot be in the Air, the Turn is to that Side (q); and if the left, it is to the left (r).

Having explained the foregoing or whole Position, turning to the left Hand, the taking some Notice of it to the right may not be improper, in this Place, beginning with the quarter Turn: For Instance, the Weight being upon the half Position or left Foot, the right, extended as aforesaid (s), begins in making a Sink or Bending of the Knee of the left Leg on which the Body rests; at which Instant the right is cast back, as was said above, into the

---

(p) See the twenty fourth Table in the Plate of Tables mark'd I. and also the List or Explanation of the said Table. (q) See the second Figure in Plate XV. (r) See the first Figure in Plate XV. (s) See the second Figure in the same Plate.

fourth

fourth Poſition behind the left (t), and preparing for the Riſe marks the firſt Note, which is made on ſetting down or receiving a Part of the Poiſe of the Body upon the Foot that was in the Air; from whence the Turn takes its Riſe, turning in a ſlow and gentle Turn to the right Side of the Room, and bearing or preſſing the Toes to the Floor, as we have already ſhewn in the foregoing, in which Turning the ſecond and third Notes are ſpent; that is to ſay, the ſecond Note is counted in changing of the Feet, which is in the Turning, as I have ſaid, for the right Foot, which was in the fourth Poſition behind, is about the ſecond Note in the ſame Poſition before the left, facing full the right Side of the Room; and the third Note is upon ſetting down the Heel of the left Foot, and taking up the right, which is extended open ſideways, as at firſt, and concludes.

A *Pirouette* with a half or three quarter Turn only differs from the *Pirouette* juſt explained, in not ending to the right Side as in that; but, inſtead thereof, the half Turn finiſhes to the lower Part of the Room, half a Turn from the upper End (u). And the three quarter Turn continues on, 'till it face full the left Side; but the whole Turn, as I have ſaid in the *Pirouette*, beginning from a whole or half Poſition, on which the Weight is equally divided, inſtead of riſing upon both Toes alike, at the End of the Step made with the right Foot, by ſinking and ſtepping backwards, as before obſerved, into the fifth Poſition behind the left Foot (v), in the Riſe or Beginning of the Turn the right Toe or Inſtep, being ſet down to the Ground in the Poſition juſt mentioned, receives one half of the Weight, the other remaining upon the Heel of the left on which the Body reſted at firſt. In the ſaid Manner half the Turn is made to the Bottom of the Room, bearing equally upon the Heel and Toe; and, when it arrives there, the remaining half is continued, by putting down the right Heel and Toe of the left Foot, which at firſt begun upon the

---

(t) See the firſt Figure in Plate IX. the ſecond Figure in Plate XI.   (u) See the firſt Figure in Plate XII.   (v) See

Heel

The ART *of* DANCING *explain'd.* 95

Heel, as the right did upon the Toe, about which Time the Feet are changed, as we have observed; that is, the right, which was stepp'd or cast into the fifth Position behind, is now first, and the left last, concluding with both Feet flat on the Floor, the Presence of the Body being to the upper End of the Room, as at commencing (w).

As to the Agreement of this Step with the Notes of common or triple Time, it is the same as already explained in the *Pirouette* beginning from the whole Position; the only Difference is, that the Weight in that, being equally on both Feet, begins directly by making a Sink and Rise, the Rise of which beats Time to the first Note of the Tune, which is the same in this Step, except that the Body, being supported by a half Position, before it can begin as in the whole Position, the other Foot which is in the Air must be cast or set down in the fourth or fifth Position; from whence this Step is usually taken, in stepping either forwards or backwards, as the Step is to be made. The remaining second and third Notes of the Measure, if to triple Time, are counted, during the said Turning, a whole Round; or, if to common Time, the fourth is included, as has been observed.

This Step, in its Performance *forwards*, is in all Respects the same as the last described *backwards*, as to its Agreement with the Notes, or its Rising, Turning on the Toes, &c. only whereas, in the two foregoing *Pirouettes*, the Manner of performing the whole Turn is not the same as the quarter, half, or three quarter Turn, in this the whole Turn is done in the same Method as the rest, except that the Step is made *forwards* into the fourth or fifth Position, instead of *backwards* as in the last explained; and, as I have already observed in the foregoing Steps, if the Turn be only a quarter or half Turn, it commences from the fourth Position (x), but if a three

---

(w) See the first Figure in Plate XI. And, if beginning with the left Foot, see the first Figure in Plate XV, and the first and second Figures in Plate XI. (x) See the second Figure in Plate IX, beginning from the second Figure in Plate XV. And, if with the contrary, see the first Figure in Plate XV, and the first Figure in Plate IX.

quarte

quarter or whole Turn the fifth (y). This Step *forwards* farther varies from the foregoing *backwards*, in that, altho' it commences with the same Foot, instead of turning to the right Hand, as in the former, in this it turns to the left, as in the whole Position; so that, comparing this with the *Pirouette* first described, it will be easily understood, in that it is the same, except in not beginning directly, as in that; but if you suppose the stepping of the Foot *forwards* to be made, and place your Feet in the fourth or fifth Position, as before observed from a whole Position, there is then no other Difference, except that the whole Turn is performed in the same Method as the other (z).

CHAP. XXXII.
Of the PIROUETTE introduced by a COUPEE.

THIS Step is taken from a half Position, as well as the two last described *backwards* and *forwards* ; but, instead of the Foot's being extended sideways in the Air, as in them, the Toe must here be pointed to the Floor, as in the Point or Beginning of the *March*, from which Position it commences.

However, before I proceed to a farther Explanation of this Step, I shall take some Notice of the *Coupee* that introduces it, which is composed of a *Half Coupee* with one Foot and a circular Motion made in the Air with the other, before its making the Point; which Step may be performed as follows, beginning with either

---

(y) See the first Figure in Plate XI, commencing from the second Figure in Plate XV; and, if with the other Foot, see the first Figure in the aforesaid Plate XV, and it concludes in the second Figure of the aforesaid Plate XI. (z) See the twenty fifth Table in the Plate of Tables mark'd E, the List or Explanation of the said Table, and also the Steps contained in Plate XV.

Foot

The Art of Dancing explain'd.

Foot, by sinking and making a *Half Coupee* or Step forwards, marking Time to the first Note, in rising from thence.

If we suppose this Step to be made with the right Foot (a), the circular Step or Motion with the left must then be made inwards to the second and third Notes, or the fourth, if common Time; that is to say, the *Half Coupee* being made with the right Foot, as aforesaid, the whole quarter of the left Leg moving in the Air, with the Knee stiff and Toe pointed, makes a circular Motion, by moving directly off sideways, as in the *Point* for a *March* (b), only more round continuing on forwards, about that Distance from the other, forming a Sort of a Circle in the Air before the right Foot on which the Body rests all this Time, in bringing the left Leg, as above directed, that is to say, the Toe pointed and Knee stiff into the third Position, so as to touch the Ancle of the right Foot (c); and then it passes on directly sideways to the left Hand making a *Point*, about the like Distance from the Foot you stand upon as the *March* (d); from whence proceeds the *Pirouette* we are about to treat of, which is performed by making an easy Sink or Bending of both Knees preparing for the Rise or Straightening of them, which resembles a Spring, only it is not from the Ground; for, in the Rise or Spring from the Sink aforesaid preparing for the whole Round, the left Foot which was upon the *Point* is taken up from the Ground, turning quite round to the left Hand in the Air, with the Leg or whole Quarter extended in the Air, the Toe pointed, and Knee stiff, as in the circular Motion, about half a Foot from the Floor (e). The Body, at the very Juncture the Rise or Spring is given, rises upon the Toe or Instep, as erect as a *Pyramid*, and turns round along with it, finishing to the upper Part of the Room as at first, only with the Toe in the Air

---

(a) See the first Figure in Plate I. (b) See the first Figure in Plate XV. (c) See the first Figure in Plate IV. (d) See the first Figure in Plate VI. (e) See the first Figure in Plate XV. If with the other Foot, see the second Figure in Plate I, the second Figure in Plate XV, the second Figure in Plates IV and VI, and lastly the second Figure in the aforesaid Plate XV.

from whence it may be continued as the *Half Coupee*, or *Bouree*, &c.

This Step usually takes up a Measure, whether of three or four Notes to the Bar; the Rise or Spring to the *Pirouette* marks the first Note, and the rest are in the Turning; but the *Coupee* and *Pirouette*, tho' frequently found together, are in themselves distinct Steps (f).

There are various other Ways of performing this Step, besides the described, as twice *round*, three Times *round*, *round* in an upright Spring beating before and behind during the Turning, and many more; which, as they are foreign to my present Purpose, I shall omit, and say something of the *Bouree before and behind*, turning, &c.

CHAP. XXXIII.
Of the BOUREE *before and behind, and behind and before, advancing in a whole Turn.*

THIS Step is composed of two *Bourees*; but, tho' in Dancing it may be performed to all Parts of the Room, or upon a Circle, an Explanation of it, commencing with the right Foot advancing to the Presence or upper Part of the Room, shall suffice, in that the rest will be comprehended thereby, since the Difference is only instead of facing, as aforesaid. The Presence or Body, for Example, must be directed to the Part or Side of the Room, to which the Step is made; whether to the right or left Hand, lower End, or on a circular Figure, it will be the very same, except that, advancing to the said Parts, as before, upon a right or straight Line, you must perform the said Step circularly or round,

---

(f) See the twenty seventh Table in the Plate of Tables marked I, and the List or Explanation of the said Table.

commen-

The Art of Dancing explain'd.

commencing either with the right or left Foot, as it shall fall out, from any of the aforesaid Parts of the Room. This will appear from the following, which, as I have above observed, is advancing to the upper End of the Room with the right Foot, in order to which the Weight must be upon the left, with the right disengaged and at Liberty in the first Position (g), which begins in making a Movement or Bending of the Knees; from whence the right makes the first Step of the three that compose the first of the two *Bourees* up the Room (h), in stepping crossways before the left, on which the Body turns a quarter Turn to the right Side of the Room, the Rise of which, whether upon the Toe or Heel, marks the Time or first Note. The second Note is in the next Step with the left Foot, on its receiving the Weight, which it does, after making a Step circularly before the right, in a quarter Turn more, now facing full to the Bottom of the Room (i); and the third and last Step with the right, which is now upon the Point in the fourth Position before the left, concludes the first *Bouree*, in pressing or sliding the Toe against the Floor into the same Position behind the left, receiving the Weight upon the third Note of the Measure, and leaving the left Foot upon the *Point* in the like Manner (j).

The first *Bouree* being thus ended, the second also begins with a Movement or Bending of the Knees, as aforesaid; from whence the left is stepped or cast behind the right, in turning a quarter Turn farther, which will then be to the left Side of the Room, the Rise of which is to the first Note or Time to a second Measure; and the second Step of this *Bouree* is with the right Foot, turning the fourth or last quarter Turn from the left Side of the Room to the upper Part or Presence thereof, the setting down or receiving of the Body upon which is to the second Note. The third Note is in the last Step of the *Bouree* made with the left, directly up the

---

(g) See the first Figure in Plate I. (h) See in some Measure the second Figure in Plate IX, only it is to turn as directed. (i) See in some Respects the first Figure in Plate VIII, only the right Toe must be, as directed, upon the Point. (j) See the second Figure in Plate XII, except that the left Toe must be pointed as directed.

Room; and upon its receiving the Weight the second *Bouree* is ended, concluding in the first Position, as at commencing.

The foregoing Step, as above described, consists of two plain *Bourees* or *Fleurets* of one Movement only, whereas it frequently is performed with two; and if so, the second must be made upon the third Step, whether on the Ground or off from thence as in a *Bound*, as has already been explained in treating of these Steps.

But sometimes in *Dancing*, instead of the second *Bouree*, a *Coupee* is found commencing with either Foot, as it shall happen; but here it is with the left crossing before the right Foot on which the Body rests (k), in a quarter Turn from the lower End of the Room to the left Side, or in a half Turn to the Presence, the right Foot or second Step of which is set to the Ground, in the Method as when introducing a *Hop* (l), or, instead of the *Coupee* aforesaid, as in the seventh and eighth Measures of the first Couplet of a *Dance* of my own Composition, named the *Suomission*, that is to say, on the *Woman's* Side. The left Foot not *coupeeing* before the right, as above, instead thereof, in turning a half Turn, receives the Weight, in rising from the Sink or Bending of the Knees in the third Position behind the right (m), which then is taken from the Floor, making a circular Motion in the Air opening to the right (n) and inclosed in the third Position behind the left (o), as in the two first Measures of the second Couplet of the aforesaid *Dance* on the *Man's* Side; and if the said Steps are with the other Foot, as on the *Woman's*, the same Method of Performance is to be observed to the left Side of the Room, as in the foregoing to the right (p). I

(k) See the second Figure in Plate XII. (l) See the second Figure in Plate X.
(m) See the second Figure in Plate IV. (n) See the second Figure in Plate XV.
(o) See the first Figure in Plate IV. (p) See the second Figure in Plate I. See in some Measure the first Figure in Plate IX, only turning to the left. See in some Respects the second Figure in Plate VIII, only the left Toe is pointed. See the first Figure in Plate XII, the first Figure in Plate X, the first Figure in Plate IV, the first Figure in Plate XV, and the second Figure in Plate IV. See the twenty ninth Table in the Plate of Tables mark'd I, and also the List or Explanation of the Characters of this Step.

have been the more particular in defcribing thefe Steps, becaufe they are of more than ordinary Grace and Variety to *Dancing*; but I fhall now proceed to the *Minuet*, the Subject of the *fecond Book* of this Work.

The End of the First Book.

THESE are to certify, that the foregoing Book, intitled the ART OF DANCING EXPLAIN'D, was designed and composed long before the Book, intitled the DANCING MASTER, appeared, as we believe; and that we have carefully examined the said Book, and found it composed and written, in the same Manner it now is, on the twenty seventh Day of January, 1727-8.

Witness our Hands.

ALEX. JACKSON,
JOSEPH JACKSON, } Dancing-Masters.

THE
ART of DANCING
EXPLAIN'D

BOOK the SECOND.

CHAP. I.
Of the MINUET STEP.

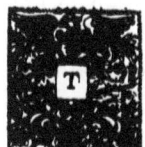HE *Minuet Step* is compofed of four plain ftraight Steps or Walks, and may be performed forwards, backwards, fideways, &c. four different Ways, to which there are the like Number of Names annexed, to diftinguifh them from one another, arifing, not improperly fpeaking, from the Placing of the Marks upon them: For Example, a Movement or Sink and Rife, being added to the firft Step of the three belonging to the *Minuet Step*, produces a *Bouree*; and the

the like to the fourth and last a *Half Coupee*, which together compose what is commonly called the *English Minuet Step*.

The second Method of its Performance is with a *Bound*; that is to say, instead of the *Half Coupee* or Movement to the last Step made upon the Floor, as in the aforesaid, you *bound* instead thereof, which is the only Variation from the foregoing.

The third Method is quite the Reverse, because, instead of the *Bouree*, the *Half Coupee* is made first and afterwards the *Bouree*, or as the *French* term it, *One and a Fleuret*, which is usually called the *French* Step.

The fourth Way of performing this Step is, by adding another Movement to the third Step of the aforesaid *Fleuret*, or the fourth of the *Minuet Step*; and it will then be notwithstanding the same Step, only of three Movements. As to the two first foregoing Steps, I shall say little concerning them, for the following Reasons: In the first Place, because they are now rarely, if ever, practised amongst Persons of the first Rank, and seem to be, for the present, intirely laid aside; not as being ungraceful, or that the *Dancer* could not give Pleasure to the Beholders, or raise to himself a Reputation, in their Performance, but merely through Alteration of Fashion, which varies in this Respect, as in Dressing, &c.

Secondly, because they have been, in some Measure, already explained in the Beginning of this Book by the *Bouree* and a *Bound*, which, from what I then observed, appears to be the same as the *Minuet Step* here treated on, except that it there answers to a Measure or Bar, but here to two, as the Time is much brisker than in the aforesaid slow Movements; and, as to their Agreement with the Notes, it is very different from what I have to say, upon that Head, to the two last Steps following: the first of which is the third of the aforesaid, namely *One and a Fleuret*, or a *Half Coupee* and *Bouree*, usually called the *New Minuet Step*, and the same that is now *danced* in all polite Assemblies (q). As it is become the *favourite* Step, my being somewhat more particular in its Description,

---

(q) See the Characters of this Step in the Plate marked O, Number I. Table the second

than

The Art of Dancing explain'd. 105

than of the foregoing, may not be lost Time; for the *Minuet* is one of the most graceful as well as difficult *Dances* to arrive at a Mastery of, through the Plainness of the Step and the Air and Address of the Body that are requisite to its Embellishment, as will farther appear from the Sequel.

But to return to the Subject in Hand; having, I say, already observed, that the *Minuet Step* is composed of four plain Steps, without shewing the Method of their Performance, or their Agreement with the Notes of the Tune, I shall now proceed to describe both of these, which are to be accomplished in the following Manner: The Weight of the Body being upon the left Foot in the first Position the right, which is at Liberty (r), begins the *Minuet Step*, by making the *Half Coupee* or first of the four Steps belonging to the *Minuet*, in a Movement or Sink and Stepping of the right Foot forwards (s), the gentle or easy Rising of which, either upon the Toe or Heel, marks what is called *Time* to the first Note of the three in the first of the two Measures, which is of triple Time or of three Notes to a Bar; the second Note is in the coming down of the Heel to the Floor (t), if the Rise was made upon the Toe, but if upon the Heel or flat Foot, in the tight Holding of the Knees before the Sink is made that prepares for the *Fleuret* or *Bouree* following, in which is counted the third and last Note of the Measure aforesaid; and the said *Bouree* or second Part of the *Minuet Step*, if I may so say, is made upon the second Measure of the Tune, as the *Half Coupee* was to the first, so that it is visible, from what has been said before, that one *Minuet Step* is of equal Value to two Measures or Bars of the Tune.

The Sink or Beginning of the Movement, that prepares for the *Fleuret* or second Part of the *Minuet Step*, for so I shall for the future call it, being made, there only remains to rise from the Sink aforesaid in the stepping forwards of the left Foot (u) to the

---

(r) See the first Figure in Plate I, Book I.   (s) See the second Figure in Plate IX, Book I.   (t) See the second Figure in Plate I, Book I.   (u) See the first Figure in Plate IX, Book I.

O   first

first Note of the second Measure, and first of the *Fleuret* or three last Steps of the four that compose the *Minuet Step*; the second Step of the said *Bouree* or *Fleuret* is made, swift forwards with the right Foot (v), to the same Note; and the third and last Step of the *Bouree*, or second Part of the *Minuet Step* with the left Foot (w), is to the third and last Note of the same Measure of the Tune, concluding the *Minuet Step* with the Weight upon the said Foot, as at first (x). It is to be noted, that it always begins with the right and ends with the left Foot; and it is performed faster or slower, according to the Tune that is played, which the *Dancer* is obliged to follow.

Having described the foregoing Step *forwards*, I shall now proceed in it *sideways* to either Hand; and, in the first Place, to the right Side of the Room, or rather obliquely, that is to say, from the upper left Corner of the Room to the right lower facing to the upper right Corner of it, or rather in the Middle between directly sideways facing the upper End of the Room and, as said above, from Corner to Corner: For Example, instead of the left Side to the upper Corner and the right to the lower, the left Side or Shoulder points about the Middle of the upper left Corner and sideways directly cross the Room; which will be easily understood by a supposed Line across the Room, for the right Shoulder consequently pointing the same Way below the Line, instead of facing the right upper Corner, as before, is now to the Middle or Space between the said Corner and directly up the Room; which will likewise be comprehended, by supposing a right Line up the Floor, and the Face a little turn'd looking towards the left Shoulder, or, more properly speaking, upon the *Gentleman* or *Lady* with whom we *dance*; and the said Turn, or rather Complaisance gives a most agreeable Twist or Contrast to the Fashion of the Body in this Step, and not a little Beauty to that Part of the *Minuet Dance* upon which it falls †; but of that more hereafter.

(v) See the second Figure in Plate IX, Book I. (w) See the first Figure in the same Plate. (x) See the first Figure in Plate I, Book I. † See the *Gentleman* and *Lady* in Plate VI.

Having

The Art *of* Dancing *explain'd.* 107

Having described the Action or Posture of the Body in which this Step must be performed, if to Advantage, I shall proceed in explaining the Motion or Stepping of the Feet upon the aforesaid Tract or Line; which is *sideways* to the right Hand, instead of *forwards,* as in the foregoing, which is the principal Difference (y). However, as it may not in all Probability be so fully comprehended by what has been said in the foregoing Step, it may not be improper to take some farther Notice of it in this Place, *viz.* That it is to be taken from the first Position, that is to say, the Weight being upon the left Foot the right, which is at Liberty (z), commences by making a Sink and Step, open off from the left Foot, on which the Body rests, *sideways* to the right (a). The Rise of the Sink marks Time to the first of the three Notes; and the rest are the same, as when done *forwards,* the *Half Coupee* or first Part of the *Minuet Step* being made to the first Measure of the Tune, as aforesaid, ending in the same Position upon the right Foot, with the left disengaged (b) to perform the *Bouree* or second Part of the said Step *sideways,* in like Manner as in the foregoing *forwards;* which it does in making a Sink and Step to the right Hand *sideways* crossing behind the right on which the Body rests (c), the Rise of which is to the first Note of the second Measure. The right Foot then makes a plain open Step, *sideways* to the same Hand (d), upon the second Note, leaving the left upon the *Point,* in the very Place the Body rested before, in Readiness to make the second Step, and is about the Distance of a *Point* in the *March.* (e); upon which the third and last Step of the *Bouree* and *Minuet Step* is made to the third Note of the second Measure of the Tune, by drawing the left Foot, pointed as it is firm to the Floor into the fifth Position behind the right (f), re-

---

(y) See the Characters of this Step in the second Table of the Plate marked O, Number II. (z) See the first Figure in Plate I, Book I. For the Action or Posture of the Body see the *Gentleman* and *Lady* in Plate VI. (a) See in some Measure the second Figure in Plate VI, Book I. (b) See the second Figure in Plate I, Book aforesaid. Action as at beginning. (c) See the first Figure in Plate XI, Book I. Action the same. (d) See the second Figure in Plate VI. Book I. (e) See the first Figure in the same Plate. (f) See the first Figure in Plate XI, Book I.

O 2 ceiving

108   *The* ART *of* DANCING *explain'd.*

ceiving the Body, and concludes in the first Position, as at first (g); and it may be continued, as long as the *Dancer* pleases.

The third and last Method of performing this Step is as follows: Instead of obliquely, as in the last explained to the right Hand, it is here diametrically or sideways crossing the Room directly to the left Hand, facing, not as in the aforesaid, but instead thereof full either up or down the Room, as it shall happen †.

This Step, in Performance, differs from the last described in this, that the right or beginning Foot, which before made the *Half Coupee* off to the right, now instead thereof makes a Sink and Step sideways to the left Hand, crossing behind the left Foot (h), which supports the Body, marking Time to the first Note of the same Measure, and filling up the remaining second and third Notes, intirely the like as in the foregoing, except that, instead of the first Position as in them, it here ends in the third with the left Foot foremost or inclosed at Liberty to perform the *Bouree*, in the same Manner to the left Side of the Room, as before to the right (i). The said *Bouree* or second Part of the *Minuet Step* begins, by making a Sink and open Step, off sideways from the right on which the Weight rests to the left Hand (k), the Rise or Receiving of the Body upon which marks Time to the first Note of the second Measure, and the right Foot makes the second Step of the *Bouree* to the second Note, in drawing it pointed (l) crossing behind the left (m), from the Place where it supported the Weight, before the first Step of the *Fleuret* was made; and the third and last Step of the *Bouree* and fourth of the *Minuet Step* is made, by stepping the left Foot open off from the right (n), in like Manner as the commencing of the *Fleuret*, only without a Sink, ending in the first Position, as at the Beginning of the Step, upon the left Foot (o),

---

(g) See the first Figure in Plate I, Book I.   † See the Characters of this Step in the second Table of the Plate marked O, Number III.   (h) See the second Figure in Plate XI, Book aforesaid.   (i) See the first Figure in Plate IV, Book I.   (k) See in some Degree the first Figure in Plate VI, Book I.   (l) See the second Figure in Plate VI, Book aforesaid.   (m) See the second Figure in Plate XI, Book I.   (n) See in some Measure the first Figure in Plate VI, the same Book.   (o) See the first Figure in Plate I, Book I.

which

which Step may be continued either diametrically or circularly, as Occasion offers.

We are now arrived at the fourth and last of the before mentioned Steps, namely, that of *three Movements* or Bendings and Risings; which is also commonly called the *New Step*, from its being used now as much, or very little less than the last explained of *two Movements* only, and more especially when performed to the left Hand sideways before and behind, in that it composes a Part of the *Minuet Dance*, as now practised, of which I shall have Occasion to speak more particularly hereafter.

In the Interim I shall proceed in describing the present *Minuet Step of three Movements*, which, as I have already said, is only the Addition of a Movement or a Sink and Rise more to the last Step of the *Bouree* or second Part of the *Minuet Step*; yet it will require a farther Explanation, by Reason that it differs very much from the last explained, in its Agreement with the Notes of the Tune; for, tho' that may properly be divided into two Parts or Divisions through the *Half Coupee*, in that it, together with the Sink which prepares for the succeeding *Bouree*, answers to the first Measure of the Tune, and the *Fleuret* or second Part of the *Minuet Step* to the second, and consequently is of equal Value, tho' no more than a single Step, with the other three remaining, it is not the like here, because the four Steps that compose the *Minuet Step* are partly of an equal Space or Distance one from the other, as in counting of one, two, three, four, and cannot so justly be divided into two Parts as the foregoing, which notwithstanding is but one *Minuet Step*, as I have said before, separated for the more familiar and easy comprehending thereof; which said Advantage we must lose in this Step, it being so intirely of a Piece that a Division here would be as unnatural, as the aforesaid is natural, as will appear by the Description I am about to give of it, which in the first Place shall be *forwards* (p): and it is to be performed in this Manner.

(p) See the Characters of this Step in the second Table of the Plate marked O, Number I. A Sink and Rise must be supposed.

The Art of Dancing explain'd.

For Example, the Weight of the Body being upon the left Foot in the first Position, the right disengaged and free (q) begins, as aforesaid, in making a Sink and Step forwards directly up the Room (r). The Rising or Receiving the Weight upon the Toe or Instep marks the Time to the first Note of the three belonging to the first Measure; the second is in the Fall of the Heel (s) and Sink which prepares for the second Step of the four belonging to the *Minuet Step*, which is made by stepping of the left Foot forwards, in the same Manner as the first (t); and the Rising or Receiving of the Body upon the Instep is to the third and last Note of the first Measure. The third Step of the said four is made with the right Foot stepping a plain straight Step forwards (u) upon the Toe to the first Note of the three in the second Measure; the second is in the coming down of the Heel of the said right Foot (v) and Sink that prepares for the fourth and last Step which is with the left Foot, in stepping forwards from the Sink aforesaid (w); and the Rising or Receiving of the Weight upon the Toe is to the third Note of the second Measure of the Tune, concluding in the same Position from whence it begun (x), in Order for a Continuance, which may be either more or less, according to the Largeness or Smallness of the Room in which the *Dance* is performed.

The two other Ways in which this Step is performed are *diametrically* or *sideways*; the first of which (y) is in the like Manner as the *Minuet Step* of two Movements, or *One* and a *Fleuret*, to the left Side of the Room, that is to say, the right Foot always crossing behind the left; but as I have already in that Step described the Method in which the Feet are to be stepped, it will be needless at present to say any more than to shew its Difference in counting to the Notes, from the former, which from what I have said

---

(q) See the first Figure in Plate I. (r) See the second Figure in Plate IX. in some Measure. (s) See the second Figure in Plate I. (t) See the first Figure in Plate IX. (u) See the second Figure in Plate IX. (v) See the second Figure in Plate I. (w) See the first Figure in Plate IX. (x) See the first Figure in Plate I. (y) See the Characters of this Step in the second Table of the Plate marked O, Number IV.

above

The Art of Dancing explain'd.

above appears to be very different from the Step now treated on, as I shall endeavour to demonstrate by the following Particulars.

In the first Place, we are to suppose a Movement added to the last Step of the *Bouree*, or second Part of the *Minuet Step*, and the first Step with the right Foot (z) to be made upon the Toe to the first Note; the second is in the coming down of the Heel (a) and Sink upon the right Foot, which prepares for the second Step made with the left (b), as was explained in the aforesaid, the Rising or Receiving of the Weight upon which marks the third Note of the first Measure, leaving the right Foot, as in the aforesaid, upon the Point (c). The Drawing or Bringing of the right Foot pointed, as it crosses behind the left (d), is the third Step, and marks Time to the first Note of the second Measure; and the second Note is in the Sink upon the said right Foot, preparing for the fourth and last Step that is made, in rising and stepping *sideways* from the said Sink upon the left Foot (e), to the third Note, concluding in the first Position (f) as at commencing.

The next Way of performing this Step only differs from the foregoing, in that, instead of the right or beginning Foot's making the first Step *behind*, as in the last, it is here made *before* (g), from whence it is called *before* and *behind*; and this crossing or stepping of the Foot *before* renders the Step much more agreeable and fuller of Variety than the aforesaid, arising by Reason of the Twists and Turns the Body naturally gives and receives in the Performance thereof.

But since this Step is much more used, in the *Dancing* of a *Minuet*, than the aforesaid, I shall endeavour to give as plain a Description of it as possible; in order to which I shall not only repeat the Stepping or Motion of the Feet, but also suppose, instead of two Bars or Measures to a Step in the *Minuet*, as in the aforesaid,

---

(z) See in some Measure the second Figure in Plate XI. (a) See the first Figure in Plate VI. (b) See in some Measure the first Figure of Plate VI. (c) See the second Figure in Plate IV. (d) See the second Figure in Plate XI. (e) See in some Degree the first Figure in Plate VI. (f) See the first Figure in Plate I. (g) See the Characters of this Step in the second Table of the Plate marked O, Number V.

only one Bar or Measure, which in Effect is the same Thing; for what matters it, whether we count three twice over, or six but once; or whether the half Time is beat to one, two, three, or to four, five, six, which last Method, in my humble Opinion, I take to be much more familiar and easy to be comprehended than the other, in that there is not any Repetition of the first or second Measure; but, however that be, I am sure, it will afford a greater Variety, and possibly may inform some of what, perhaps, they were ignorant of before.

But to proceed in the Description of the Step now treated on: For Instance, the Weight and Position, as aforesaid (h), facing either to the upper or lower End of the Room, it begins in making a Sink and Step sideways, with the right Foot crossing directly before the left (i) to the same Side of the Room, and producing a Twist or Turn of the Body towards the said Step (j) which receives the Weight upon the Toe, marking Time to the first of the abovementioned Notes. The second is in the coming down of the right Heel, in the third Position before the left (k) and Sink for the succeeding Step, which is made by stepping the left Foot, open off sideways from the right on which the Body is, to the left Side of the Room (l); the Rising or Receiving of the Body either upon the Toe or Heel marks the third Note, leaving the Toe of the right Foot upon the Point (m), in the same Place the Body was before the second Step was made. In the Stepping of the left Foot last mentioned it is to be observed, that the Body is convey'd or rather, more properly speaking, makes a becoming Feint in the Air not much unlike that made in the *Minuet* Step of *One*, and a *Fleuret* to the right, only there the Bend or Sway the Body makes in the Air was to the right (n) upon the *Half Coupee*, or first of the four Steps which compose the *Minuet Step*; but here it is upon the

---

(h) See the first Figure in Plate I, Book I. (i) See the first Figure in Plate XI, Book I. (j) See in some Measure the Twist or Turn of the Body in the said Figure. (k) See the second Figure in Plate V, Book I. (l) See the first Figure in Plate VI, Book the same. (m) See the second Figure in Plate VI, Book I. (n) See in some Measure the Sway or Twist of the Body in the first Figure of Plate XI, Book I.

second

second to the left, and the Look or Turn of the Head, which in the former was to the left, is in this to the right (o): The Toe, I say, being left pointed, as aforesaid, makes the third Step in the *Minuet*, by being drawn pointed crossing behind the left Foot, and receives the Body in a Twist upon the fourth Note or half Time, as above (p). The fifth Note is in the Sink that prepares for the last Step of the four which compose the Step we now treat of, and is made in like Manner as the second Step with the left Foot to the third Note, in rising and stepping open off sideways (q) from the Sink aforesaid upon the left Toe to the sixth and last Note, except that the right Toe is not left pointed as in the former, but ends in the first Position as at Beginning (r); and the lastMethod of counting the Notes or Time to the Step will bear, as well throughout all the *Minuet Steps* before described as the present.

Having explain'd the *Minuet Steps* which form the Circle of this *Dance*, I shall next take Notice of some of the most remarkable Steps used, by Way of Embroidery or farther Grace thereto, as the *Hop, Double Bouree,* or *Fleuret* advancing or in the same Place, *Balance, &c.*

CHAP. II.
Of the HOP in the MINUET.

THE *Hop* in the *Minuet* needs little farther Explanation, since it has been already described in the *Rigadoon Hop* of two Springs; I shall therefore refer to that, because it is the very same as the *Hop* under Consideration, only, when performed in

---

(o) See also in some Degree the Twist or Sway of the Body in the second Figure of Plate XI, Book I. (p) See the second Figure in Plate XI, Book I. (q) See in some Measure the first Figure in Plate VI, Book aforesaid. (r) See the first Figure in Plate I, Book I.

a *Minuet*, there muft be a *Bound* added and a different Method in counting of the Notes; for, inftead of performing the firft and fecond Springs to one Bar or Meafure, as in the aforefaid, they are divided, that is to fay, the firft *Spring* or *Hop* is to the firft Bar of the *Minuet Tune*, and the next Spring and the Bound which is added are to the fecond. They are all here to be reckoned but as one Step †, which is in its Performance thus: For Example, the Weight and Pofition being as aforefaid (s), the Spring is made in like Manner upon the firft Note; but, inftead of the right or advanced Foot's being fet down upon the fecond Note, it is now put down to the third (t), the fecond being counted in the Progrefs the right Foot made in the Air, concluding one half of the *Hop* in the Sink upon the aforefaid third Note, that prepares for the fecond Spring which is made, as in the aforefaid, to the fourth or beginning Note of the fecond Meafure by taking of the left Foot up from the Floor into the third Pofition behind the right and advanced Foot upon which the Weight of the Body now is (u). The left being upon the Point and at Liberty makes the *Bound*, as was fhewn in treating of that Step, the Sink or Preparative for which marks the fifth Note; and the fixth is in the *Spring* or *Bound* upon the left Foot, by rifing or fpringing off from the right on which the Weight refted before the faid Spring was made, concluding as at firft (v).

This *Hop* in the *Minuet* may be performed *backwards*, in the fame Manner as defcribed *forwards*, except that, inftead of commencing with the right Foot from the third Pofition behind, it muft be from the fame Pofition before (w); but the reft being intirely the fame there needs nothing more to be faid of it here, fince it has been fully explained in the *Rigadoon Step* of two Springs *forwards*, by which it may be eafily underftood how it is performed *backwards* (x).

---

† See the Characters of this Step in the third Table of the Plate marked O, Number I. (s) See the firft Figure in Plate V, Book I. (t) See the fecond Figure in Plate IX, Book I. (u) See the fecond Figure in Plate V, Book aforefaid. (v) See the firft Figure in Plate V. Book I. (w) See the fecond Figure in Plate IV, Book I. (x) See the Characters of this Step in the third Table of the Plate marked O, Number II.

CHAP.

The Art of Dancing explain'd. 115

CHAP. III.
Of the Double BOUREE upon the same Place.

THIS Step is taken from the third Position before and ends in the same behind, answering to two Measures of the Tune, the same as the *Minuet Step*, and is here esteemed but as one Step; tho' it is otherwise when it is performed in a *Saraband*, or such like slow Movement, for then one of them alone is to a Measure without any Dependence on the other, beginning with either the right or left Foot, as Occasion offers. But it is not so in the *Minuet*, for the first *Bouree* or *Fleuret* must commence with the right Foot, as an Equivalent to the *Half Coupee*; and the second *Bouree* to the remaining *Fleuret* or second Part of the *Minuet Step*, as usual, with the left Foot, compleating six Steps in the same Space of Time as the foregoing *Minuet Step* of four, and consequently much swifter in its Performance †, which is thus: The Weight of the Body being upon the left Foot in the third Position, the right inclosed before it and disengaged (y) begins in making a *Sink* or *Bend* of both Knees, from whence the right in rising steps directly open off sideways, either more or less according to the Tune: For Example, if to the above-said slow Time, it may then be the Length of a Step in Walking, or of a *Point* in the *March* (z); but not so now, by Reason of the Quickness of the Tune. Therefore, about half the Length of the said Step, receiving the Weight of the Body upon the Instep or Toe of the right Foot to the first Note, the left on which the

---

† See the Characters of this Step in the third Table of the Plate marked O, Number III. (y) See the second Figure in Plate IV, Book I. (z) See the second Figure in Plate VI, Book aforesaid.

Weight was remains in the same Place, only the Toe is pointed (a); the second Note is in the Raising of the said left Toe and setting down or receiving of the Weight upon the left Heel, and also leaving the right Foot upon the Point where it marked the first Note (b); from whence it is drawn swift into the third Position behind the left (c), at the same Time pressing the Toe strong to the Floor, the receiving of the Weight upon which is to the third Note, concluding the first *Bouree* and Measure in a smooth easy Sink upon the right Foot, and bending the left the same Instant the right receives the Body in order to begin the second *Bouree*.

The second *Bouree* is like the aforesaid, in rising from the Sink by stepping of the left Foot off sideways to the same Hand (d), receiving the Weight upon the Toe or Instep to the fourth Note and Beginning of the second Measure of the Tune, and leaving the right Toe upon the Point as aforesaid (e); the fifth is in the Raising the said Toe and setting down or receiving the Weight upon the right Heel, leaving the left Toe pointed, as in the first *Bouree*, or where it marked the fourth Note (f); from whence it is drawn swift into the third Position behind the right Foot (g), pressing the Toe strong to the Floor at the same Instant; the receiving of the Weight upon which is to the sixth Note, and concludes the second Measure of the Tune in the same Step of the *Dance*, in the Position as at commencing.

It must be observed, that if this Step is performed twice over, as in that under Consideration, the Sink falls upon the sixth Note of the second *Bouree*, the same as upon the third in the first.

Having described the foregoing Step *upon the same Place*, it may perhaps be acceptable to the Reader, if I add thereto the said *Bouree running* or *flying* along the Room (h), it being often used in

---

(a) See the first Figure in Plate VI, Book I. (b) See the second Figure in Plate the aforesaid. (c) See the first Figure in Plate IV, Book I. (d) See in some Respects the first Figure in Plate VI, Book I. (e) See the second Figure in the same Plate. (f) See the first Figure in the same Plate. (g) See the second Figure in Plate IV, Book I. (h) See the Characters of this Step in the third Table of the Plate marked O, Number IV.

The ART of DANCING *explain'd*.

Dancing of a *Minuet* by those who have attained to such a Perfection in this Art, as to render them capable of judging the most proper Places of making use of it; and it only differs from the former by *advancing*, instead of being upon the same Spot of Ground.

The *running Bouree* may be performed either from the Position treated on in the foregoing Step, or from the first as Occasion offers; but I shall at present only explain it from the latter, that is to say, the first Position: The Weight being upon the left Foot, as in the aforesaid (i), it begins by making a Sink and Step with the right Foot forwards (j). The Rise or Receiving of the Body upon the Toe marks the Time or first Note; the second Step, made with the left Foot (k) plain upon the Toe, marks the same Note; and the third Step, with the right Foot (l) plain in the like Manner upon the Toe, marks the third and last Note, concluding the first *Bouree* in the same Position upon the right Foot (m), in a Readiness to begin the second *Bouree*. The latter *Bouree* commences by sinking upon the third Note and Step of the former, from whence it steps forwards, as the aforesaid (n), the Rise of which upon the left Toe is to the fourth Note; the second Step plain with the right Foot (o) marks the fifth in the like Manner, and the third Step plain with the left Foot (p) the sixth; and it concludes in the first Position as at first (q), from whence it may be continued.

(i) See the first Figure in Plate I, Book I. (j) See in some Measure the second Figure in Plate IX, Book I. (k) See the first Figure in the same Plate. (l) See the second Figure in the same Plate. (m) See the second Figure in Plate I, Book I. (n) See in some Measure the first Figure in Plate IX, Book I. (o) See the second Figure in the same Plate. (p) See the first Figure in Plate IX, as aforesaid (q) See the first Figure in Plate I, Book I.

CHAP.

CHAP. IV.
Of the BALANCE.

THE *Balance* is compos'd of two plain Steps, to which are added two Movements or Sinkings and Risings commencing from two different Positions, namely, the first and second Position or *Point*, as in the Beginning of a *March*; and the said Steps and Movements are equal in Value to one *Minuet Step*, and fill up two Measures of the Tune the same as in that (r).

The *Balance* is performed thus: For Instance, the Weight of the Body being in the first Position, as above, upon the left Foot (s), the right disengaged makes the first Movement and Step by sinking or Bending of the Knees, and stepping with the right Foot directly opening off sideways (t), facing either to the upper or lower Part of the Room, as it shall happen. The Rising or Receiving of the Weight upon the Toe or Heel marks Time to the first Note; and, if upon the Toe, the second is in the Coming down of the Heel (u); or, if made upon the Heel, it is in the tight Holding of the Knee after the Rise to the first Note is made, leaving the left Toe upon the Point (v), on the very same Place the Body was at the Beginning of the Step (w). The third Note, which concludes the first Measure and Part of the Step, is in the Sink that prepares for the second Step of the *Balance*, namely, with the left Foot from the Point aforesaid, in which it touches the Heel of the right Foot (x) and then steps open off sideways (y), receiving the Weight

---

(r) See the Characters of this Step in the third Table of the Plate marked O, Number V. (s) See the first Figure in Plate I, Book I. (t) See in some Degree the second Figure in Plate VI, Book I. (u) See the first Figure in the same Plate. (v) See the same Figure in Plate VI, Book I. (w) See the second Figure in Plate VI. (x) See the second Figure in Plate I, Book I. (y) See the second Figure in Plate VI, Book I.

of

The Art of Dancing explain'd.

of the Body, either upon the Toe or Heel to the fourth Note, in the same Place from whence it was brought from the Point. The Coming down or Fall of the left Heel is to the fifth Note, if the Rise be made upon the Toe; if not, in the tight Holding of the Knee, as aforesaid, ending in the first Position, as at Beginning (z). The sixth Note is in the Sink or Preparation for the succeeding Step, whether it be the same or any other; and, when this Step is performed with a quarter or half Turn, as it frequently is, it must always be turning to the left Hand, if commencing with the right Foot, as it does in the present.

CHAP. V.
Of the two COULEES or MARCHES.

TO perform two *Marches*, instead of a *Minuet Step*, in a suitable and proper Place in *Dancing* of a *Minuet*, I take to be an agreeable Variation or Change; but, as the Manner of performing a *March* has been already shewn, I shall refer to what has been before observed upon that Step, and only take Notice, that it must begin with the right Foot to the first Measure, and with the left to the second. The first of these is to be made upon One, Two, and Three; and the second upon Four, Five, and six, in the like Method as already explained in the Step of this Name (a).

(z) See the first Figure in Plate I, Book I. (a) See the Characters of this Step in the third Table of the Plate marked O, Number VI.

CHAP.

CHAP. VI.

Of the SLIP behind and HALF COUPEE forwards to the right and left Hands, each to a MINUET STEP.

THIS Step is composed of three plain Steps, as the *Bouree*, which are generally done to a Measure, as that, in other *Dances*; but otherwise here, in that it is equal in Value to a Step in the *Minuet*, and consequently, like that, takes up two Measures or Bars of the Tune (b). It is performed facing either, up or down the Room, as in *Dancing* of the *Minuet* it shall fall out, but usually to our *Partner*, and may be taken from the third or first Position: For Instance, the Weight being upon the left Foot, with the right at Liberty resting upon the Heel of the said left Foot, as in the *March* (c); or, if from the first, instead of behind, as we have observed, it is equal to the Foot on which the Body is, facing to the upper End of the Room, which shall here suffice as an Example (d), and begins the *Slip*, or first and second Steps of the three that compose this Step, by making a Sink and Step sideways open off to the right Side of the Room (e), rising upon the Toe or Heel to the first Note, and leaving the left Foot on which the Weight was (f) upon the *Point* in the same Place (g). It rests there, during the counting the second Note; and the third is in the swift Drawing of the said left Foot pointed cross behind the right (h), concluding the second Step of the three to the first Measure, in receiving

---

(b) See the Characters of this Step in the third Table of the Plate marked O, Number VII. (c) See the first Figure in Plate V, Book I. (d) See the first Figure in Plate I, Book I. (e) See the second Figure in Plate VI, Book I. (f) See the first Figure in Plate I, Book I. (g) See the first Figure in Plate VI, Book I. (h) See the first Figure in Plate XI, Book I.

The ART *of* DANCING *explain'd.* 121

the Body in an agreeable Twist or Turn (i) with both Knees bent; that is to say, in the crossing, as aforesaid, the left Shoulder, in bringing forward before the right, is more raised by the lowering or falling of the other.

The first Movement being thus ended, with the Knees bent upon the third Note, in Order to the Performance of the *Coupee*, or second Part of this Step, which is made to the second Measure by rising from the Sink aforesaid and stepping of the right Foot forwards (j), the Rising or Receiving of the Body on the Toe or Heel marks the fourth or beginning Note of the second Measure; and the fifth is in the Coming down of the said Heel to the Floor, if the Rise was upon the Instep in the first (k) or third Position (l), with the left Foot at Liberty the same as the right at commencing. The sixth Note is in the Sink which prepares for the same Step with the other Foot; and you are likewise to observe that, in the Performance of the *Half Coupee* or second Part of the foregoing Step, the Body returns from the said Twist in bringing the right Shoulder, which was behind and somewhat inclined downwards, to be equally forwards to the left and the same in Height: For Example, when we stand in a natural and erect Posture.

But to return to the *Slip* to the left Hand, which is the very same as to the right already explained, it begins in rising from the Sink aforesaid, stepping open off sideways to the left Hand (m); and the rising upon the Toe or Heel of the left Foot marks the first Note, leaving the right Toe upon the Point (n), as the foregoing did the left, making a Pause or Rest whilst the second Note is counted. The third Note is in the drawing or crossing of the right Foot behind the left (o), receiving the Body in the aforesaid Twist (p) and bending of both the Knees, in which the right Shoulder is

---

(i) See the Contract or Sway in the first Figure of Plate XI, Book I. (j) See in some Measure the second Figure in Plate IX, Book I. (k) See the second Figure in Plate I, Book aforesaid. (l) See the second Figure in Plate V, Book I. (m) See in some Measure the first Figure in Plate VI, Book I. (n) See the second Figure in the same Plate. (o) See the second Figure in Plate XI, Book I. (p) See the Sway or Twist in the second Figure of Plate XI, aforesaid.

Q   raised

raised in advancing, as in the foregoing, to the right Hand the left Shoulder (q) was on concluding one half of the Step to the first Measure of the two; and the second is in the *Half Coupee* that is made as in the aforesaid, by rising from the Sink which fell upon the third Note and stepping of the left Foot forwards (r). The Rise Receiving of the Weight upon the Toe is to the fourth Note of the next Measure; the fifth is in the Falling of the Heel (s), and the sixth in the Sink for the succeeding Step, concluding upon the left Foot, as at beginning, in one of the said Positions (t).

Having now shewn the Method of performing this Step in *Dancing* of a *Minuet*, both to the right and left Hands (as indeed it cannot be done to one without the other by Reason they both change the Feet but as one *Minuet Step*, two *Bourees*, or two *Marches*) since this Step is much used in Tunes of common and triple Time, as *Rigadoons*, *Bourees*, *Sarabands*, and *Paffacailles*, &c. and also, instead of being performed to two Measures, as in this *Dance*, is often found to one Bar only (u) and of Consequence varies in the Method of counting from the aforesaid, it will not be improper to say something of it here, especially as it has hitherto been omitted: For Example, in *Bourees* and *Rigadoons* the Rise of the first Movement marks Time to the first Note, as in the foregoing; but the second differs in this that, instead of the Toe's being pointed during the counting of the second Note, it is drawn swift behind the Foot on which the Weight is full upon the said Note, receiving the Body in the Twist (v) and Bending of the Knees, as aforesaid. The Rise of the *Half Coupee*, which in the foregoing was to the second Measure, is now to the third Note, and the fourth Note falls in the Sink for the succeeding Step; or if done to two Measures here, as in the *Minuet*, then, instead of counting only upon the Point, the second Note before its drawing behind the third must also be

---

(q) See the first Figure in the Plate XI, Book I. (r) See the first Figure in Plate IX, Book I. (s) See the first Figure in Plate I, Book I. (t) See the first Figure in Plate I, or first Figure of Plate V, Book I. (u) See the Characters of this Step in the third Table of the Plate marked O, Number VIII. (v) See the first and second Figures in Plate XI, Book I.

reckoned,

The Art of Dancing explain'd. 123

reckoned, immediately upon which the *Slip* is made, as in the foregoing, to the fourth and laſt Note. The Riſe to the *Half Coupee* marks Time to the firſt Note of the ſecond Meaſure; the ſecond is in the Fall of the Heel, the third in the Reſt the Body makes upon it, and the fourth in the Sink for the ſucceeding Step.

But if to the above Tunes of triple Time it be performed to two Bars, it is much the ſame, as in the *Minuet*, only more ſolemn and grave, and the Foot that is upon the Point follows the Riſe in a ſlow Progreſs, preſſing the Floor upon the ſecond Note and Beginning of the third; but before the Expiration thereof it is brought ſwift behind the Foot on which the Weight is, concluding the firſt Meaſure as in the *Minuet*; and the *Half Coupee* is to the ſecond Meaſure the ſame only, as I have ſaid, more grave and ſlow.

When this Step is performed to one Meaſure, as in the aforeſaid Tunes of triple Time, the eaſy Riſe from the firſt Step made open off ſideways is upon the firſt Note; and the Point or ſecond Step attends the ſaid Riſe in a ſlow Progreſs, during the counting of the ſecond Note, and then is drawn ſwift behind, before the Expiring of the ſaid Note in a full Sink or Bending of the Knees; and the third is in the Riſe of the *Half Coupee* made from thence by ſtepping forwards, as aforeſaid, half of which is borrowed in the Sink for the next Step in the Movements laſt mentioned. This Step is ſometimes done to both Hands, as in the *Minuet*; but it is often found ſingle.

CHAP. VI.

Of DANCING the MINUET in general.

Having explained the different Ways in which the Steps of a *Minuet* are to be perform'd, I shall now say something of that *Dance* in general and proceed to shew, how the said Steps form the Circle or Figure thereof by linking them one to another in Order as they fall; and in the first Place observe, that the *Minuet* now in Use is compos'd of three different Steps that form the Figure of it, which is mostly circular or in the Shape of an S reversed or an Z (w), upon which said S or Z the abovenamed Steps present themselves, as follows: That is to say, after making our Honour or Courtesy to the Presence (x) or upper Part of the Room in which we *dance*, and afterwards to our *Partner* (y), the *Dance* begins directly. Instead of stepping back again into your Place, as the Custom was formerly, and also instead of standing to wait the Close or Ending of a Strain of the Tune, begin upon the first Time that offers, in that it is much more genteel and shews the *Dancer*'s Capacity and Ear in distinguishing of the Time, and from thence begets himself a good Opinion from the Beholders, who are apt to judge favourably of the following Part of his Performance; whereas the attending the concluding or finishing of a Strain has the contrary Effect.

However the latter is by much the safer Way for those whose Ear is not very good, the concluding of a Strain of the Tune being much more remarkable than the middle Part; for, if they should happen to begin out of Time, it is a thousand to one if they

---

(w) See the second and fifth Divisions of the Plate marked U. (x) See the *Gentleman* and *Lady* in Plate II.   (y) See the *Gentleman* and *Lady* in Plate IV.

recover

The Art of Dancing explain'd.

recover it throughout the *Dance*. But on the other Hand, had they waited a remarkable Place of the Tune, and taken the Time at Beginning, they might have come off with Reputation and Applause; for many *dance* the *Minuet Step* in true and regular Time, tho' out of Time to the *Music*, which is occasioned by not hitting with it right at first; and not being able to recover it afterwards, they *dance* the whole *Minuet* out of Time. Their *dancing* on this Account loses its Effect upon the Beholders; for, if the Steps and the Notes do not perfectly agree, in their performing, one with another, they can produce no Harmony, and if no Harmony, no Pleasure to those they design to entertain.

But to the Step and Figure, as aforesaid, the Honour or Courtesy being made as above, the *Lady* faces the *Gentleman*, who, just before the *Dance* commences, presents his right Hand, or makes a Motion as tho' he would if he was not at too far a Distance, and begins the *Dance* in making the *Half Coupee* and *Fleuret* (and rest of the Steps leading to what I call the *Introduction*) open off sideways to the right Hand in the Manner already described, facing the *Lady* or right Side of the Room, who performs the same to the left (1); and in the following Step they return again in two *Minuet Steps* of three Movements to the left, all behind, the last of which ends to the upper Part of the Room (2) to which both advance in *One* and a *Fleuret* (3). About this Time the *Gentleman* presents his right Hand to the *Lady* (z) and performs four more of the said Steps (4); the first whereof is either advancing, as the foregoing, or sideways open off to the right Hand facing the Presence or upper End, as aforesaid, the rest turning gradually the same Way, 'till he arrives at the left upper Corner of the Room facing the Bottom thereof (a). During this he hands or introduces the *Lady* into the *Dance* in the

---

(1) See the Characters or Steps marked 1 in Plate IV, or first Division of this Dance in the Plate distinguished by the Letter U, Book II. (2) See in Plate IV, or first Division of the Plate distinguished by the Letter U, the Steps or Characters marked 2, and 3. (3) See the Characters or Steps marked 4 in Plate IV, or first Division of the Plate marked U. (z) See the *Gentleman* and *Lady* in Plate V. (4) See the Characters or Steps marked with the Figures 5, 6, 7, 8, in Plate V, or in the first Division of the Plate marked U on the *Man*'s Side. (a) See the *Gentleman* or first Figure in Plate VI.

most

most agreeable Manner he possibly can, by leading or conducting her in the Circle round him in her Performance of the like Number of Steps (5), that is to say, of *One* and a *Fleuret* forwards; and, about the End of the second or third Step after giving Hands, he breaks off or lets go the (9) *Lady* who continues on a Step more to the lower right Corner of the Room, and then makes a *Half Coupee* and *Bouree* to the same Hand sideways to the upper End of it (7), provided the Break or Letting go of the Hands was upon the second Step (8), as I have observed; but, if on the third (9), the *Half Coupee* and *Bouree* or fourth of the Steps aforesaid is made directly facing the upper Part of the Room (10), as I have said (b), concluding the first Division or Part of the *Minuet Dance* in the Hat's being put on in a graceful Manner.

There is no general Rule in the Performance of this *Dance*, as to its Length or Shortness; however I shall reduce and divide it into six Parts or Divisions (c), by Way of Distinction one from another, each consisting of eight *Minuet Steps*, which to a *Minuet* Tune of the like Numbers of Bars will answer the first Strain played twice over ✝.

CHAP. VII.
Of the Figure of S reversed or second Division.

Having explained the Introduction or first Part of this *Dance*, I shall now proceed to the second; which in Figure is circu-

---

(5) See the Steps upon the *Lady*'s Tract marked 5, 6, 7, 8, in Plate V, or in the first Division of the Characters or Steps contained in the Plate marked U. (6) See the Characters or Steps marked 6 and 7 in Plate V, and first Division in Plate marked U. (7) See the Character or Step marked 8 in Plate V, and Division aforesaid. (8) See the Character or Step marked 6 upon the *Lady*'s Tract or Figure in Plate V. (9) See the Character or Step marked 7 in Plate V. (10) See the Step marked 8. (b) See the *Lady* in Plate VI. (c) See the whole Dance included in the Plate marked U. (✝) See the Music contain'd in the fourth and fifth Plates or first Division in the Plate marked U.

lar

The ART *of* DANCING *explain'd.* 127

lar or, as I have said, in the Form of an S reverfed, or Z, upon which fall the Steps that adorn this Part of the *Dance*, and are performed as follows: For Inftance, the *Gentleman* at the upper left Corner of the Room faces the *Lady* who is at the lower right in the third Pofition, where the foregoing ended with the right Foot difengaged and inclofed before the left (d), and they commence in performing about four of the *Minuet Steps* of three Movements before and behind fideways croffing the Room to the left Hand; that is to fay, the *Gentleman* performs to the right Side of the Room and the *Lady* to the left (1), who by turning a fmall Matter gradually upon the third and fourth of the faid Steps meet in the Middle of the Room facing one another (e), and pafs obliquely upon the right Hand of each other, that is, the *Lady* to the uppermoft right Corner, and the *Gentleman* to the lower left †, continuing on the remaining half Circle or Figure in four *Minuet Steps* of *One* and a *Fleuret* forwards (2). The *Lady*, as I have said, paffes on round by the right upper Corner 'till fhe arrives at the left, looking full to the Bottom of the Room (f).

The laft of the forefaid Steps (3) may alfo be made open off fideways to the right Hand, turning a quarter of a Turn the fame Way; that is, the *Lady* from facing the left Side of the Room (g) turns down it, concluding in the third Pofition as above. The *Gentleman* does the fame, paffing by the lower left Side in his Way to the right, and concludes as aforefaid, only up the Room (h).

But, inftead of either of the former Ways, this Part of the *Dance* is frequently performed in making the firft of the four Steps forwards, after paffing each other, and then not continuing the remaining Circle on forwards, or to the laft *One* and a *Fleuret* open off to the right Hand fideways, as before; but inftead thereof three

---

(d) See the *Gentleman* and *Lady* in Plate VI. (1) See the Characters or Steps marked 1, 2, 3, 4, in Plate VI. (e) See the *Gentleman* and *Lady* in Plate VII. † See the Tract or Figure in Plate VII, or fecond Divifion in Plate U. (2) See the Characters or Steps marked 5, 6, 7, 8, in Plate VII, or fecond Divifion of the Plate marked U (f) See the *Lady* in Plate VIII. (3) See the Character or Step in Plate XIII, marked 8. (g) See the *Lady* and *Gentleman* in Plate XIII. (h) See the *Gentleman* in Plates VII and XIII.

of the said *Minuet Steps* are made directly opening off sideways to the right Hand, by making half a Turn upon the *Half Coupee*, or Beginning of the first of them, from the upper End of the Room, the rest continuing on to the upper left Side facing the lower End. The *Gentleman* performs the same Way except that, after the half Turn from the Bottom, he makes the said three Steps to the lower right Side of the Room facing the *Lady*, or up it, answering the playing of the second Strain of the Tune twice over, †, which now has been played once through, and concludes the second Division of the *Dance*; and it is likewise to be observed that, in the Performance of these eight *Minuet Steps*, the *Gentleman* and *Lady* only alternately change Places (k).

CHAP. VIII.
Upon PRESENTING the right Arm or third Part.

THE second foregoing Step being explained we enter upon the third, which consists in the Ceremony of *presenting* or giving the right Hand; and in it there is no small Beauty and Air, as to the graceful and easy raising of it, in Order to take Hands, and also the gentle and natural Fall on Letting them go. As for the Tract or Figure it varies from the former, in its being circular but particularly towards the latter End, upon which Tract the Steps we now treat of are to be performed, as follows: For Example, the *Gentleman* at the lower Part of the Room on the right Side, and the *Lady* at the upper left Side, facing each other (l), begin the first

---

† See the Music contained in Plates VI and VII, or second Division in the Plate marked U. (k) See the *Gentleman* and *Lady* in Plate VIII. (l) See the Plate aforesaid.

Step

The ART *of* DANCING *explain'd.* 129

Step either obliquely open off sideways to the right Hand, or else instead thereof make four *Minuet Steps* of three Movements before and behind crossing the Room to the left Hand; that is to say, the *Gentleman* to the left Side of the Room and the *Lady* to the right 6), turning a little upon the third and fourth *Minuet Steps*, so as to face each other near the Middle of the Room (m). Instead of passing forwards to the cross Corners, as in the second Division, they turn a quarter off to the upper and lower Ends of the Room upon the last Movement of the fourth *Minuet Step:* For Instance, the *Gentleman* to the Presence or upper Part, and the *Lady* to the lower (n), to which each advance pursuing their respective Tracts in taking as large a Circumference, as the joining of Hands will admit.

In performing the four remaining *Minuet Steps* forwards (7), which are of *One* and a *Fleuret*, the right Arm is to be raised in the Manner before observed, about the turning off or ending of the fourth *Minuet Step* of three Movements (8), as a Sign or Warning to the *Lady* of the *Gentleman's presenting* his Hand, which is given by an easy Bending of the Elbow before it is presented near the End of the fifth *Minuet Step*, continuing on round the sixth and seventh *Minuet Steps* until the *Gentleman* faces the upper right Corner of the Room and the *Lady* the lower left. About this Time the Hands are let go and the Arm falls gently to the Side, whilst the eighth Step is perform'd obliquely off sideways to the right Hand (o) and lower right Corner of the Room, the *Gentleman*'s Head being a little turn'd looking upon the *Lady* who does the like to the upper left Corner, concluding in the third Position as at commencing this Division, only much nigher to each other, and the Shoulders pointing to the upper and lower right and left Corners of the Room, as was already shewn in the Explanation of this Step;

---

(6) See the Characters or Steps marked 1, 2, 3, 4, in Plate VIII, or third Division of Plate U. (m) See the *Gentleman* and *Lady* in Plate XI. (n) See the *Gentleman* and *Lady* in Plate IX. (7) See the Characters or Steps in the said Plate IX marked 5, 6, 7, 8, or third Division of Plate U. (8) See the last Step in Plate VIII, marked 4; and first of Plate IX. (o) See the *Gentleman* and *Lady* in Plate VIII.

R which

which Part or Division of the *Dance*, as here treated on, falls upon the first Strain of the Tune, the second Time of playing, and answers to the Strain twice over (†).

As for the Taking off or Keeping on the Hat I shall not take upon me to determine, leaving it to every one's Choice to act as they shall think most agreeable, since it intirely depends upon Fashion and Fancy; but, as I have a Right as well as others humbly to offer my Thoughts on this Point, I shall declare in Favour of the former, in that it has the Appearance of much more Complaisance and Air than Keeping the Hat upon the Head, which in my humble Opinion seems more flat and disrespectful; and the Taking off and Putting on of the Hat with a good Air likewise gives a singular Grace to the *Dance*, which is all lost by its remaining upon the Head.

But if it should be objected, that it is inconvenient and troublesome to take off the Hat with the right Hand, by Reason it must be changed to the left before the right can be at Liberty to present to the *Lady: I answer*, it is easy to be done; or it may be taken off with the left Hand as well as the right, and then once changing will serve, which may be upon the letting go or breaking off Hands, that is to say, in making *One* and a *Fleuret* open off to the right Hand. The said Step finishes the Part of the *Dance* now treated of; and the Hat is to be taken off with the left Hand on giving the right falling naturally and slow down to the Side, and holding the Hat at Arms Length during the Time of changing, as was above observed.

---

† See the Music to the Steps in Plates VIII. and IX

CHAP.

CHAP. IX.

Of the FOURTH DIVISION or PRESENTING of the left ARM.

AS the laſt explained treated of the *preſenting* or giving the right *Hand*, the preſent or *fourth Diviſion* is upon *preſenting* of the left, which in its Performance is thus: For Inſtance, being upon the left of each other, the Hat in the right Hand, the Poſition and Preſence of the Body the ſame as at the Beginning of the third Part, only, as I have ſaid on the Concluſion thereof, ſomething nighr together, and the Body a little more turned to the right, the *Gentleman* who faces the upper Part will be to the ſame Side of the Room, but the *Lady*, as ſhe faces the lower Part, is to the left (p); to both of which each advance in eight *Minuet Steps*, returning upon the ſame Circle or Tract that conducted them hither, which is enlarged by the aforeſaid turning (9) and making the firſt *Minuet Step* which is of *One* and a *Fleuret* forwards; and on the commencing thereof the left Arm is raiſed (q) in a ſlow and eaſy Motion, in Order to be *preſented* or given, which is much upon the ſecond *Minuet Step* by a gentle bending of the Elbow, as in the aforeſaid.

But, inſtead of the ſecond's being a *Minuet Step* of *One* and a *Fleuret*, you may make the *Minuet Hop*, which, if well executed, is an agreeable Variation proceeding round in the Continuation of three *Minuet Steps* more of *One* and a *Fleuret*, at the full Extent or Length of the Arms, 'till arrived very near the Place of ſetting out,

---

(p) See the *Gentleman* and *Lady* in the Plates VIII and X. (9) See the Steps in Plate X, marked 1, 2, 3, 4, 5, 6, 7, 8, or the fourth Diviſion of Plate U.
(q) See the *Gentleman* and *Lady* in Plate X.

that is to say, whilst the *Gentleman* faces to the upper right Corner of the Room and the *Lady* the lower left (10); upon which Hands are broke off or let go, and, extended as they are, gently fall to their proper Places. The Hat is put on again with the right Hand, upon the Ceremony of the Arms being ended; and the three remaining *Minuet Steps* are performed obliquely open off to the right Hand sideways (11), as upon the last Step of the preceding Division (r), or directly across the Room to the right and left Sides, concluding in the Position and Place from whence the third Division of three Movements to the left begun; or, instead of the eighth and last's being made, as I just observed the *Double Bouree* was performed, it would fall very naturally here and be no small Embellishment to this Part of the *Dance*, or any other Steps to fill up the Time (12). I mean when performed by such as have arrived at a Capacity of doing it perfectly, otherwise it is better omitted; but nothing can be more graceful than the former, as appears from what has been said in the Explanation of that Step; and it affords a farther Variety, in that the Tune has now been twice played through on the Conclusion of the Division or Part now treated of (s), which was to the second Strain both Times over (t).

---

(10) See the Steps marked 3, 4, 5, on the different Tracts in Plate X, or in the fourth Division of Plate U. (11) See the Characters or Steps marked 6, 7, 8, in Plate X, or fourth Division of Plate U. (r) See the Action of the *Gentleman* and *Lady* in Plate VIII. (12) See the Characters of this Step in the third Table of the Plate marked O, Number 3. (s) See the Music to the first, second, third, and fourth Divisions in Plate U. (t) See the Music to the Part of the *Dance* contained in Plate X.

CHAP.

CHAP. X.

Of the fifth DIVISION or second S

AS this Part of the *Dance* has been already explained by the second *Division*, which in Figure and Step is altogether the same, except that, instead of the *Gentleman*'s being at the upper End of the Room as in the foregoing Part, the *Lady* is now there and the *Gentleman* at the lower (u), from whence both commence as in the aforesaid, I might here refer to what I formerly said, in that a farther Explanation seems entirely needless, since it will easily be comprehended from the former as some may imagine, it being no more than to perform the said Steps in the Method above described; yet, for the better understanding thereof, if I accompany the *Dancer* or *Reader* through this Part of the *Dance* a second Time, it will not I hope be thought a tedious or unnecessary Repetition. The *Gentleman* and *Lady*, situated as was already observed, both commence in performing the said four *Minuet Steps* of three Movements before and behind sideways crossing the Room to the left Hand; but the *Gentleman* now, instead of moving to the right Side of the Room, as in the second Division, moves to the left, the *Lady* doing the same to the right (1); and as I have said, by turning a small Matter gradually upon the third and fourth of the said *Minuet Steps*, they meet in the Middle of the Room, as in the aforesaid, facing one another (v) and pass obliquely upon the right Hand of each other, *viz.* the *Gentleman* to the upper right Corner and the *Lady* to the lower left, continuing on the remaining half Circle or Figure in four *Minuet Steps* of *One* and a *Fleuret* as afore-

---

(u) See Plate VIII. (1) See the Characters or Steps mark'd 1, 2, 3, 4, in the said Plate VIII, or fifth Division in Plate U. (v) See the *Gentleman* and *Lady* in Plate XI.

said

said forwards (2), the *Gentleman*, as I have said, passing on round by the right upper Corner until arrived at the left facing down the Room (w).

The last of the said four Steps may also be made open off sideways to the right Hand, turning a quarter of a Turn the same Way as the *Gentleman* from facing the left Side of the Room (†) down it, and finishing in the third Position (‡); and the *Lady* the like, passing by the lower left in her Way to the right Side and concluding, as aforesaid, only up the Room (*†).

But, instead of either of the foregoing Ways, this Part of the *Dance* is usually perform'd in making the first of the four Steps forwards after passing each other (4), and then not continuing the remaining on a Circle forwards, or to the last *One* and *a Fleuret* open off to the right Hand sideways, as before (5), but instead thereof three of the said *Minuet Steps* are performed directly opening off sideways to the right Hand in making half a Turn upon the *Half Coupee*, or Beginning of the first of them, from the upper End of the Room, the remaining continuing on to the upper left Side facing the lower End. The *Lady* does the same, except that after the half Turn from the Bottom she performs the said three Steps to the lower right Side of the Room, looking up it or to the *Gentleman*; and, having again alternately changed Places as before, the *Gentleman* is left at the upper left Corner or Side of the Room and the *Lady* at the lower right (*‡), concluding to the first Strain of the Tune twice over which is now begun a third Time.(*)

---

(2) See the Characters or Steps mark'd 5, 6, 7, and 8, in Plate XI, or the fifth Division of Plate U. (w) See Plate VI. † See the Action in Plate XIV, and also the Character or Step marked 8. (‡) See in some Measure Plate VI. (*†) See the aforesaid Plates IV, and XIV. (4) See the Character or Step in Plate XIV, mark'd 5. (5) See the Steps or Characters in Plates XIII or XIV, mark'd 6, 7, and 8. (*‡) See the *Gentleman* and *Lady* in Plate VI. (*) See the fifth Division of Plate U. or the under written Music to Plates VIII, and XI.

CHAP.

The ART *of* DANCING *explain'd.* 135

CHAP. XI.
Of the sixth DIVISION or PRESENTING of both ARMS and Conclusion.

THE sixth and concluding Part of the *Minuet Dance* principally consists in the Ceremony of *presenting* or giving *both Hands*, as the third and fourth Parts did in giving the *single Arm*, and they are much alike in Figure and Form: For Instance, the *Gentleman* and *Lady* facing each other in the third Position, where we left them in the three last explained (x) *Minuet Steps*, begin in the Performance of the like Number of Movements sideways each to the left Hand, the *Gentleman* to the right Side of the Room and the *Lady* to the left; and, near the End or Finishing of the said three *Minuet Steps*, both turn off to the same Hand to which they were performed †, as in the fourth *Minuet Step* of three Movements belonging to the third Division, opening gracefully in Order to enlarge the Figure and *present both Hands* (1) as the other was for *One*, only making the fourth *Minuet Step* which is of *One* and a *Fleuret* forwards to that Part of the Room to which the Presence of the Body is directed; that is to say, the *Gentleman* to the *lower* and the *Lady* to the *upper* (y), upon the Beginning of which said Step both Arms are raised in the easy Gracefulness observed in the single Arm, as the Sign or Warning of giving both Hands, (z) which is done upon the commencing of the fifth or succeeding Step.

(x) See the *Gentleman* and *Lady* in Plate VI pursuing their different Tracts or Figures to the Steps marked 1, 2, 3, and 4. † See the Character or Step in the sixth Division of Plate U marked 3. (1) See more particularly the Steps marked 1, 2, 3, and 4, in the sixth Division of Plate U. (y) See the *Gentleman* and *Lady* in Plate XII. (z) See the Action in the Figures of Plate XII.

In

136 *The* ART *of* DANCING *explain'd.*

In this Part of the *Dance* there may be a *Minuet Hop,* inſtead of *One* and a *Fleuret,* continuing on round upon the right Side of each other, until the *Gentleman* faces the upper Part of the Room and the *Lady* the lower (a), which will be about the Concluſion of the ſixth *Minuet Step*; during which the Arms are raiſed near the Height of the Shoulder, and the Elbows a little elevated or raiſed forming a Circle or whole Round.

In this Poſture the ſeventh and eighth *Minuet Steps* are alſo performed, the *Gentleman* making *One* and a *Fleuret* backwards, or rather a ſmall Matter to the right, whilſt the *Lady* performs the ſame Steps forwards (2), upon which the Hands are let go; and the *Gentleman*, in making the Slip or Beginning of the eighth *Minuet Step*, takes off his Hat with the right Hand which falls gently down to the Side, as aforeſaid, in Order to make the Reverence or Bow to the Preſence or upper End of the Room, which is upon the third and fourth *Minuet Step.* At the ſame Inſtant the *Lady* coupees to the *Gentleman* in a half Turn to the right from the lower Part of the Room facing up it, and leaves the right Foot upon the Point † finiſhing the remaining half of the *Step* and *Dance* in the Reverence or Courteſy made in drawing the ſaid right Foot behind the left, on which the Body reſts, into the third or fifth Poſition (‡); after which the Honour or Reſpect is made to each other and the Ceremony ended (b), as alſo the Tune which has now been played three Times over (*†).

As to the Hat I ſhould rather approve of its not being taken off here till the breaking off or letting go of both Hands; however this is likewiſe ſubmitted to the *Dancer*'s Choice, as well as the Preſenting of the ſingle Arm, whether he takes it off, or keeps it on, throughout the whole *Dance.*

(a) See in ſome Meaſure the *Gentleman* and *Lady* in Plate IX. (2) See the Steps marked 5, 6, 7, and 8, in Plate XII, or Steps with the ſame Figures in the ſixth Diviſion of Plate U. (†) See the ſecond Figure in Plate VI, Book I. (‡) See the firſt Figure in Plate IV, or ſecond of Plate XI, Book I. (b) See the ſecond, third, and fourth Plates. (*†) See the Muſic to the Steps of Plates VI and XII, or laſt Diviſion of Plate U.

CHAP.

The ART *of* DANCING *explain'd.*

CHAP. XII.

Of the MISTAKES *in* DANCING *of a* MINUET, *with their* OCCASIONS *and* RULES *to prevent them.*

IN the foregoing Chapters I have shewn the Method or Manner in which the *Minuet Dance* is to be performed, when reduced to a just and regular *Dance*; yet in Effect it is no more than a voluntary or extempory Piece of Performance, as has already been hinted, in Regard there is no limited Rule, as to its Length or Shortness, or in Relation to the Time of the Tune, since it may begin upon any that offers, as well within a Strain as upon the first Note or commencing thereof. It is the very same with Respect to its ending, for it matters not whether it breaks off upon the End of the first Strain of the Tune, the second, or in the Middle of either of them, provided it be in Time to the *Music*; but nevertheless there are frequently *Mistakes*, in the Performance of this *Dance*, arising from Want of a just Notion of the Figure and some certain Rule in performing the Steps upon the said Figure, and more particularly those Steps which are designed by Way of Ornament or farther Grace, which instead of that often prove its Disgrace. Nothing is more common than to see the *Gentleman* or *Lady* detained in the Performance of some Step, in Order to illustrate the *Dance*; and so consequently not reaching that Part of the Room, on which the crossing is made, Time enough (c), instead of performing *One* and a *Fleuret* open off sideways to the right Hand (d),

---

(c) See the *Gentleman* and *Lady* in Plates VII, and XI. (d) See the *Gentleman* and *Lady* in Plates VI, and VIII.

or some such like Step, or making a Feint off to the right Hand in the same *Minuet Step* quite round forwards falling into the *Minuet Step* of three Movements all behind facing the right or left Side, as it shall fall out, by which Time the former will be arrived at the Place of crossing which will then be in its due Time; whereas the running in either before or behind our *Partner*, as before, would have caused a Confusion.

This Disorder also frequently happens in performing the common *Minuet Step*, as when one of the *Dancers* does not fill out the Room and Figure in the Performance of an equal Number of Steps to the other; for, if this be not observed, it will produce the like Effect as the former; or if, as I have observed, in presenting the right Hand or giving of both, a sufficient Warning is not had by raising of the Hand or Hands, as aforesaid, one *Minuet Step* before the Hands are given (†), the *Dancers* are often nonplus'd and put out of the Figure, while on the contrary a Presence of Mind with the Observation of these *Rules* will prevent all such Blunders and Confusions.

There is yet one Observation more, with which I shall conclude what I have to say upon this Head, which may be of some Service in preventing the said Accidents, *viz.* The marking whether the *Minuet Step* of three Movements before and behind sideways to the left Hand, which introduces or leads to the giving the right Hand, was facing up or down the Room, because in going the Circle or Figure round to the right you certainly come to the same Place (e), whether it be facing to the upper or lower Part of the Room, ending the Division in the *Minuet Step* of *One* and a *Fleuret* obliquely off sideways to the right Hand and looking the same Way as described in that Step; and also the like in the Performance of the *Minuet Steps* round to the left, in which the said Hand is given (f).

---

† See the Divisions or Chapters which treat of giving the Hands. (e) See For Example the *Gentleman* and *Lady* in Plate VIII. (f) See the Beginning in the *Gentleman* and *Lady* in Plate X, concluding in Plate VIII.

The ART *of* DANCING *explain'd.*

As the foregoing are the principal Places, in which young *Dancers* usually mistake, I thought the making some Observations on the *Occasion*, and the *Rules* or *Methods* to be observed in preventing them, might not be unacceptable; for, admitting that *Masters* may have frequently taught their Scholars the same Lesson, yet according to the old Saying, *Words soon pass into Oblivion, but what is put down in Print remains more strongly fix'd upon the Mind.*

There is much more that might be said upon this Subject; but, as the aforesaid is sufficient, to avoid being tedious I shall only proceed to the making a few farther Observations, in Regard to the foregoing described Steps, which as yet have not been introduced into the *Dance* above explained nor any Place assigned them therein: For Instance, the *March*, *Balance*, *Slip* behind and Step forwards being to the right Hand, and the same to the left and a *Double Bouree* forwards, every one of which Steps, as was already observed, depend upon Fancy, as there are some Parts of the *Dance* much more proper than others, it may not be foreign to my present Purpose to take Notice of them; and in the first Place introduce the *March*, which seems to claim three Places in the said *Dance*, the Choice of which rests in the Performer, for it is to be observed that no Step of this Sort is ever performed more than once or twice in *Dancing* of a *Minuet*. For Example, should the said *Dance* be perform'd in one Assembly or Company twice or thrice over, its Steps ought to be varied as much as possible, that is, provided the *Dancer* is capable thereof; otherwise, as I have already observed, it is much better performed plain; but to what I was saying the two *Marches* will be agreeably made advancing upon the seventh *Minuet Step* of the second Division, the first of the three Ways there described, that is, of *One* and a *Fleuret* continuing all round forwards.

The eighth *Minuet Step* may be of *One* and a *Fleuret* open off sideways to the right Hand, as aforesaid, facing either to the upper or lower End of the Room, as it happens; the next Place it challenges is the second Measure of the fourth Division, instead of the *Hop* which is then left out; and the third is upon the last Step but one of the fifth Division or second $, intirely in the same Method described in the second Division.

The *Balance* is also frequently made much about the same Place or eighth *Minuet Step*, either sideways facing each other, or advancing and retiring; and the next is the *Slip behind* and Step forwards to the right and left Hands, each to a *Minuet Step* and Fall in their Performance upon the aforesaid second and fifth Divisions, only in the second of the three Methods explained in the second Part of the *Dance*, by breaking off the *Minuet Step* of *One* and a *Fleuret* upon the Ending of the sixth *Minuet Step*, instead of a seventh it makes the said Slip to the right Hand turning to each other from the contrary Sides of the Room, and the *Slip* to the left Hand is instead of the eighth *Minuet Step*.

This Step may also be performed with no small Advantage to the *Dance*, instead of the seventh and eighth *Minuet Steps* of the fourth Division which are there obliquely; and the *Double Bouree* forwards may be made upon the seventh *Minuet Step* of the second or fifth Divsion, concluding the eighth *Minuet Step* in *One* and a *Fleuret* to the right Hand, as aforesaid, or instead of the fifth *Minuet Step*, after which the remaining are as described in the second Division or $.

The third Way of this Step's Performance is by a half Turn upon the *Half Coupee* or Beginning of the sixth *Minuet Step* of *One* and a *Fleuret*, opening off sideways to the right, or in the sixth Division after the *Hop* instead of the *Minuet Step*.

The foregoing Graces or Steps being now united and brought into the aforesaid *Dance*, and having their proper Places assigned therein, I shall conclude with one Observation more, *viz.* that it is in its Performance longer or shorter, according to the *Dancer's* Pleasure. In Order to this instead of performing the second Division but once, as in the *Dance* before described presenting the right Hand, it may be performed twice or thrice, only it must be noted that the fifth Division upon breaking off the left Hand is performed the like Number of Times; that is to say if the second twice, the fifth the like, and if thrice the same after giving the single Hand;

but

The ART *of* DANCING *explain'd*   141

but the shortest Way is once, as described in the foregoing *Dance*.

The said *Dance* and its Steps, as I have already observed, altogether depend on Fancy, and are in their Performance various and uncertain; for it is left to the Pleasure of every one to perform them in the Order here set down, in any better Method of their own, or without any Steps. Indeed, it must be confessed that the Steps well performed in a *Minuet* are great *Ornaments* to that *Dance*, in filling it with Variety; yet at the same Time it must be owned the performing the plain *Minuet Steps* alone is extremely graceful, if well accompiished, and in Effect the most *Gentleman-like*, or at least the safer of the two.

CHAP. XIII.

Of TIME *or some Account of what* TIME *is, with Rules to be observed in Keeping it.*

TIME is a large Space or Distance without Variation or Change; and, as it has been from the Beginning of all things, it will remain 'till a Period be put thereto and it ceases to be. This mighty Space the great Author thereof, in his exceeding Wisdom, has divided or measured into equal Parts and Proportions, as Days into Hours, Months into Weeks, Quarters into Months, Years into Quarters, &c. which Divisions or Parts move or travel round in a continual but just and regular Motion or Pace, succeeding each other without ceasing until they arrive at the utmost Limits or Confines of *Time*, which will then be no more.

But leaving these sublime Thoughts to draw more closely to the Point or Subject in Hand, I shall endeavour to illustrate it by one Day or Measure of the foregoing *Space* or *Time*, in supposing every Hour therein to be Bars or Measures of a Dance or Tune; and that they are as short in Length or Time, as Measure in common or triple Time. I shall likewise shew, that by one Hour may be
compre-

comprehended the Scale both of common and triple Time: For Inftance, the former thus.

COMMON TIME.

$$\left\{\begin{array}{l}1\\2\\4\\8\\16\end{array}\right.\begin{array}{l}\textit{Semibreve.}\\\textit{Minims.}\\\textit{Crotchets}\\\textit{Quavers}\\\textit{Semi-quavers.}\end{array}\mathrm{------}\left\{\begin{array}{l}1\\2\\4\\8\\16\end{array}\right.\begin{array}{l}\textit{Hour.}\\\textit{Half Hours.}\\\textit{Quarters of the Hour.}\\\textit{Half Quarters of the Hour.}\\\textit{Half half Quarters of the Hour.}\end{array}$$

The above is the whole *Proportion* of *Common Time* or of four to the Meafure, as ufually found in Books of *Mufic*; yet we often find in Pieces of *Mufic* the fixteen *Semi-quavers* doubled two and thirty *Demi-femi-quavers*, and then the Hour will be divided into the like Number of Parts.

In *Triple Time* the Hour muft be fuppos'd to be divided into three Thirds or Parts, by Reafon it only confifts of three in a Bar or Meafure: The Example is as follows.

TRIPLE TIME.

$$\left\{\begin{array}{l}1\\3\\6\\12\end{array}\right.\begin{array}{l}\textit{Prick'd Minim.}\\\textit{Crotchets.}\\\textit{Quavers.}\\\textit{Semi-quavers.}\end{array}\mathrm{------}\left\{\begin{array}{l}1\\3\\6\\12\end{array}\right.\begin{array}{l}\textit{Hour in three Thirds.}\\\textit{Thirds or Parts of the Hour.}\\\textit{Half Thirds or Parts of the Hour.}\\\textit{Half half Thirds or Parts of the Hour.}\end{array}$$

This is the *Proportion* of *Triple Time* or three in a Meafure, as ufually put down; yet fometimes it amounts to twenty four *Demi-femi-quavers*.

Having now fhewn that the Hours of the *Day* may be efteem'd as fo many Meafures of a *Tune* or *Dance*, it muft confequently be underftood that a *Day* of twelve Hours contains the like Number

The Art of Dancing explain'd.

Measures; and, admitting that the *Tune* or *Dance* consisted of seventy two Bars, six Divisions or *Days* would compleat it. This Comparison may possibly be thought by some foreign to the Purpose, tho' it is indeed very just and suitable; and I question not but upon farther Consideration it will appear so to the judicious Reader, for since the Subject in Hand is *Time* and there is Nothing more certain than the *Day* and its *Hours*, the latter will of Course imprint in the Mind stronger and juster Ideas of the former.

However, it may perhaps be objected and at first View with great Show of Reason, that the *Time* in *Dancing* is various and liable to be changed to faster or slower, according to the Performer's Fancy; whereas the *Day* and *Hours* are immutable or without any Change. I answer, for this very Reason, as I have just observed it will give them a truer Notion of the Justness of *Time*, and be a Means to prevent their starting from or dragging behind it, which is often done by such whose Ears are pretty good, as well as by those who have very bad Ears, tho' it is the natural Fruit of the Want of an Ear which of all other Things is most difficult to cure, it being more a Gift of Nature than Art. This caused the *Ancients* to say, the *Gods* gave a *Genius* to *Music* and *Dancing*; and it is of that Importance in the latter as to render it impossible to please without Keeping *Time*, nor is it to be called *Dancing* without it.

From what has been said it appears, that to have a just and true Idea of *Time* is of no small Consequence in order to *dance* well, and that too much cannot be said upon this Head; which is, I think, a sufficient Motive for me to proceed in a few farther Observations upon it, which if duly consider'd, I am confident, will be found of remarkable Service.

In the first Place then, you are to take Notice, that of the foregoing *Proportions* of *Time* one is *common* and the other *triple*, from whence arise all the Times and Movements made use of in *Dancing*. From the former of these flow very slow *Entrees* containing two Steps in each Measure call'd, *Quadruple* or of two Times on Account of their Slowness or admitting of a suppos'd Bar in the Middle of the said Measure; but the rest as *Allemaignes*, *Gavots*, *Galliards*,

liards, *Bourees*, *Rigadoons*, &c. are only of one Time, as not allowing of more than one Step to a Measure by Reason they are much lighter Movements than the aforesaid *Quadruple*, of which they are esteem'd but as half a Measure. The latter consists of *Louvres*, or slow *Jigs*, *Courants*, *Sarabands*, *Passacailles*, *Chaconnes*, *Minuets*, *Passepieds*, &c. the first of which namely *Louvres* or slow *Jigs* are of two Times or Steps to a Measure and agreeable with *Quadruple*, so that in Effect there are three Sorts of *Times* in *Dancing*, *viz.* common, triple, and quadruple proceeding from the two former; yet they are all reckon'd but as *common* and *triple Time* and only beat as such, except that some are slower and others quicker, which is the Subject I am now about to explain.

Common Time, for, Instance, is of four Notes to the Bar or Measure, as has already been observed in the *Explanation* of the Steps upon that *Time*; and the Rise or Beginning of the Step, in *Dancing*, from a Sink always marks *Time* to the *Tune*, as well as the fourth or last Note is in the Sink or Preparative for the Rise or beating Time to the succeeding Step, which no sooner is perform'd than the *Dancer* proceeds to the next, as in *Walking*; and so on 'till the *Dance* is compleated, keeping a just and equal Distance or Space between every Beginning and Ending of a Measure of the *Dance*, as has been observed by the *Hours* of a *Day*, which is call'd *Time*, the same Way, as not making the Rise or marking of the *Time*, from a Sink upon the first Note which in all Measures is out of *Time*, and also performing the Steps of a *Dance* sometimes faster or slower than at others; but this is as morally impossible for one of a good Ear, as it wou'd be for a *well timed Watch* to go out of *Time*. *Dancing* may justly be consider'd as a *Watch*; for as, when the latter is set a going by the Springs, the Wheels move round measuring out the *Hours* or Divisions of a *Day* in certain and equal Spaces, during the Time it goes: So the Springs and Steps of a *Dance* ought to be continued after it is put in Motion by *Music*, 'till the Whole is ended, which may easily be accomplish'd. But the Difficulty arises here; for Example, supposing a Person, would set his *Watch* a going at Twelve at Noon, having no Rule nor any

Thing

The ART *of* DANCING *explain'd.* 145

to direct him in it but beholding of the *Sun*, is it not a Thousand to One but he wou'd be either before or after the Time? The Case is the very same in *Dancing*, as to those who have not a *Genius* or *Ear* to *Music*; and tho' I durst engage to make such a One acquire the former, namely to *dance* in just and regular *Time*, yet I wou'd not answer for his commencing upon the right Time by Reason, as I have observed in the Comparison of the *Sun*, it is a Point of a very nice Nature and in Reality not to be done with any Certainty, if the *Ear* is not first helped and improved by a Knowledge of that *Science*; no more than the former without a Skill in *Dialling*.

Having by the going of a *Watch* shewn the true and exact Time in which the Steps of a *Dance* ought to be perform'd, and the Difficulty of suiting the Movement of the *Dance* to that of the *Tune*, I shall proceed to give the Rules to be observed in beating or keeping Time to the foregoing Proportions of Time, which I take to be the first Step in the Affair under Consideration; and I shall begin with the *Gavot*, upon which Movement the *Time* is sometimes beat directly upon the first of the four Notes belonging to the Measure; but most usually after letting pass or slip half a Measure, that is to say, the third and fourth Notes. For the better Understanding of this I shall name two or three *Dances* of the latter Sort, *viz.* the *Princess Royal* compos'd by Mr. *L'Abbee*, the *Princess Ann* by Mr. *Siris*, and the *Gavot* to the *Dance*, named the *Prince Eugene*, of my own Composition, and they all begin with odd Notes to which in the *Dance* a plain Step or Walk is made, whilst the Person who beats *Time* raises the Heel or Toe on playing the odd Notes of the *Tune*, in Order to strike full upon the *Time* or first Note of the ensuing Measure; which is done in the Fall or Coming down of the Heel or Toe, either of which remains upon the Floor during the Counting of the first and second Notes or half Measure. While the third and fourth Notes, or concluding Half are counting the Heel or Toe is raised to mark Time to the succeeding Bar, as at first, and so on 'till the whole *Tune* or *Dance* is ended, keeping an exact and equal Motion up and down neither faster nor slower, and counting the said first, second, third, and fourth Notes successively over and

T   over

over during the same; so that the Heel or Toe rises upon the third Note, remains in the Air the fourth, comes down to the first, and rests the second, &c. as before.

The *Galliard* Movement is intirely the same, as to the beating Part, but not as to the odd Notes, for instead of two, as in the foregoing, there is only one here; an Instance whereof we have in Mr. *Isaac*'s *Galliard*, upon which the Heel or Toe is raised to beat the Time upon the first Note, as aforesaid. These two Movements are rather more solemn and grave than the following, namely, *Allemaignes, Bourees, Rigadoons, &c.* but with Regard to the Method of beating *Time* the very same, for they usually begin with an odd Note; and if not, 'tis only borrowing the last Note of the foregoing Measure for raising the Heel or Toe, as aforesaid.

It is here to be noted, that it can never be reckoned out of *Time*, whether the said four Notes of the Measure be counted faster or slower, provided they are continued through the *Dance*, as begun at first; for tho' the Fancy of *Masters* often differs upon this Point, yet every Movement has its proper *Time*.

From what has been said it fully appears, that the first Note or Beginning of a Bar is the *Time* or Mark the *Dancer* must hit; and in Order thereto, as the Performer in *Music*, in playing of the *Tune*, prepares for beating *Time* by taking up of the Toe or Heel, so does the *Dancer* in making a Sink or Bending of the Knees to beat or mark *Time* to the *Tune*, as well as to perform the first or introducing Step of the *Dance*; but whether it be done by a Rise upon the Toe, a Hop, or any other Step, it matters not, in that it is to be observed, the Rise from a Sink beats *Time* in *Dancing*, as the Fall of the Heel does in *Music*.

Before I proceed to *triple Time*, it will be necessary to say something farther of *quadruple*, which from its Graveness is reckoned as two Times, as was already observed; and I know no more proper or suitable Method of explaining it, since in Time and Value it is equivalent to two Measures of *common Time*, than the Counting every Note double as One One, Two Two, Three Three, Four Four, and supposing them, what in Effect they really are, four *Minims*, for

in

The Art of Dancing explain'd. 147

in this Sort of *Time* the *Crotchets* are of equal Length to the *Minims*, and wou'd be as before obferved, if the *Time* was beat in the Middle of the Meafure. For Inftance, on the commencing of the third *Minim* it is no longer *quadruple* but *common Time*; from whence it follows, that the *Minims* muft be beat in their *Timing*, as one Meafure, the fame as the *Crotchets*, tho' in Length and Value double to them.

Tunes of *quadruple Time* rarely, if ever, begin with odd Notes, as the foregoing *Tunes* of *common*; and, for an Example, I fhall name a *Tune* or two of this Kind, as the *Entree d' Apolon*. But as that *Dance* may not probably be known to fuch as this *Book* is principally defign'd for, I fhall name a fecond of the fame Sort, namely the *Godolphin*, compos'd by the late Mr. *Ifaac*, upon which may be practifed the *Time* of this Movement; to which End the Heel is raifed to mark the *Time*, as already explain'd, after which it remains on the Floor the playing of the firft and fecond *Minims* or half Meafure. The third and fourth *Minims* are in the two Motions the Heel or Toe makes in rifing, in Order to mark the enfuing Meafure: For Inftance, the firft Rife is made ftrong and brifk upon the Beginning of the latter half of the Meafure or third Note; the fecond Rife is made farther up into the Air, in the fame Manner as the firft, to the fourth and laft Note; upon the Expiration whereof the Toe or Heel comes down marking the *Time* to the next Bar, counting One One, Two Two, &c. as before, whilft the whole *Tune* is compleated.

Having fhewn how the *Dancer* fuits his Steps to the Notes of the *Mufic*, it will be of no Ufe to fay any thing farther of that here; and therefore I fhall only obferve, that as there are in this Sort of *Tunes* two Steps to each Meafure, the firft is beat, as ufual, down, but the fecond is marked up in the Air, on the Beginning of the third *Minim*, as above explained.

Being now arrived at *triple Time* or of three in a Meafure, I have little to fay, having already in the foregoing Proportions of *Time* defcribed the Manner of beating or marking *Time*; for it is altogether fuperfluous and unneceffary to enlarge, fince it is intirely in

the

148 *The* ART *of* DANCING *explain'd.*

the same Method, except to make a few Observations touching the most material Difference in the Movements thereof; and first observe, that the *Courante* is a Sort of *quadruple* Movement which consists of three *Minims*, instead of the like Number of *Crotchets*, as in the rest following; which *Minims* are usually divided into double the Quantity of *prick'd Crotchets* and *Quavers*, mix'd or blended promiscuously together, according to the *Composer's* Fancy, producing this Movement and play'd as three *Minims*, which renders it very solemn and grave; and, in its counting or beating in Time it is the same as the foregoing *quadruple*, only it is a *Minim* less and generally begins with an odd *Quaver* or half Note. Upon this the Heel or Toe is raised, as aforesaid, to mark the *Time* or first Note in the Coming down of the Toe or Heel, counting One One, Two Two, during which, two Thirds of the Measure the Foot rests upon the Ground. In the third and remaining *Minim* or Part the Heel or Toe is raised in Readiness to mark the Measure following, which is perform'd successively on, in like Manner, keeping just and regular *Time*, &c. as was shewn before; but, for an Example, I shall name the *La Burgogne* by Mr. *Pecour* and *Brawl* of *Audenarde* by Mr. *Siris.*

The next grave Movements are *Sarabands*, *Passacailles*, and *Chaconnes*, each of three *Crotchets* to a Measure, and every one a Degree lighter than the other: Nevertheless the Method of beating *Time* is the same as described above in the *Courante* Movement, only instead of *Minims* to *Crotchets* and of the *Time's* commencing after an odd Note, it is mark'd directly as in *quadruple*; that is to say, excepting *Chaconnes*, which always begin with odd Notes. Examples of the two former Sorts are the *Princess Ann*, the *Follie D'Espaigne*, and *Passaca:lle D'armid*, all which *Dances* were compos'd by Mr. *L'Abbee*; and also of the latter the *Princess Ann's Chaconne* by the same Author is an Instance, where a whole Measure is let slip beforethe Time commences.

The next *Minuets* and *Passepieds* are still brisker, the first being of three *Crotchets* to a Bar or Measure, and the second of three *Quavers*; and the first usually begins without odd Notes, but the second

cond never. The *Time* of these Movements, in *Dancing*, ought never to be beat after every Bar but every other Measure, by Reason, as has been said, one *Minuet Step* takes two Measures of these Movements; and it is to be noted that, as in *quadruple*, the *Time* is to be mark'd the first Measure down, and the second up, instead of twice down. It must be farther observed that if the Strains of the *Minuet* or *Paſſepied* consist of eight, as they most frequently do, four *Minuet Steps* are equivaleut to a Strain once over; from whence it follows, that the Beginning of a Strain, whether the first or second it matters not, is always the *Time* the *Dancer* is to mark or hit, and from thence to proceed on from one second Bar to another upon the *Time*, neither varying to faster nor slower, than at first setting out, during the Performance of the whole *Dance*; and if the *Minuet* or *Paſſepied* is of more Measures, it is nevertheless performed in the same Manner. There is Plenty of Examples of the former Kind, as is of the latter the *Royal George*, that is, the Conclusion and Beginning of the *Bretagne*; the first by Mr. *L'Abbee*, the second by Mr. *Pecour*, to which I shall add one more of my own Composition, namely, the *Paſſepied Round*.

As to *Tunes* of *triple Time* agreeing with *quadruple*, viz. *Louvres* or slow *Jigs*, they are of two Measures, or of six *Crotchets* in the Bar, the first three whereof are beat down and the remaining up, each answering to a Measure of a *Saraband*, and a Movement usually beginning in odd Notes. For Instance, the *Entree Espagnol* and *Paſtoral Dance*, the latter by the late Mr. *Iſaac*; and the *Union* by the same Author is of this Nature, tho' it does not begin with odd Notes as the *Dances* aforesaid. As the foregoing Discourse shews that *Louvres* or slow *Jigs* are agreeable to *quadruple Time*, I shall next proceed to observe, that *Jigs* and airy light *Tunes* of the like Number of Notes to the Measures, as the aforesaid, agree with *Rigadoons* in *common Time*, and beat as such in marking the first three down, and the remaining up; as for Example, in *Jigs* or *Forlanes*, the *Princeſs Amelia* compos'd by Mr *L'Abbee*, and the *Dance* of that Movement by Mr. *Pecour*; and the *Shepherdeſs* compos'd by my self is likewise an Example of this Sort.

There

There is yet another Movement that occurs to my Memory, namely, the *Canary*, which is of a very brisk Nature, consisting only of three or six *Quavers* in a Measure, but usually the latter, slipping before the *Time* is beat three *Quavers* or half a Measure, and marking the three first down and the rest up; and the last Movement of the *Royal Galliard* by the late Mr. *Isaac* is an Example of this Kind.

There is still a Movement unobserved, of the like Quantity of Notes to a Measure, *viz.* the *Hornpipe*, which is of three *Minims* or six *Crotchets* in the Bar, and, in marking or beating *Time*, agrees with a *Tune* of *triple Time* or of three, as for Instance a *Saraband*, in which the Foot remains down, during the counting of One, Two, and upon the third rises to mark the ensuing Measure *&c.* The second Parts of the *Union* and *Richmond* are both *Dances* of a *Hornpipe* Movement, and of the late Mr *Isaac*'s Composition.

Besides the foregoing Rules of beating *Time* it may be of Service to such as have but *indifferent Ears*, when they are about to *dance* in any Assembly or private Room, or in their *Dancing*, to hearken to the *Tune*, that they may know the *Time* in which the *Dance* is to be perform'd; which they may more easily do by Reason the *Music* rarely fail of beating *Time* to the *Tune* they are playing, or at least ought not, because hearing the beating or striking of the Toe or Heel against the Floor are visible and certain Marks of the *Dancers* commencing.

Moreover in *Dancing*, if the *Partner* with whom we *dance* be a good Performer, we should take Care to keep our Steps and Figure agreeable with theirs; and I am of Opinion, if a Person has the least Notion of the Steps he is performing, it will be very easy for him to observe, whether they begin and end together, which I believe may be useful in *Dancing*.

However, as I have said before, the most sure Method I take to be, *listening* to the *Music* and *Time* beat thereto, tho 'that itself is uncertain, nothing being more common than the *hearing* of a *Tune* begun in one *Time*, and, before it is ended, to be near as fast again; which renders it impossible for the best *Dancers* whatsoever

to

to *dance* as they ought, for instead of their finding the Note upon which they should step, it is push'd or drove from under their Feet during every Step they take, and of Consequence causes them to lose that natural and careless Air so agreeable in *Dancing*, notwithstanding they keep up with the *Tune*, as being never certain of its *Time*. Indeed, it must be own'd to be the *Dancer's* Business to *dance* to the *Tune*; yet it is nevertheless the *Music's* Part to beat and keep constant and true *Time*, as well at the latter Part of a *Tune* as at first. By this Means the *Dancers*, sure of the *Time* they *dance* to, perform not only with Pleasure and Ease to themselves, but also give a double Satisfaction to the *Spectators* in beholding the *Dancers*; for altho' the latter are at a considerable Distance from each other, yet the former will observe, that every Movement or Sink and Rise the *Dancers* make is exactly the same in one as well as the other; the former in Order to mark *Time*, and the latter in marking of it. Moreover every Turn, Step, Spring or Bound seen in one will be at the same Instant observed in the other, in such an exact Symmetry and Harmony of the Parts agreeing with the Notes of the *Music*, as to cause the most agreeable Surprize in the Beholders of the two *Dancers*; or admitting a Dozen or more in Number, by observing them all to move as only one Person. This is the natural Effect of good *Dancing* adorn'd with all its Beauties, in that the *Music* seems to inspire the *Dancing*, and the latter the former; and the Concurrence of both is so requisite to charm those who *behold* them, that each of them in some Measure suffers by a Separation. For Example the *Eye* can receive no Pleasure in the *Music* any more than the *Ear* in *Dancing*; but in Conjunction there is at once an Attack upon both these Senses.

Tho' this is only an imperfect Draught of *fine Dancing*, yet it may serve to shew how frequently this Art suffers by the *Unskilfulness* of its *Performers*, whether it arise from the Want of a true Knowledge of the Steps, a bad Ear, or from any other Cause; and this it was that gave Birth to my Treatise on *Dancing*, in which the principal and most remarkable Steps in that *Art* are described and taken in Pieces. I have also shewn how the Steps of each Measure

are

are made to *common* or *triple Time*; and in the *Minuet* I have given an Explanation of all the Steps of that *Dance*; and shewn, tho' in Effect it is not so, how it may be reduced into a regular *Dance*. In discoursing upon *Time*, I have given Examples in the most known *Tunes* of every Movement, upon which it may be practised or beaten; and in the Rules for the same I have fully made appear, how the Steps of the foregoing Discourse, altho' in Pieces, are there united and set together again, moving in just *Time* to the Sound of *Music*, as the *Watch* is put in Motion by its Springs. Upon taking some farther Notice of the Elevation, Movement, and graceful Fall of the *Arms*, together with some Observations concerning *Country Dancing*, I shall conclude this Work, in Hopes that, as the chief, nay only Motive of undertaking it was the *Publick Good*, it may answer the desired End; the accomplishing whereof will be a sufficient Recompence for the great Pains, Trouble, and Expence I have been at in compleating the same; and, as there never hitherto appeared in the World, at least in our Language, a Piece of this Nature, I flatter my self it will meet with the more Acceptance.

CHAP. XIV.
Of the Movement of the *ARMS* in *DANCING*.

HAVING shewn the Method in which the different Steps are to be taken and perform'd, I shall now proceed to shew how the Movements of the *Arms* ought to accompany the said Steps in *Dancing*; lest this Work should be compared to the Legs and Body of a Man without *Arms*.

However as on the one Hand, I shall make it my Study to omit Nothing that can contribute to compleat this *Work*, I shall at the same Time, on the other, only observe what I apprehend to be material

The ART *of* DANCING *explain'd.* 153

terial, without tiring the *Reader*'s Patience on a Subject which cannot be compleated without the very best *Masters*. The Correspondence of the *Legs* and *Arms* in *Dancing* is a Point of so nice a Nature that any Awkwardness or improper Movements therein would destroy the Beauty of the whole, since that *Dancing* cannot be good which is decrepid or lame in any of its Parts, any more than a *Gentleman* or *Lady* can be justly esteem'd compleatly genteel who are naturally and easily disposed in some Parts and disagreeable in others; so that in fine it is the very Polish and finishing Stroke.

For the better comprehending of this we must first take Notice that, in whatsoever Position we stand before the Elevation or Raising of the *Arms*, the Palms or Insides of the Hands are to our Side in a genteel easy Shape or Fashion, the whole *Arms* hanging from under the Shoulders without Force downwards, or too much Relaxation upwards, but natural and easy in a Readiness for the Elevation †.

The next Observation relates to the Position of the Hands after their Elevation or being raised; and we should find them with the Palms of the Hands to the Presence or right forwards with the Arms both open or extended, in the like Manner we have described them by the Sides, neither too much raised nor too much sunk beneath the Shoulders, but graceful and easy, and being so disposed ready to perform the first Motion, which in the Movement of the *Arms* above corresponds with the Sink or Bending of the Knees below ‡. This is done by moving or raising the whole *Arms*; and, in the Fall of the said *Arms* to their first Situation after their Elevation, the Palms of the Hands, instead of right forwards as before, are now to the Floor; which is effected by a slow and easy Turning of the said Wrists during the Motion of the said *Arms* downwards compleating the Movement or Motion of the *Arms*, from whence all other Movements take their Rise or Beginning; so that, if the graceful Raising or Elevation of the *Arms* from the Sides to the Palms right forwards be by a slow and even Raising of the Wrists, turning outwards or backwards till they arrive at their proper Height as before described ‡, their becoming Fall must in like

† See the Figures in Plate I, B. I. ‡ See Plates II and XV in B. I.

Manner

Manner * be in the Turn of the Wrists and Palms of the Hands downwards in a slow and even Motion inwards, or forwards, whilst the Palms are to the Sides, as at first ‡, greatly resembling the Fall of a Feather or the Coming down of a Bird, their Fall is so smooth and easy; and it is a wonderful Grace to *Dancing* when well performed.

To avoid being tedious or overloading this Subject with too many Observations I shall reduce the various Movements of the *Arms* to three or four, *viz.* first, the Movement of the Wrists from the *Elbows* round upwards (a). Secondly, the *Movement* of the *Arms* inwards in their Motion upwards (b). Thirdly, the compleating the said *Movement* of the *Arms* inwards by the *Movement* of the *Wrists* round upwards mentioned before (a). And fourthly, the irregular or *contrary Movement* (c).

Now, as to the Method of Performance and Timing of the *Movement* of the *Wrists* round upwards, it is by a slow and even Motion or Movement of the *Knuckles* or *Forefingers* and *Thumbs* upwards round from a small Bend of the *Wrists* and *Elbows* corresponding therewith (b). The Commencing is upon one, the *Movement* round backwards (b) finishing in a Flirt or careless Motion of the *Wrists* and *Arms* in their Return to their former Situation, as in the Position of the *Arms* after their Elevation; upon two (a) and three if to triple Time, in the Motion or Preparative for the *Movement* of the *Arms* next ensuing, as it will conclude in like Manner upon four, if to *common Time*.

*The next *Movement* is made by the easy Fall of the *Elbows* at the same Time or Instant; and the *Knuckles* or *Forefingers* and *Thumbs* lead the Way in a smooth and easy Motion from below upwards forming a quarter or half Circle or Bow †. The *Hands* in a handsome Fashion may be supposed the Ends or Points of the said half Circle or Bow; and it is to be noted that this Movement is on-

---

* See the Plates XV, and II; B. I. ‡ See the Figures in Plate I, B. I.
(a) See Plate XV, B. I. (b) See Plate X, B. I. (c) See Plates IV, V, VI, IX,
XII, XIII, XIV. B. I. † See the Figures in Plates X, and XI, B. I.

The ART *of* DANCING *explain'd.* 155

ly about the one Half of the aforesaid. But as that begun by forming the Circle round upwards above the Position of the *Arms*, the *Elbows* during the *Movement* of the *Wrists* remaining elevated until the Flirt or Finishing is made; on the other Hand in this *Movement* of the *Arms* the half Circle, or Motion the *Wrists* make, is below the Position of the *Arms*; and, instead of the *Elbows* remaining elevated, as before, together with the whole *Arms*, they fall or sink down in a slow, smooth, and easy Motion, whilst the *Forefingers* and *Thumbs*, as aforesaid, at the same Time move upwards in the like slow and deliberate Manner, finishing together with the *Hands* above and the *Elbows* below in Order to the throwing the Arms open off again, as in *Hops*, *Chaffees*, and the like, for which these are the proper *Arms*. The bringing them in on the Conclusion of the foregoing Step, as just described ‖, is in Order to the said throwing them out on the Time or Beginning of the next Step † for which this is the Preparative, tho' the *Movement* of the *Arms* to the Palms of the *Hands* downwards must always be first made by Way of farther Preparation, concluding open and extended, 'till the Measure is expired; and from hence it appears, that these two Movements usually answer each separately to a Measure or Step, forming together much about a whole Circle. The former Half, as I have said, moves under the Position of the *Arms*, and the latter Half above in the *Movement* of the *Arms* round upwards in the Form and Manner above described; and these are the second and third *Movements* I proposed to explain.

The *irregular* or *fourth* and *last Movement* is produced from the two former, *viz*, by the Fall of the *Elbow* of one *Hand* as the Knuckle moves upwards, whilst the other at the same Time performs the Motion of the *Arm* round upwards, which compose a fine *Contrast*, concluding both at the same Time (d) with one Hand bended and the other extended (d). This beautiful *contrasted* Movement changes, every Step alternately, first one Hand and then the other, and is the proper *Movement* of the *Arms* in *Half*

‖ See the Figures in Plates X and XI, B. I.   † See Plate XV, B. I.   (d) See Plates IV. V, VI, IX, XII, XIII, XIV. B. I.

156 *The* ART *of* DANCING *explain'd.*

Coupees, Marches, Bourees, and the like; only it muſt be obſerved that the bended *Arm* is the contrary *Arm* to the beginning *Foot* in any of the Steps (e) aforeſaid, excepting backwards or ſidways, becauſe then the *Oppoſition* or *Contraſt* is between the ſame *Hand* and *Foot*, as was already ſhewn in treating of *Walking* (f). The *Movement* of the *Arms* round upwards † is made uſe of in *Pirouettes, Bourees* with a *Bound*, and all ſuch like Steps.

Altho' there are various other Methods or Manners of *moving* the *Arms* in *Dancing,* yet as theſe, like the five *Poſitions* with Regard to the *Feet*, are as it were the principal, it is needleſs (nor indeed is it agreeable to my preſent Deſign) to enlarge, eſpecially on a Subject which, as I have already ſaid, cannot be ſufficiently deſcribed by *Words* but muſt be compleated by the very beſt *Maſters*; and therefore to avoid Trifling, as I have deſcribed and given ſome Hints of the Method or Manner of *moving* the *Arms* which will agree with all the Steps made Uſe of in genteel *Dancing*, I ſhall refer the reſt to the perſonal Inſtructions of a *Maſter* properly qualified, who muſt compleat what is here wanting, not only in Relation to the *Movements* of the *Arms* but alſo thoſe of the Feet between which there is, as I have already obſerved, a perfect Connexion and Harmony. The *Fingers* and *Toes, Wriſts* and *Ancles, Elbows* and *Knees, Shoulders* and *Hips,* in *Dancing* muſt move all of a Piece; and in fine the Compleating of this is the End I had chiefly in View in compoſing this *Work.*

CHAP. XV.
Of COUNTRY DANCING.

THO' my original Deſign was only to have ſpoke of genteel *Dancing*, yet as *Country Dances* are at all *Aſſemblies* or *Balls* introduced as it were a Part of or belonging to the former, (and

(e) See Plates IV, VI, IX, XII, XIV. B. I. Plate XV, B. I.   (f) See Plate XIII, B. I.   † See

indeed

The ART of DANCING explain'd.

indeed I think it may very properly be efteem'd as a luxuriant or carelefs Branch growing out from the other) and is become as it were the Darling or favourite Diverfion of all Ranks of People from the Court to the Cottage in their different Manners of *Dancing*, and as the Beauty of this agreeable Exercife (I mean when perform'd in the *genteel Character*) is very much eclipfed and deftroyed by certain *Faults*, or *Omiffions*, in the *Performers* not hitherto, if I remember right, taken Notice of in any *Books*; I fhall, at the Requeft of fome Perfons of Figure my Subfcribers, endeavour to point out tho'e *Neglects* which render this Diverfion, to fine *Dancers*, either altogether difagreeable, or much lefs pleafant, becaufe one or two Couples either through *Carelefnefs*, or *Want* of *better Inftructions*, will put the whole Set in Diforder.

This will always be occafioned by the *Couples* below thofe who lead up the *Dance*, when they omit moving up into the firft *Couple*'s Places, on their cafting off, and down again in their cafting up to their Places as at firft; or the like, if the firft or leading *Couples* crofs over and figure in. In a Word, whenever the leading *Couples* move downwards, the *Couples* coming up to lead the *Dance* fhould move upwards and, when they move up again, the *Couples* who do not lead the *Dance* ought to move down again, attending the Motion of the *Dancers* going down with the *Dance*, who in Return will attend them in like Manner, when they arrive at the upper End to *dance* in their Turns. The nice Obfervation of this prefents to the *Beholders* an agreeable Profpect of the whole Company in Motion at once, inftead of the Confufion that happens when this is neglected; as when in giving the right Hand and left in going round downwards from above, or upwards from below, inftead of continuing on and giving firft the right and then the left Hand to thofe you meet, you turn back, or if in Converfation with your *Partner*, or otherwife, you be not attentive and ready to begin at the Conclufion of any Part or Divifion of the *Dance*; which frequently falls out for, when the coming up *Couples* have concluded the *Dance* with thofe going down, they often forget that they are immediately to begin again with the next above them,

them, and so for *Want* of *Attention* breed Confusion and at the same Time expose themselves to the *Spectators*.

Indeed good Breeding, in Regard to those with whom we *dance*, requires our not being *careless*; and yet my *fair Readers* and others I hope will excuse me, if I tell them I fear this is too often the Case, since with due Circumspection and Care it is impossible not to follow almost any *Country Dance*, tho' I must own when I was a *Youth* I thought it *Conjuration*. If we place ourselves at the Bottom, and, instead of Talking, take a Survey of the *Dance*, whatever it is in its Performance, over and over again, first with one *Couple* and then with another, it is impossible, I say, but we must be able to go down with it, when it comes to our Turns, as well as avoid Disorders in our gradual Ascent to the upper End; it being only to observe and distinguish one from another the Things of of which the different Parts of all *Dances* whatsoever are composed whether *Casting off* or *up*, *Figuring in*, *Hands across* or *round*, *Right Hand and Left*, *Flying*, *Pursuing*, *Clapping of Hands*, *Heys*, *Leading up* or *down*, *Back to Back*, *Changing of Places*, *Falling back*, *Meeting again*, or whatever it be, by dividing one Part of the above Catalogue from the other. And with a little Practice you will soon be able not only to follow *Country Dances* but also lead them up, tho' you never *danced* them before: For Instance, if a *Gentleman* or *Lady* at the upper End propose a *Dance* to their *Partner* unknown to one of them, you need only ask how it begins, and they will acquaint you, and whether it be *Falling Back*, *Meeting again*, *Crossing over*, or whatsoever else, you will readily perform it. For this Reason I would advise all *young People* and *others* who are not perfect in *Right Hand* and *left*, *Figuring in*, *Heys*, and the like, before they attempt to *dance* in Public, to make themselves well acquainted with and able to perform all the different Parts or Divisions of *Country Dancing*; which they may privately learn amongst one another, if they don't care to practise in Public, and thereby not only render this Diversion more agreeable to themselves, but also more pleasing to those who accompany them in this Exercise.

Besides

The ART of DANCING explain'd.

Besides as I have before hinted, instead of giving a confused Idea to the *Beholders* it will afford an agreeable Landscape or Prospect of so many Pairs of fine *Gentlemen* and *Ladies* gracefully in Motion to the Sound of *Music*, and compleating each Part of the *Dance* in *Time* to the Measure, or Strains of the *Tune*, as it were of one Accord: As of even Rows longwise when falling back and meeting again; half Circles, when casting off or up again; Figures of Eight or Binding of a Hedge, as in Figuring in, or the Heys; irregular Figures, when one flies and the other pursues; round Circles, when Hands are joined; cross Figures, when the right or left Hands are joined moving round; Beating Time in Contrast, as when Hands are clapped first in Time with their own, and next crosswise with their right Hand against their *Partner*'s, or others again clap their own Hands, and afterwards strike the left in Contrast; Leading crosswise in Rows, in Order of marching up the Room and the like down, with various other beautiful Circles and Figures. If a fine Picture, beautiful Fields, crystal Streams, green Trees, and imbroider'd Meadows in Landscape or Nature itself will afford such delightful Prospects, how much more must so many well shap'd *Gentlemen* and *Ladies*, richly dress'd, in the exact Performance of this Exercise, please the *Beholders*, who entertain them with such a Variety of living Prospects.

Having in the above Sketch or Draught attempted to raise some noble Ideas of *Country Dancing*, when performed in a proper Manner, and in the foregoing *Instructions* pointed out and removed all the most material *Faults* and *Omissions* in the Performance of this Branch of our *Art*, which either obstruct the Pleasure of the *Dancers*, or *Beholders*, I think I have finished what I designed, viz. the Improvement and Pleasure of others. I shall therefore conclude this *Work*, not in the least questioning but my good Intentions will meet with a favourable Reception from the Public, especially from those who receive Benefit or Profit thereby.

FINIS

THESE are to certify, that the foregoing or Second Part of the Work entitled, the ART OF DANCING EXPLAIN'D, was designed and composed long before the Treatise entitled, the DANCING MASTER, appeared as we believe and that, having carefully perused and examined the same, we found that, on the twenty seventh Day of January, 1727-8, it was written in its present Form.

   Witness our Hands,

        ALEX. JACKSON, } Dancing-Masters.
        JOSEPH JACKSON,

BOOK I

The following CUTS represent the Figures of Gentlemen standing in the different Attitudes or Postures, from whence the Steps of Dancing are to be taken & performed; and the Steps are also described in Characters as going to be made by the said Figures, or as having been already performed by them.

The CUTS were originally designed not only for the better Explanation & Understanding of my Printed Book, intitled The ART of DANCING explained by READING and FIGURES, but likewise to be proper Furniture for a Room or Closet, being of themselves an intire and independant Work, for if put in Frames with Glasses, they will not only shew the various Positions or Postures at one View, but be very agreable & instructive Furniture.

The PLATE marked A. contains the Plan of Rooms in different Positions, shewing the upper & lower Ends, and the proper Place at which the Dancer ought to begin. The PLATES E.I. contain Tables of the Steps which the said Figures are supposed to perform in their regular Order, as treated on in ye first Book which bears the Title aforesaid.

The Price of the CUTS belonging to the first and second Books without ye Printed Part, is Two Guineas, and those who are willing also to purchase the latter, viz. the Printed Part, may have it of the AUTHOR at the Red and Gold Flower Pot next Door to Widow EDWARDS's Coffee House, over-against the Bull and Gate in Holborn, for Half a Guinea, pursuant to my Printed Proposals wherein I assured the Public, that the whole Work, except to Subscribers, should not be sold under Two Guineas and a Half.

June 26. 1735.

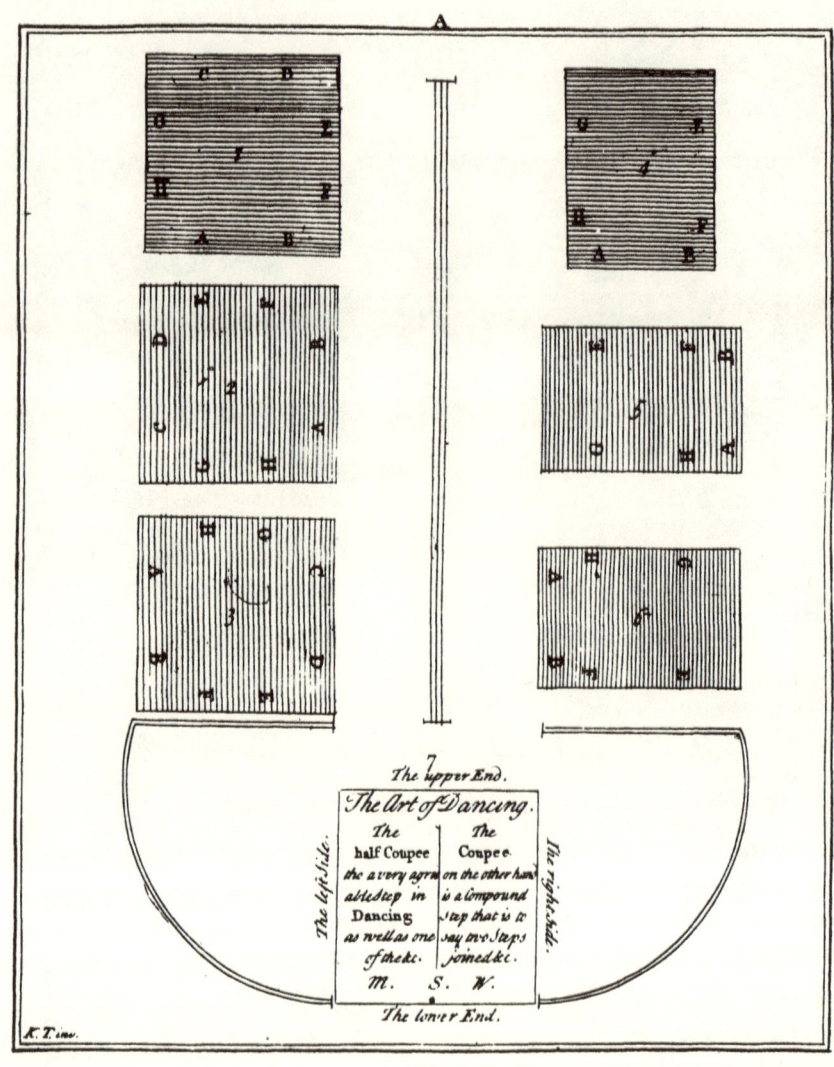

To my much Honoured Scholar the R.t Hon.ble the Lord Howard, Son to the Earl of Stafford; This PLATE is humbly dedicated by his Lordships most obliged Servant Kellom Tomlinson.

Those who understand Musu and ye Characters of Dancing will hear the former by the Sight of the Notes, & See ye various Turnings and windings of ye latter in ye Characters below; & in ye Figures ye graceful Attitudes of ye Dancers, forming together not only a compleat Entertainment of Musu & Dancing but also a fine picture.

To the Honourable Charles Talbot and the Honourable John Talbot, Sons to the late Earl of Shrewsbury, this PLATE is humbly inscribed by their Honours most obliged Serv.ᵗ K. Tomlinson

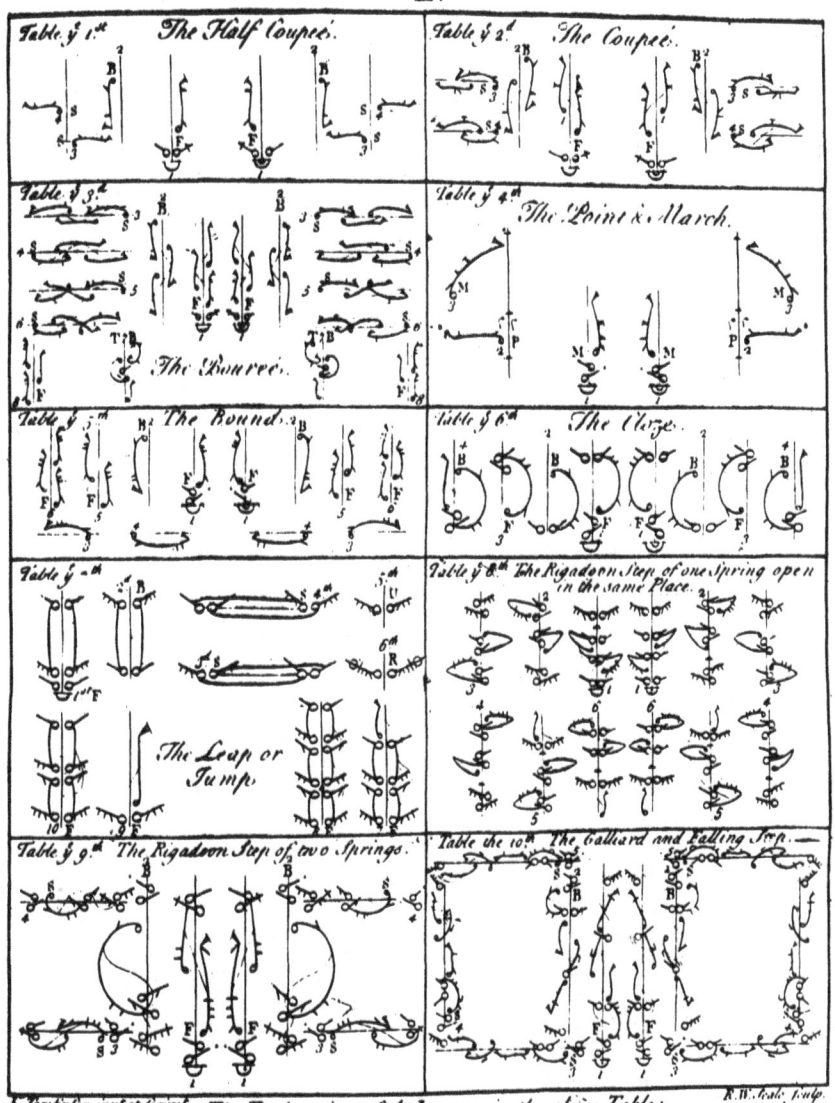

I.

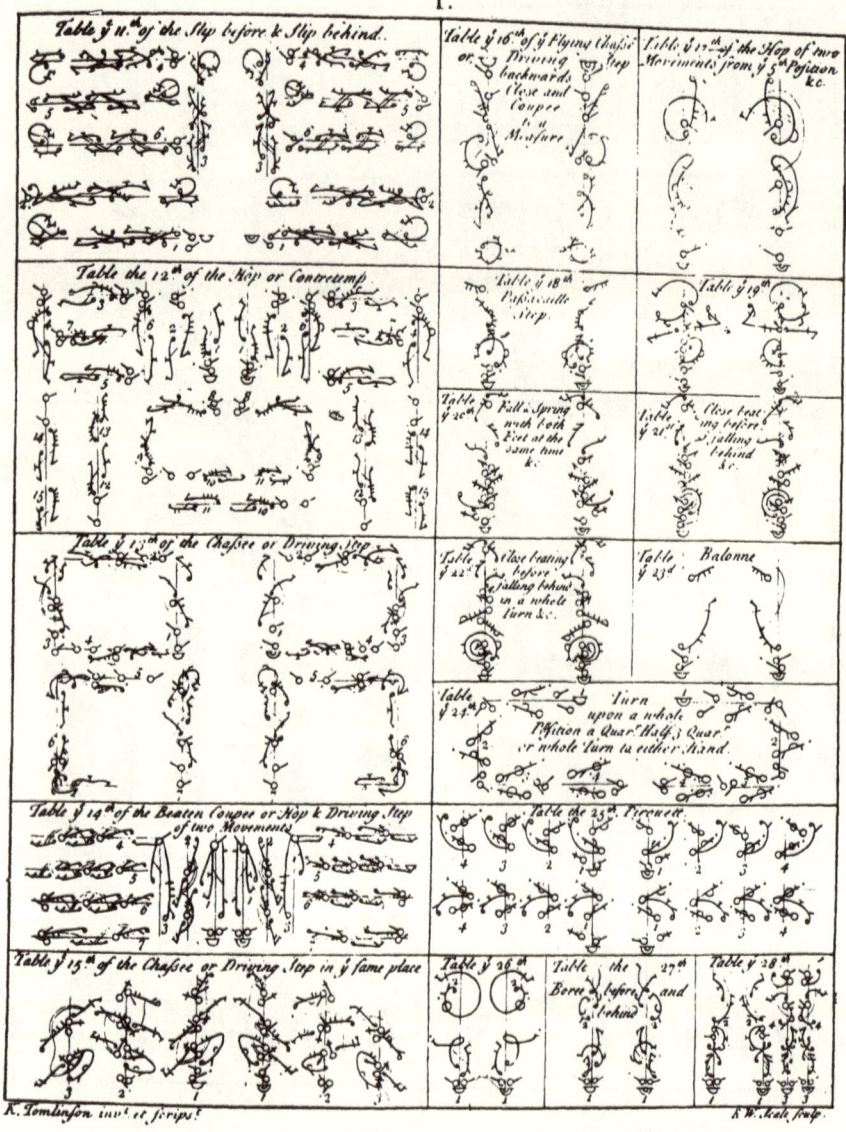

Whilſt Tuneful *Muſic* gives the Ear Delight,
And Graceful *Dancing* charms ẏ raviſh'd Sight;
They give a double Force to Cupid's Dart;
Which through ẏ Eye, makes Paſſage to ẏ Heart.

BOOK II.

The following CUTS repreſent the Figures *of* Gentlemen *and* Ladies, *one of each in a* Plate, *as* Dancing *a* Minuet, *beginning from ẏ* Reverence *or* Bow *and proceeding regularly on 'till the whole is finiſhed; ſhewing the beautiful Attitudes and graceful Deportments of the Performers in the different Figures and Circles of that celebrated* Dance, *they being of themſelves an intire and independant Work.*

Theſe Prints *are alſo deſign'd as proper* Furniture *for a* Room, *as well as for the better* Explanation *of the* ſecond Book *entitled,* The ART of DANCING Explain'd *by* READING *and* FIGURES; *and when hung up in their regular Order in* Frames *with* Glaſſes, *they will be a beautiful and inſtructive Repreſentation of the whole* Dance *at one View.*

The PLATE *marked* O *is a* Specimen *or* Explanation *of the* Characters *of* Dancing; *and that marked* U *contains the whole Form of the* Minuet *written in* Characters *in the Order deſcribed in the* ſecond Book *under the Title aforeſaid.*

NB. Both Sets of Cutts *were invented and cauſed to be delineated from the Life by* KELLOM TOMLINSON *Dancing-Maſter.*

To my once honoured Scholar the Right Honourable the Lady Elizabeth Heathcote, Daughter to the late Earl of Macclesfield, and Thomas Heathcote Esqr her Ladyships Eldest Son, this Plate is most humbly inscribed by her Ladyship's ever obliged Servant
Kellom Tomlinson.

To Corbet Owen of Ynysmaingynne *MERIONETHSHIRE* and Riwsason *MONTGOMERYSHIRE* Esq. and my ever respected Scholar Miss Elizabeth Owen his Sister, this *PLATE* is gratefully inscribed by their most obliged Servant *Kellom Tomlinson*

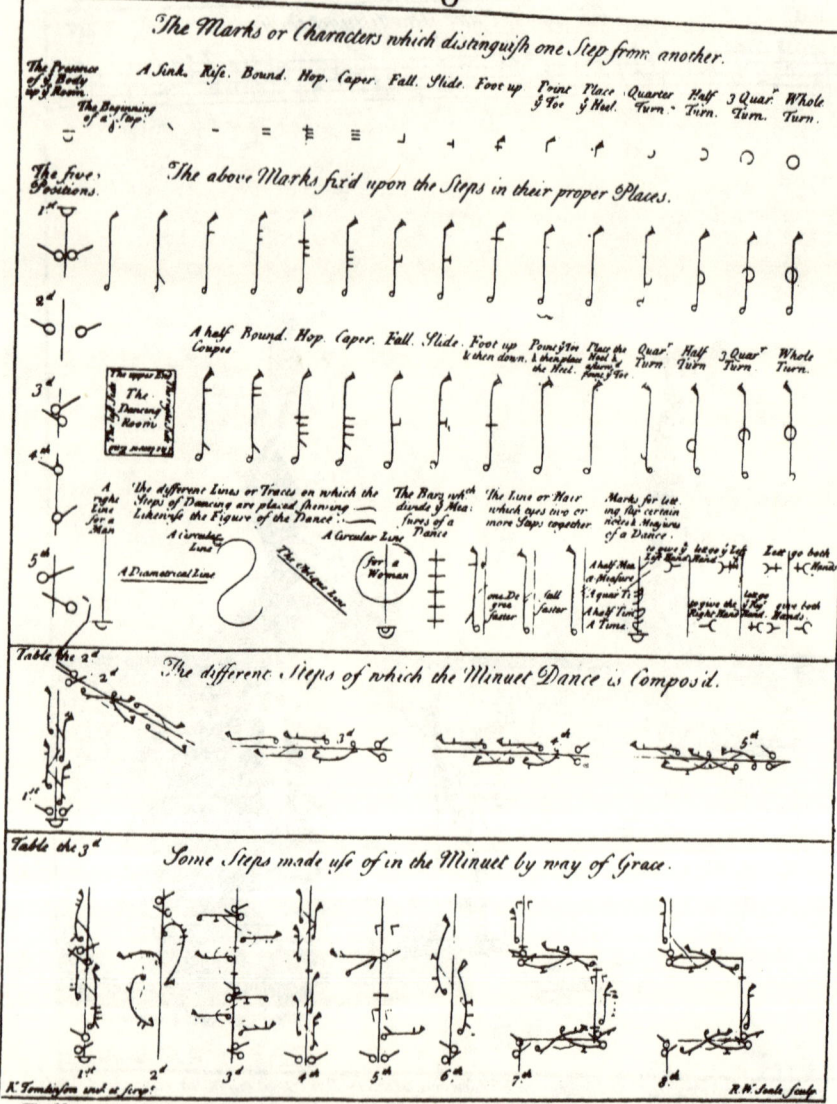

The NOBILITY and GENTRY, who are desirous their Children should learn the *Characters* of DANCING, of which the above is a Specimen, and willing to honour the *Author* in learning of him, shall pay no more than ye usual Prises for *Dancing* only, viz at their own Houses one *Guinea* and an *half* 12 Lessons: and in Proportion, if they are pleased to come to him, for in his humble Opinion teaching to *play by Ear* and to *Dance without Book* are equally wrong, & ought to be discontinued. Young *Dancing Masters* also may be instructed in the Art of *Dancing* & *Writing* by *Characters*.

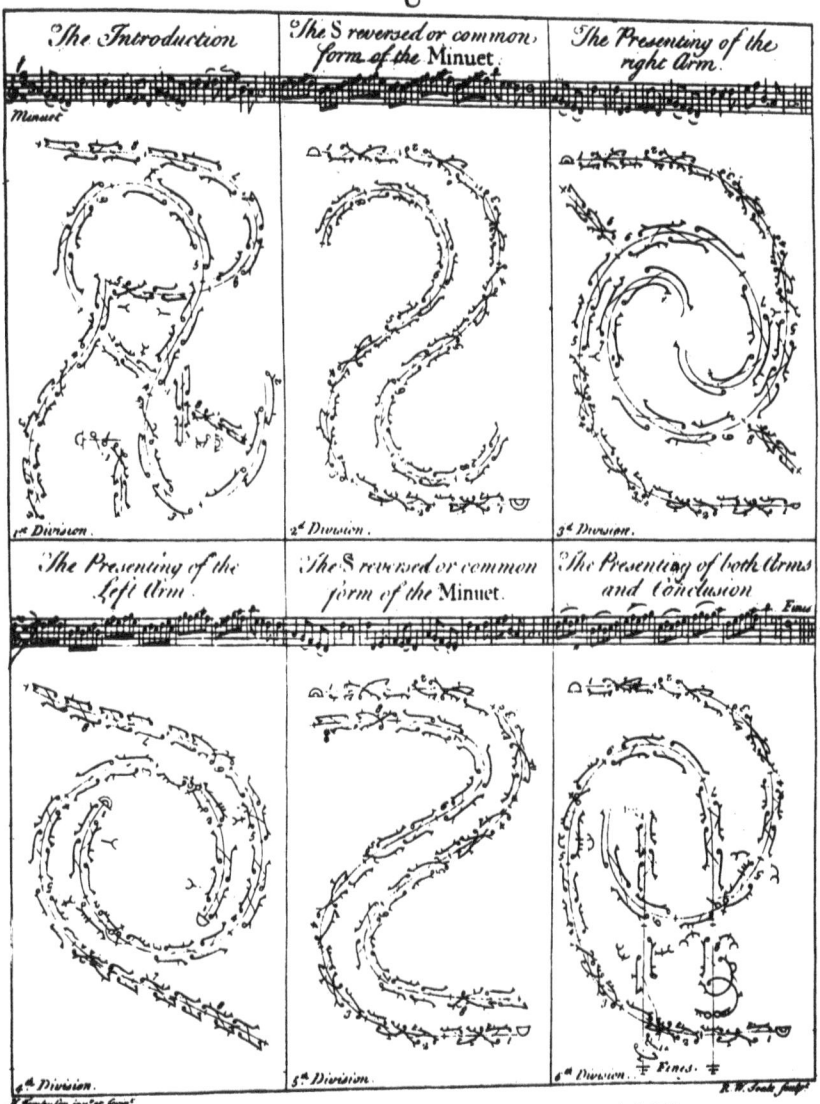

SIX
DANCES
COMPOS'D
By Mr. *Kellom Tomlinson.*
BEING
A COLLECTION of all the Yearly DANCES, publish'd by him from the Year 1715 to the present Year, *viz.*

      I. *The Passepied-Round O.*
     II. *The Shepherdess.*
    III. *The Submission.*
    IV. *The Prince Eugene.*
     V. *The Address.*
    VI. *The Gavot.*

The SUBMISSION writ, as it was perform'd at the *Theatre* in little *Lincoln's-Inn-Fields*, by Monsieur and Mademoiselle *Salle*, the Two *French* Children.

To be had only of the Author at his House in *Devonshire Street*, the last but one on the Right Hand going to *Queens-Square*, by *Ormond Street.*

Price of the Set, one Guinea and an Half.

To the LADIES.

THAT *the* Art of Dancing *is, at this Time, improv'd to (almost) a* Period of Perfection, *is a* Truth *which no* judicious Person *will go about to dispute.*

It is likewise as evident and undeniable, that the Advancement of that Art is owing to the Favour *and* Protection *of the* FAIR SEX, *under whose auspicious Smiles,* DANCING *has been* cultivated *and* improv'd, *from* Motions *and* Gesticulations wild *and* irregular, *to an agreeable and artful Movement of the* Body, *in a Manner no less* decent *than* delightful.

It is you, LADIES! *who have done* Honour *to this* Art, *and given a* Sanction *to its* Professors, *by making it a* Branch *of* Education; *and by admitting it as an* innocent Diversion *in* Conversation. *Encourag'd by this, our* ablest Masters *have labour'd (not in vain) to Number among other* Arts *and* Sciences, ORCHESOGRAPHY, *or the* Art *of* Dancing *by* demonstrative Characters; *by which, the various* Turns *and* Movements *of the* Body, *are plainly* directed *and* express'd; *which* Art *is now become* equal, *and of the* same Use, *with* Notes, &c. *in* Musick.

'Twere pity this Art should be a Secret *to you,* LADIES, *whose* Favour *and* Encouragement *have nourish'd it, from its* Infancy, *to its present* Perfection! *I my self, lament the* Prevalence *of* Custom, *which has hitherto depriv'd you of learning to dance* by Book; *and (notwithstanding all the* Jests *and* Reflections *which may be thrown*

DEDICATION.

thrown upon me) am resolv'd to instruct such Ladies, whom I have the Honour to teach at present, *and those who may become my Scholars* hereafter, *(their Inclinations concurring) in the aforesaid Art of* Dancing by Characters; *which, when they have attain'd, will not only enable them to know the true* Foundation *of what they have already learnt, and to perform it* correctly, *but will likewise render what they shall learn* hereafter, *abundantly more* facil *and* pleasant; *besides, if at any Time the* Memory *shall chance to* fail, *the* Character *will still be a* ready *and* certain Remembrancer, *and prevent their having Recourse to those who (perhaps) may* know *less than* Themselves.

That you, LADIES, *have a* Capacity *of acquiring any* Art *or* Science, *to which you shall apply your Selves, is a* Truth *too* notorious *for* Contradiction: *The many* living Instances *of* FEMALE EXCELLENCE, *which are now among us, make* Envy *it self confess it: Why then,* LADIES, *should the* Characters of Dancing, *alone be conceal'd from you? In my humble Opinion,* teaching to Play by Ear, *and to* Dance without Book, *are equally* absurd. *I could say a great deal more* upon this Head, *but am not willing to* press *too much upon your* Patience; *I chuse therefore rather to be* Silent, *than* tedious, *being ambitious of no greater Honour, than that of* subscribing my self,

LADIES,

Your most Obedient,

Humble Servant,

Kellom Tomlinson.

THE GAVOT,

A
NEW DANCE,

COMPOS'D
For the YEAR 1720.

BY

Mr. KELLOM TOMLINSON.

For the Use and Improvement of his Schollars, writ into CHARACTERS, and Publish'd by him for the further Encouragement of DANCING.

N. B. The following DANCES Compos'd by Mr. *KELLOM*, are likewise printed, *viz.*

The Address.
The Prince Eugene.
The Submission.
The Shepherdess.
The Passepied Round O.

To be had only of the Author, at his House in *Devonshire Street*, the last but one on the Right Hand going to *Queens-Square*, by *Ormond Street*.

Price Five Shillings.

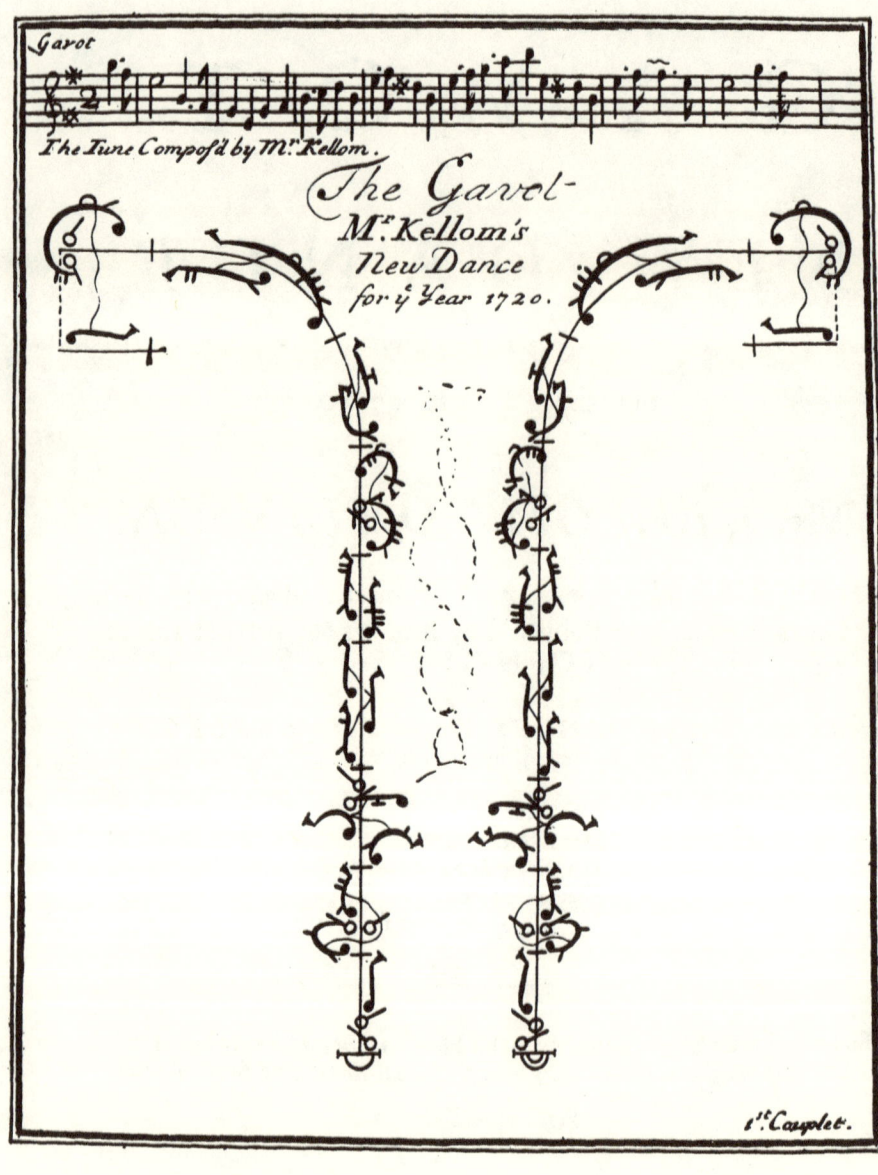

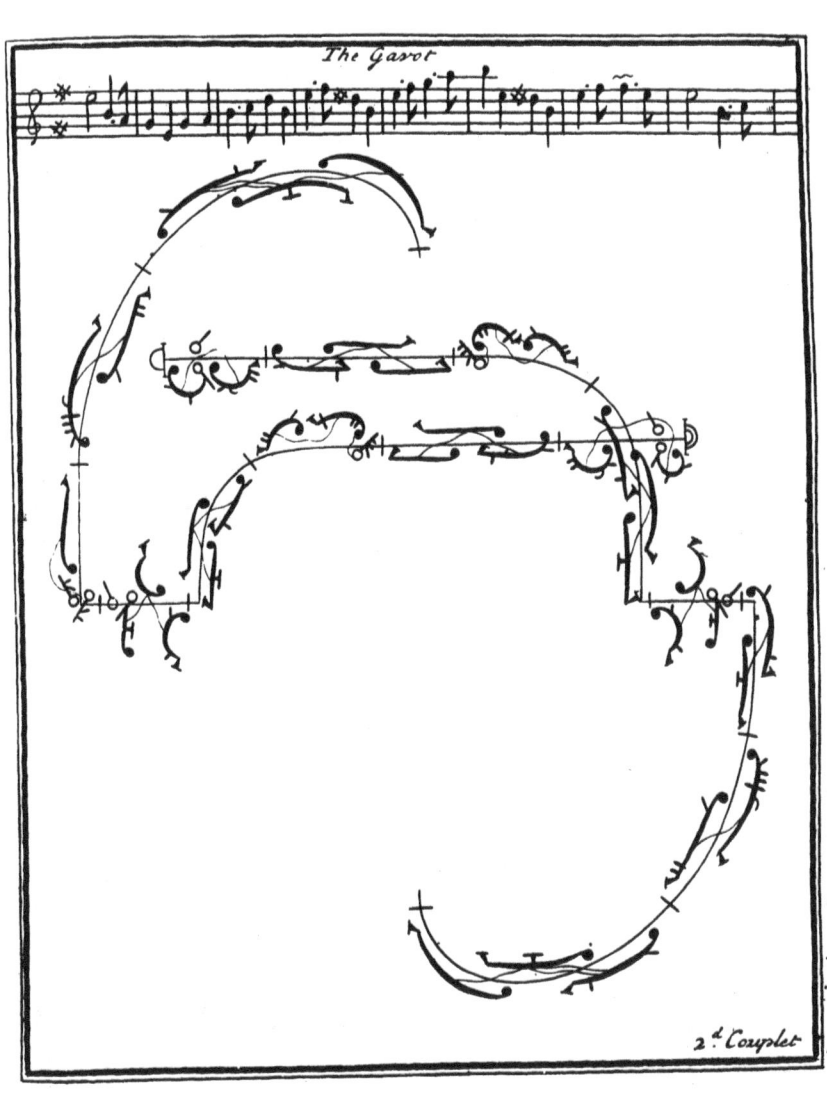

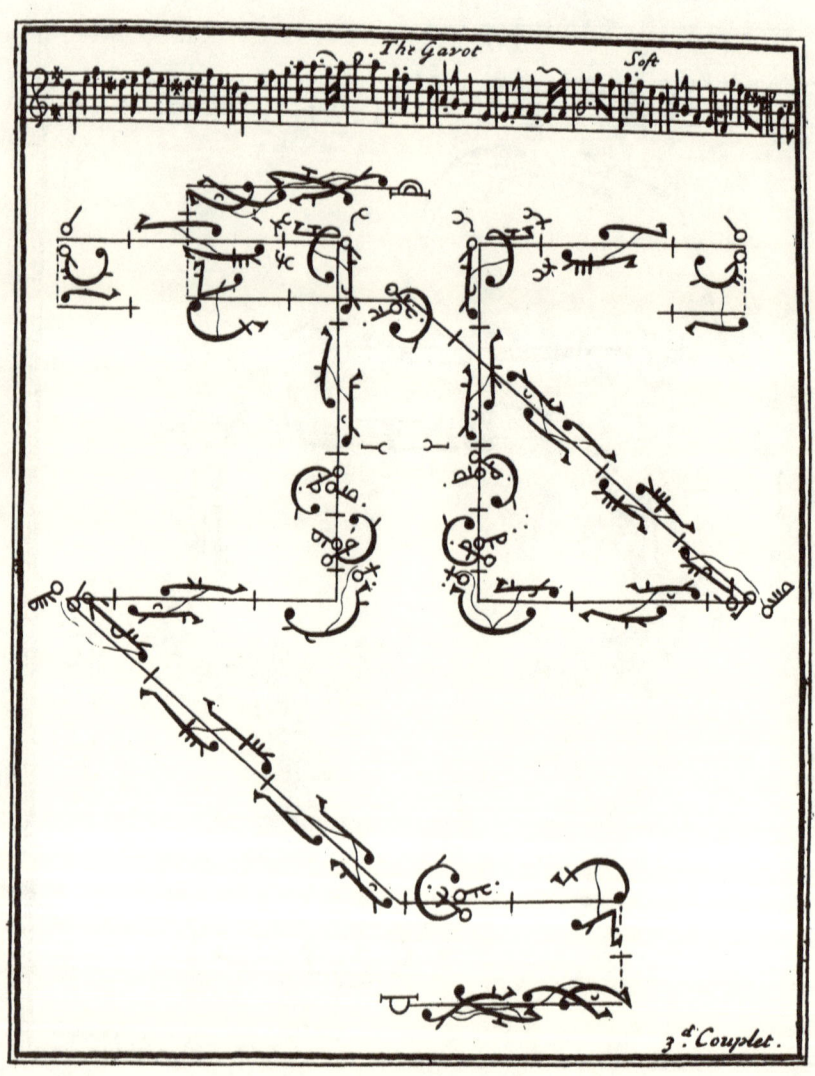

The ADDRESS a New RIGADOON

Compos'd for the Year 1719 by

M^r: Kellom Tomlinson

For the Use and Improvement of his Scholars; writ in Characters & Publish'd by him for the further Encouragement of Dancing.

N.B: The following Dances Compos'd by Mr Kellom are likewise Printed, viz.

The Prince Eugene.
The Submission.
The Shepherdess.
The Passepeid Round O.

To be had only of the Author, at his House in Devonshire Street, the last but one on y^e right hand, before you Enter into Queens Square, near Ormond Street.
Price 5 Shillings.

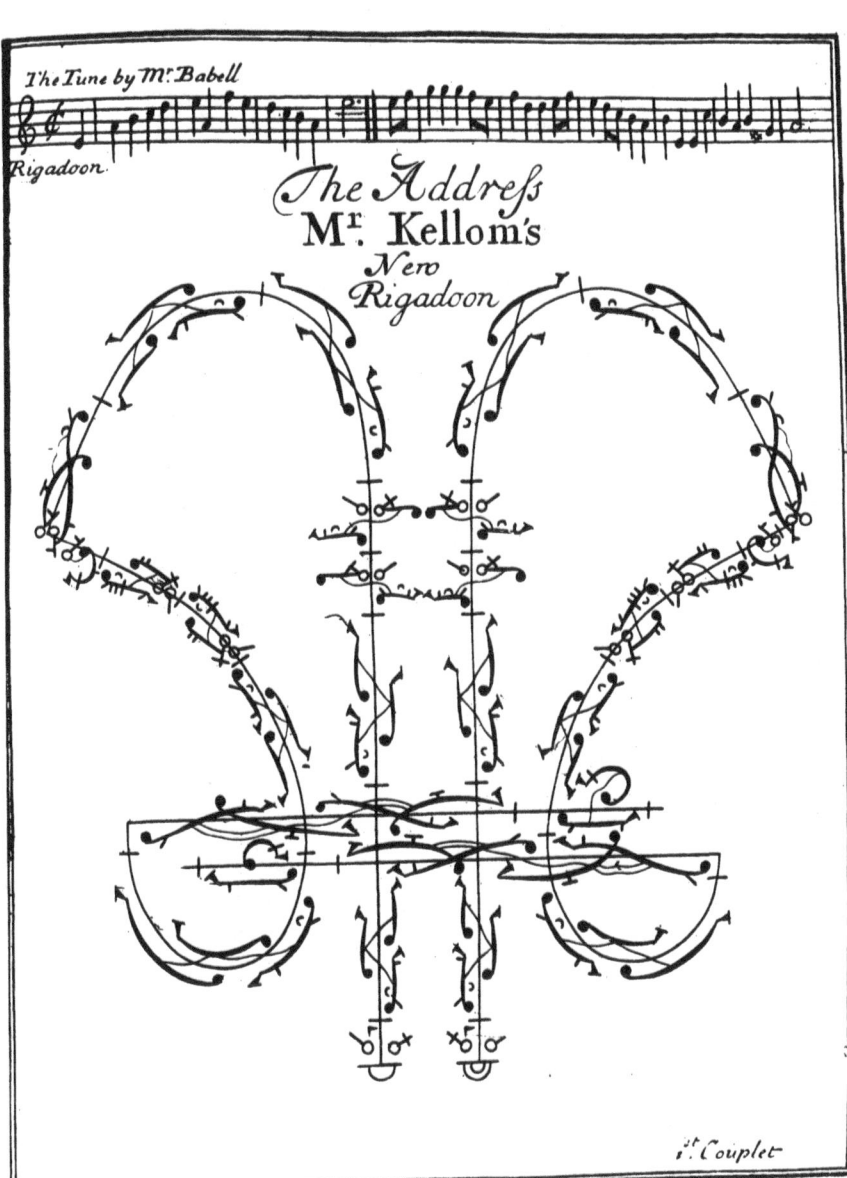

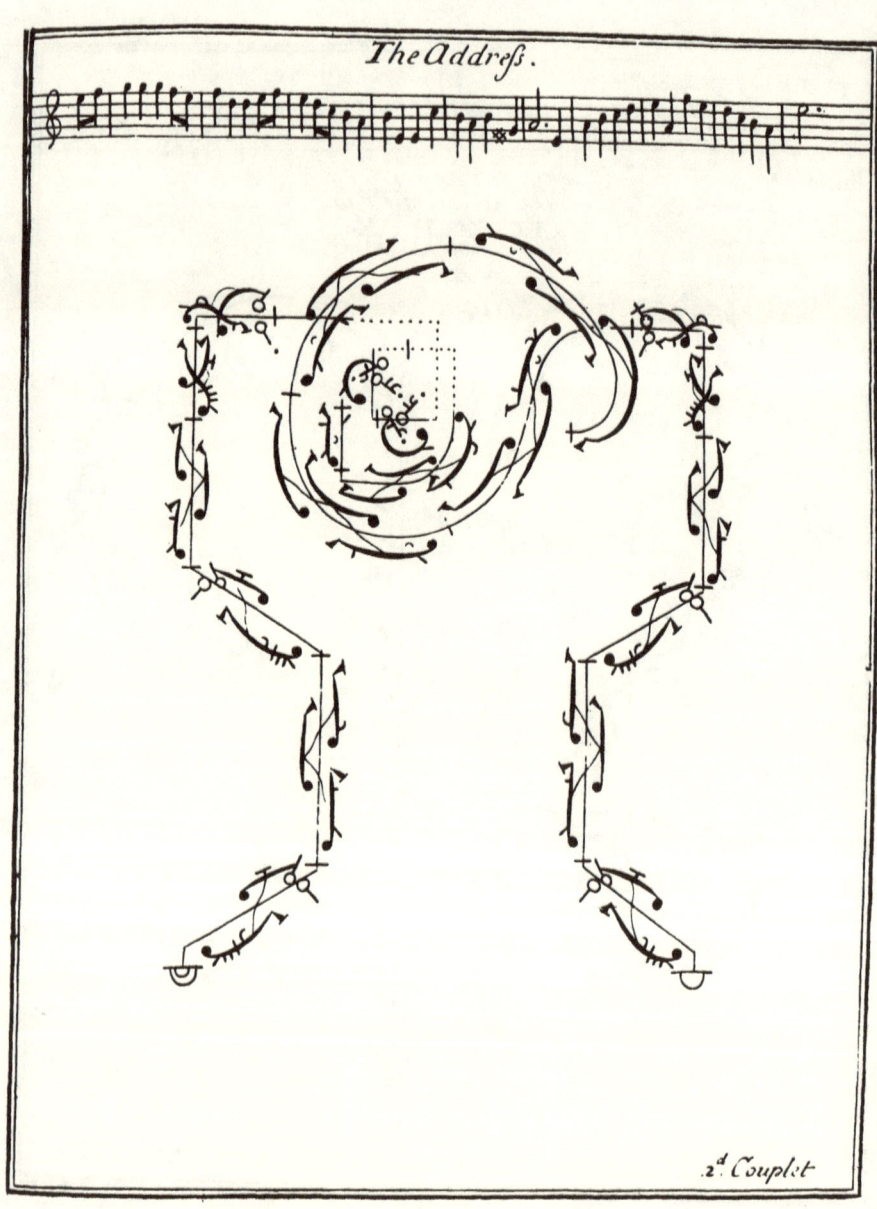

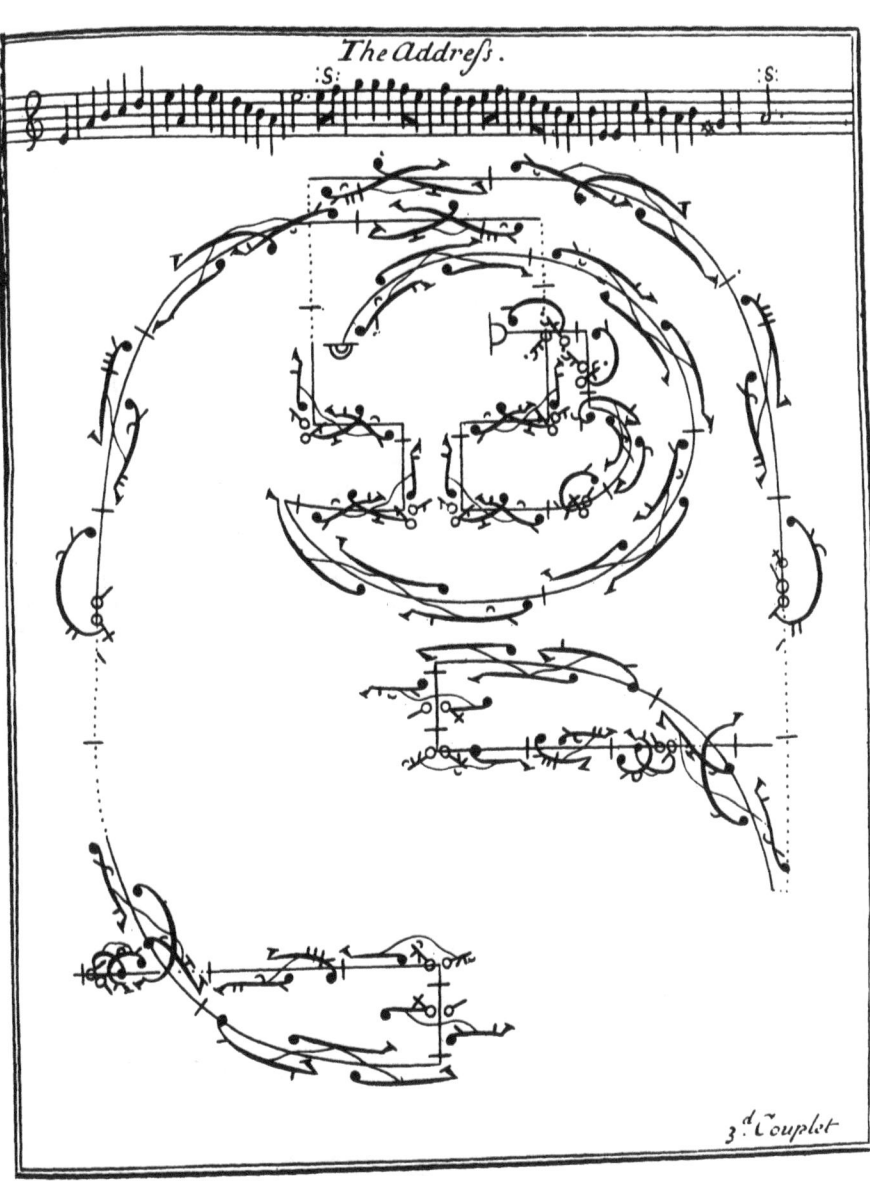

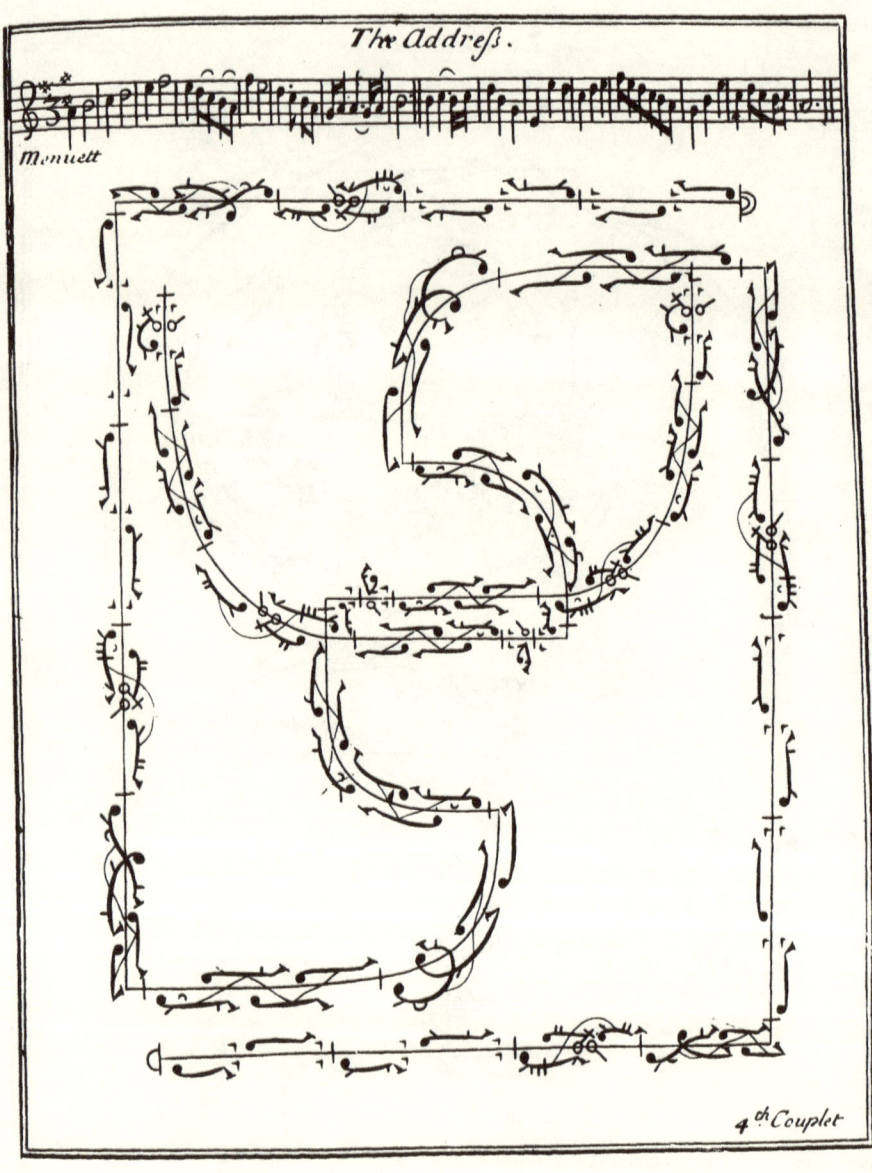

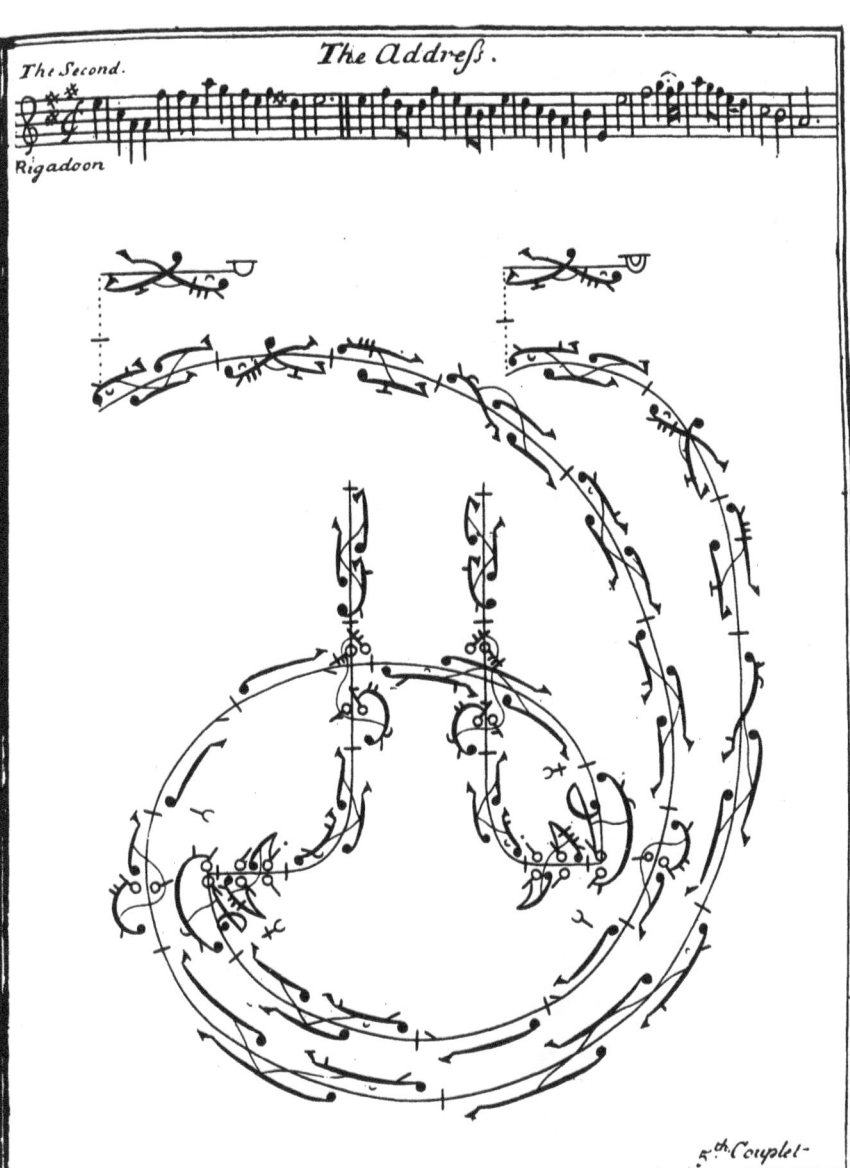

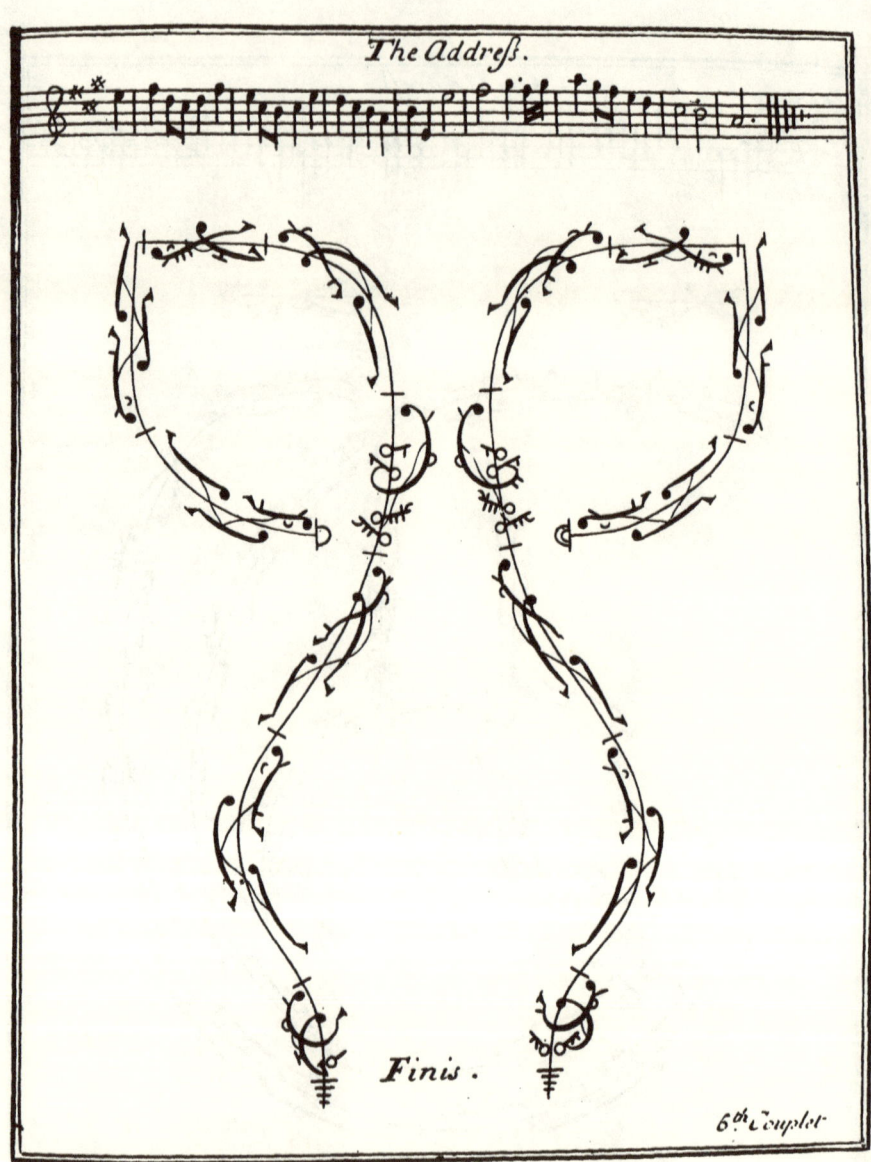

THE

Prince *EUGENE*,

A

NEW DANCE,

Compos'd and Written into *Characters* and *Figures*,

In the Year 1718.

By KELLOM TOMLINSON,

FOR

The Use and Improvement of his Scholars; Publish'd for the further Encouragement of DANCING.

N. B. The following Dances by Mr. *Kellom* is also printed, *viz.*

The *Submission*,
The *Shepherdess*,
The *Passepied Round O*.

To be had at the Author's in *Southampton Street*, the Fifth Door from *Holbourn*, on the Left Hand going up to *Bloomsbury* Square.
Price five shillings.

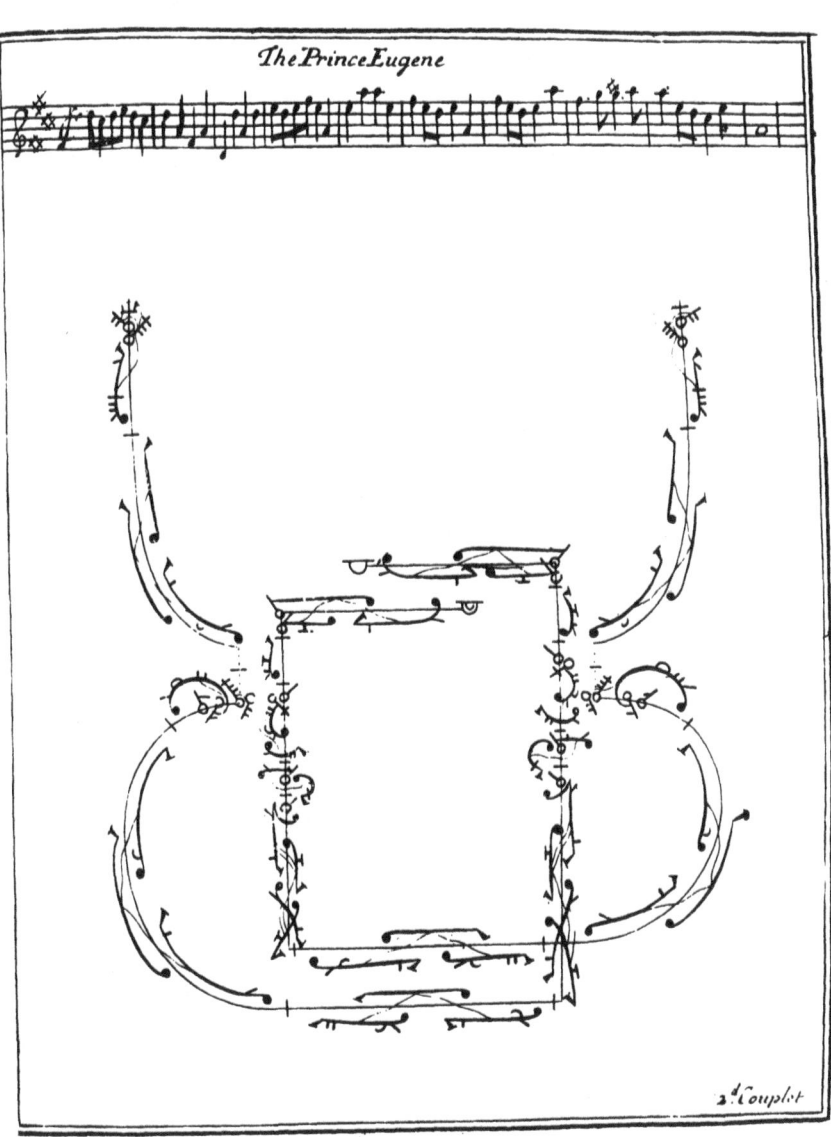

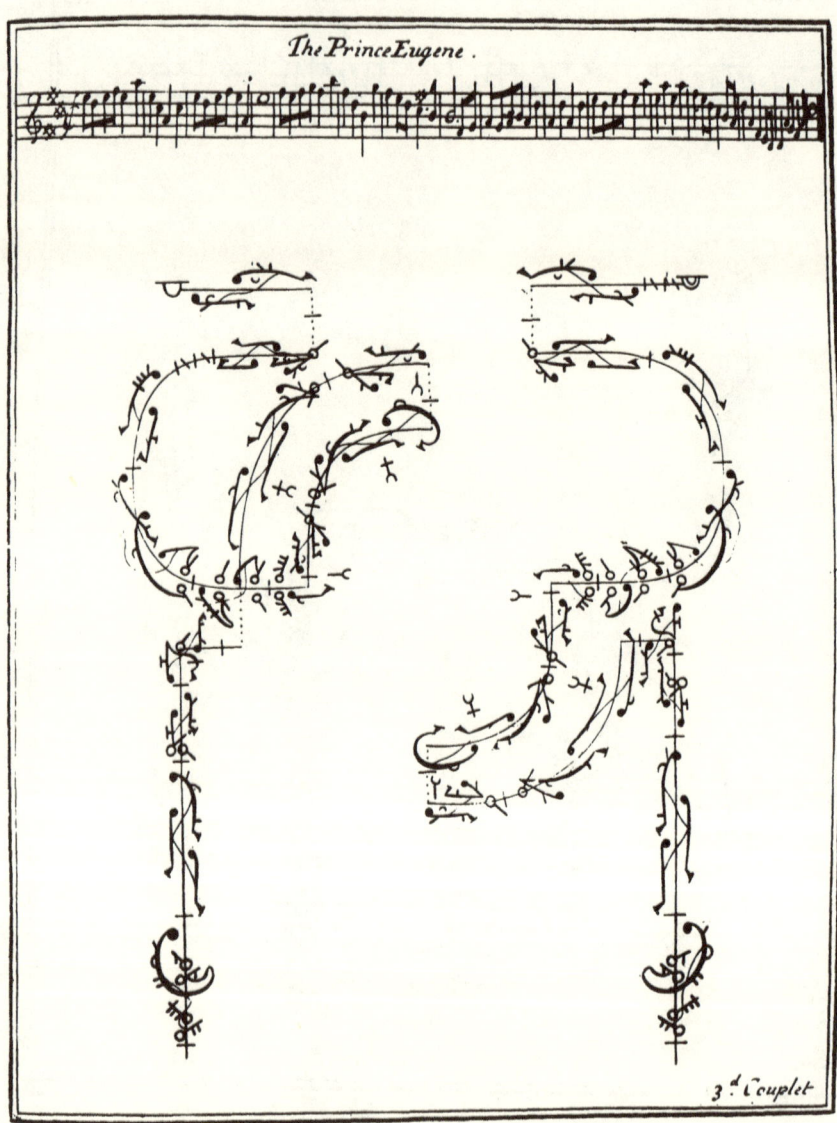

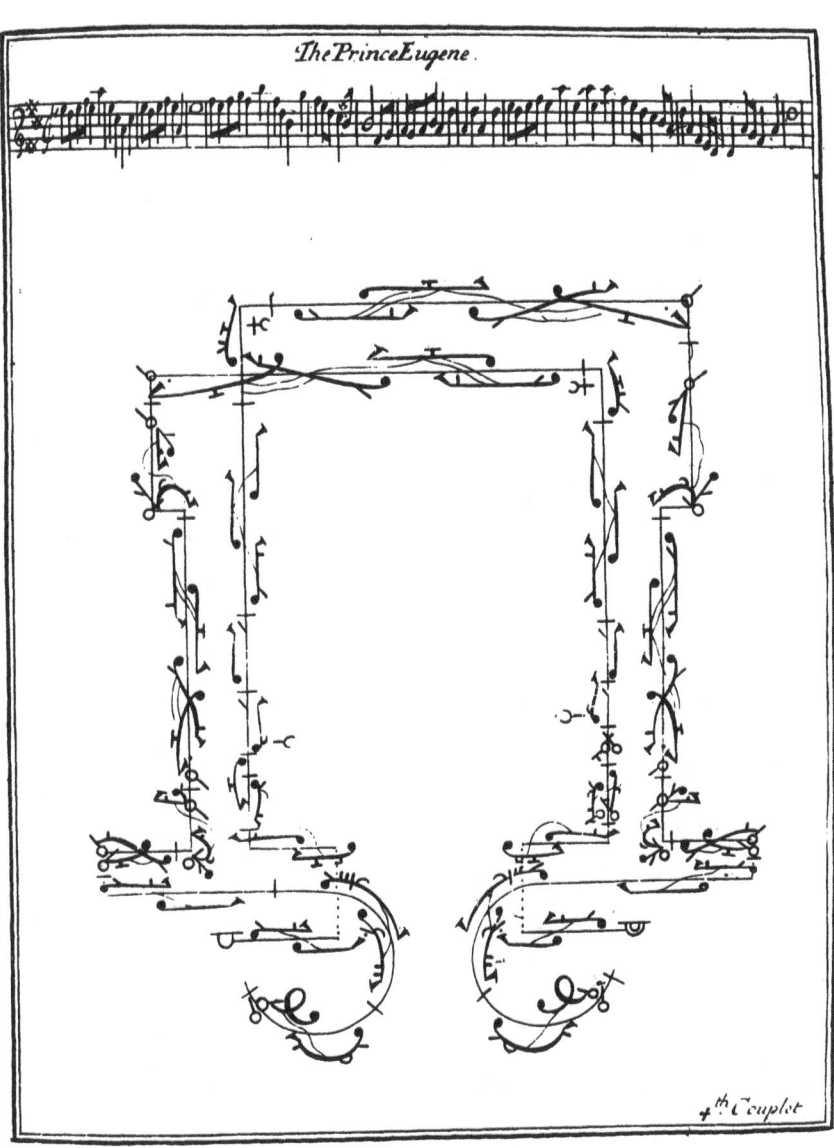

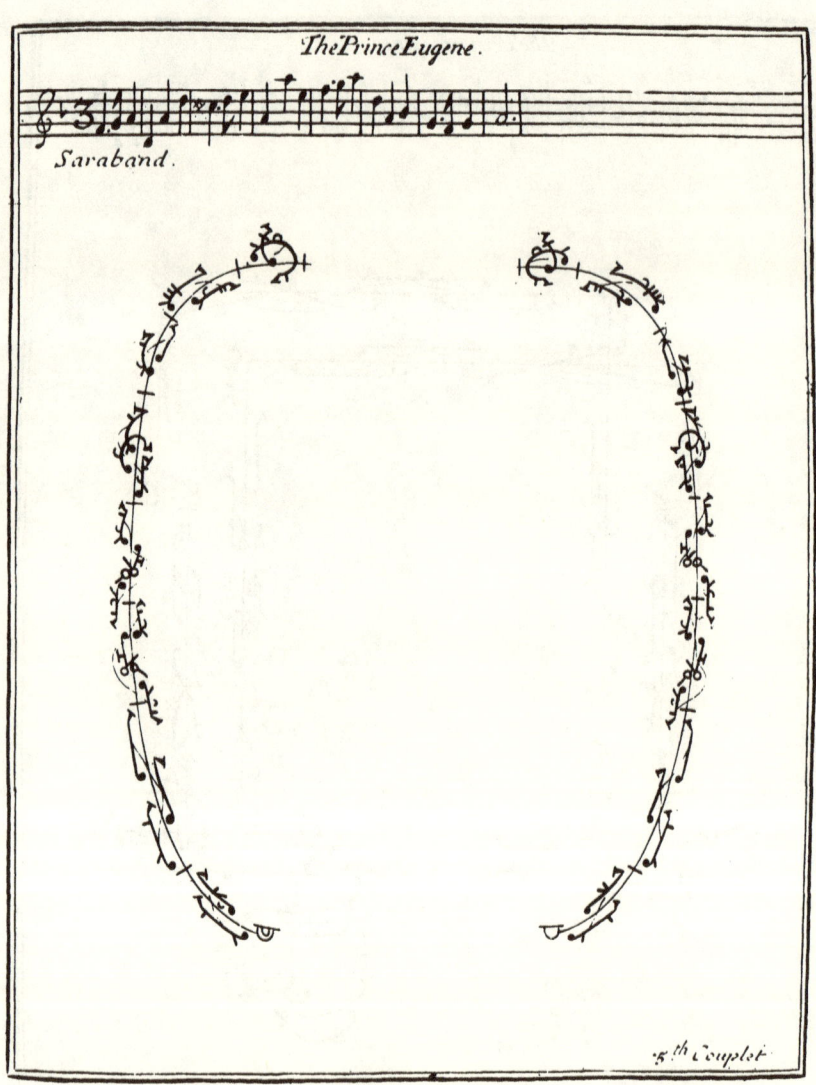

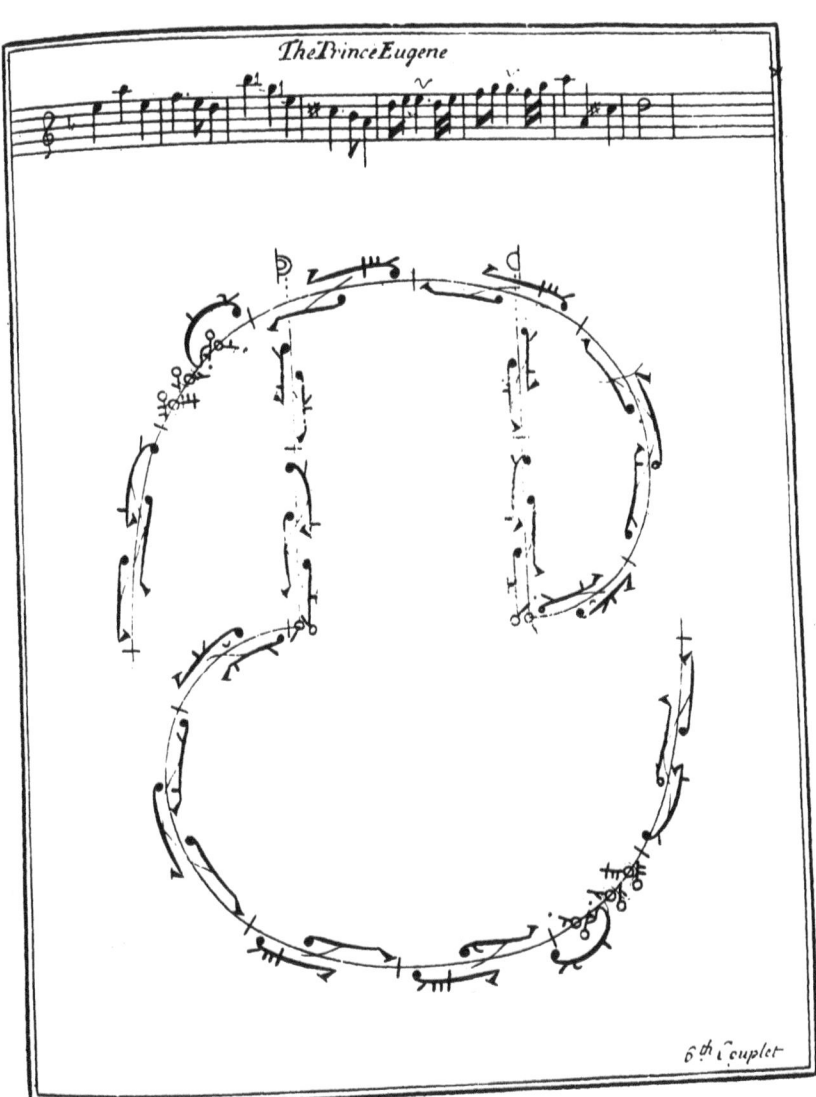

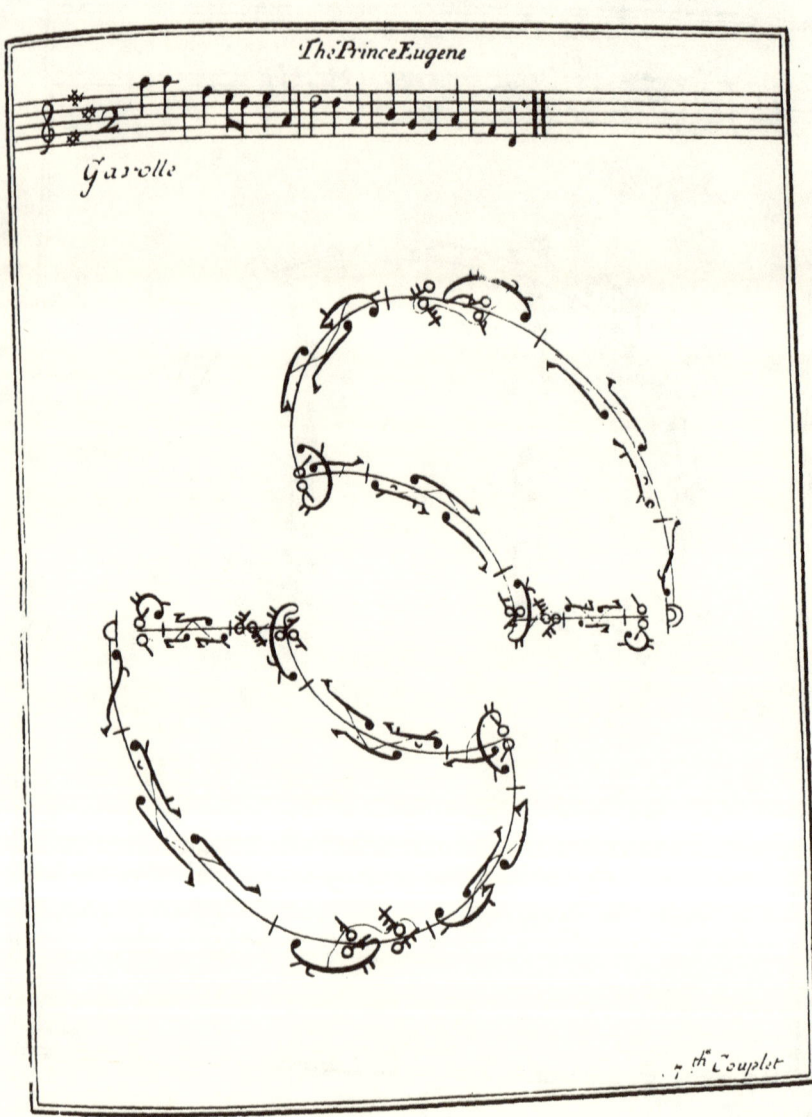

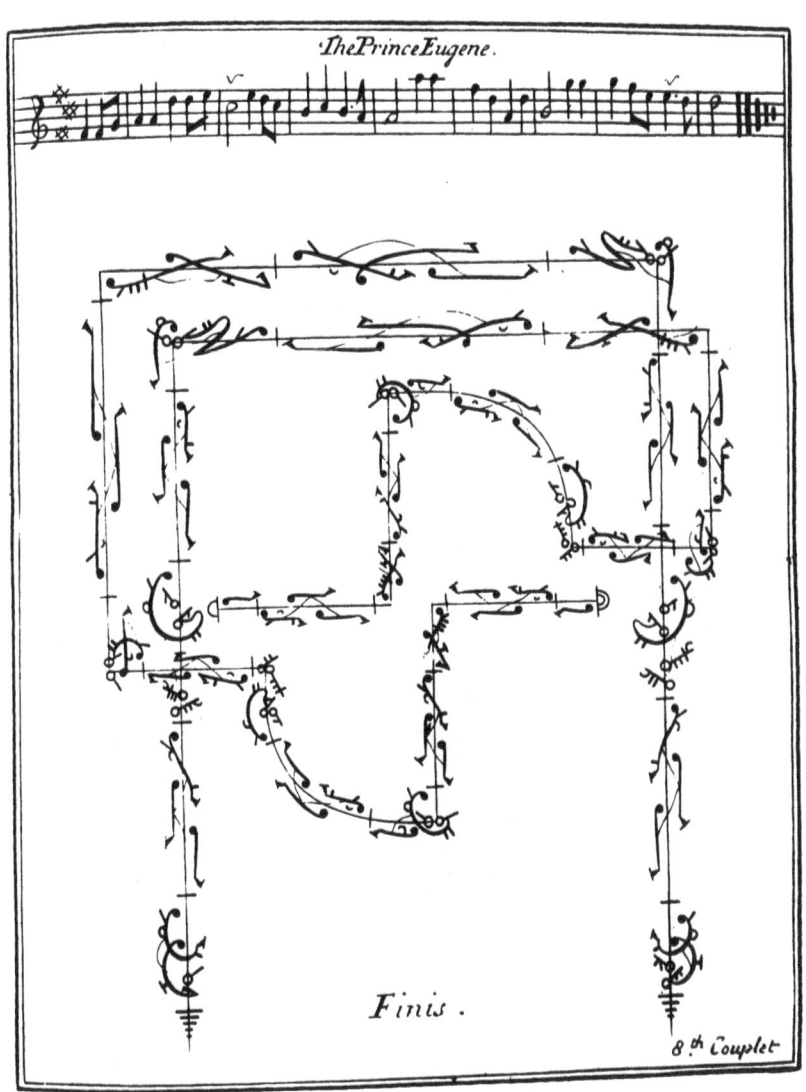

THE SUBMISSION,

A

New BALL DANCE,

Compos'd and Written into Characters and Figures,

In the Year, 1717,

By *Kellom Tomlinson*, Dancing-Master.

For the Use and Improvement of his Scholars; Publish'd for the further Encouragement of Dancing.

To be had at the Author's Lodgings at Mr. *Smith*'s a Coach-maker, the Corner of *King*'s *Gate Street Holbourn*, or at Mr. *Walsh*'s, at the *Harp* and *Hautboy*, in *Catherine-Street* in the *Strand*.
N.B. The following Dances by Mr. *Kellom* are likewise Printed, *viz*. The *Shepherdess* and *Passepeid* Round O.

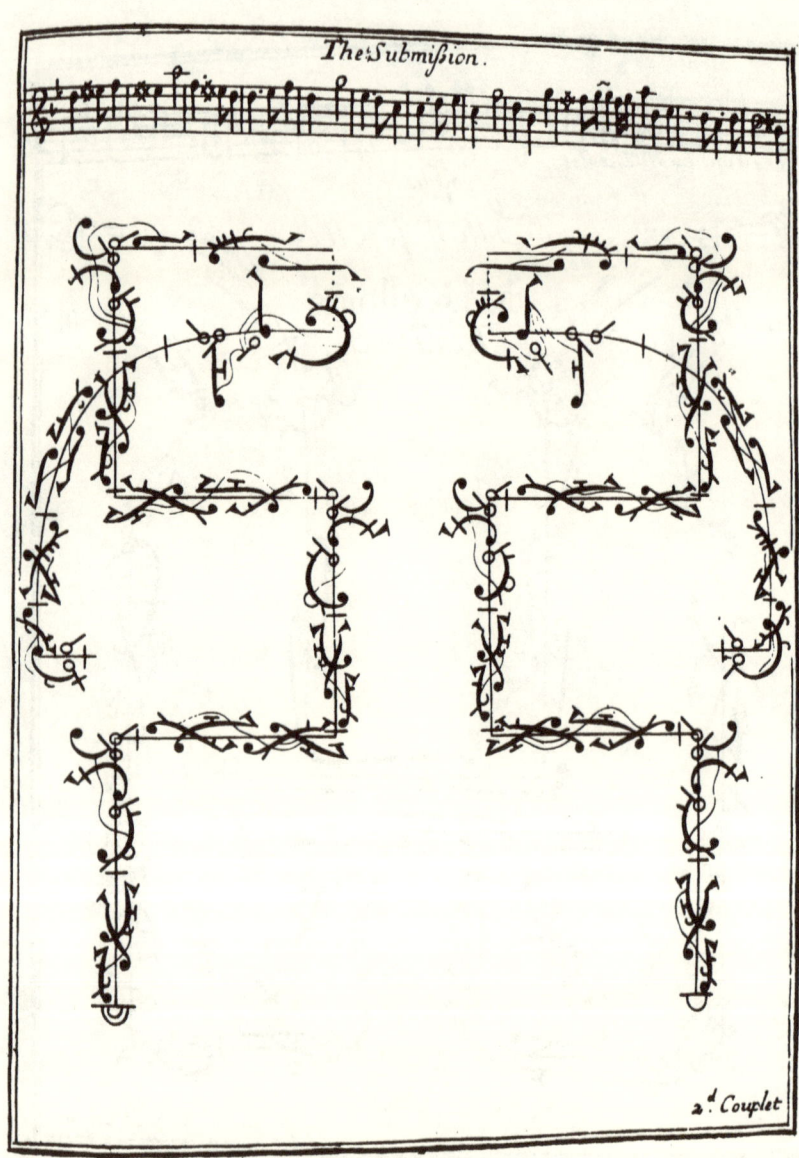

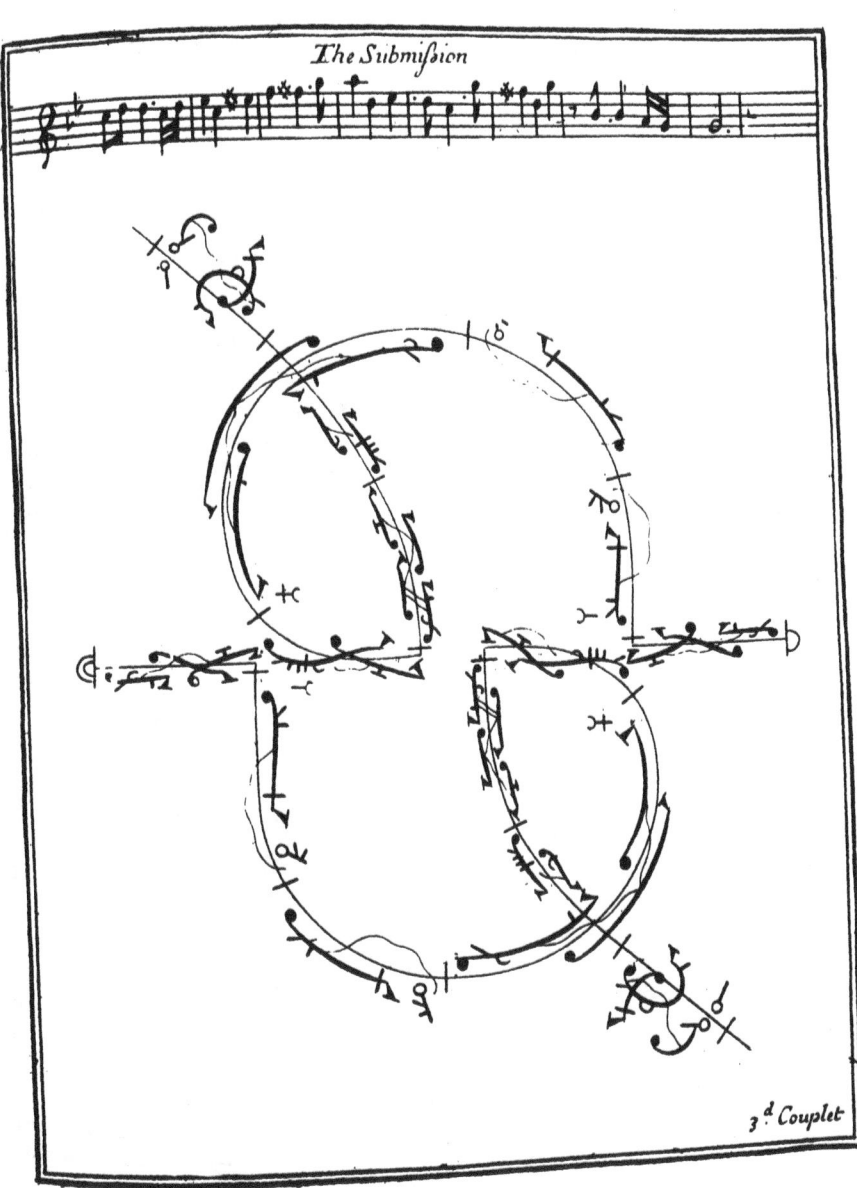

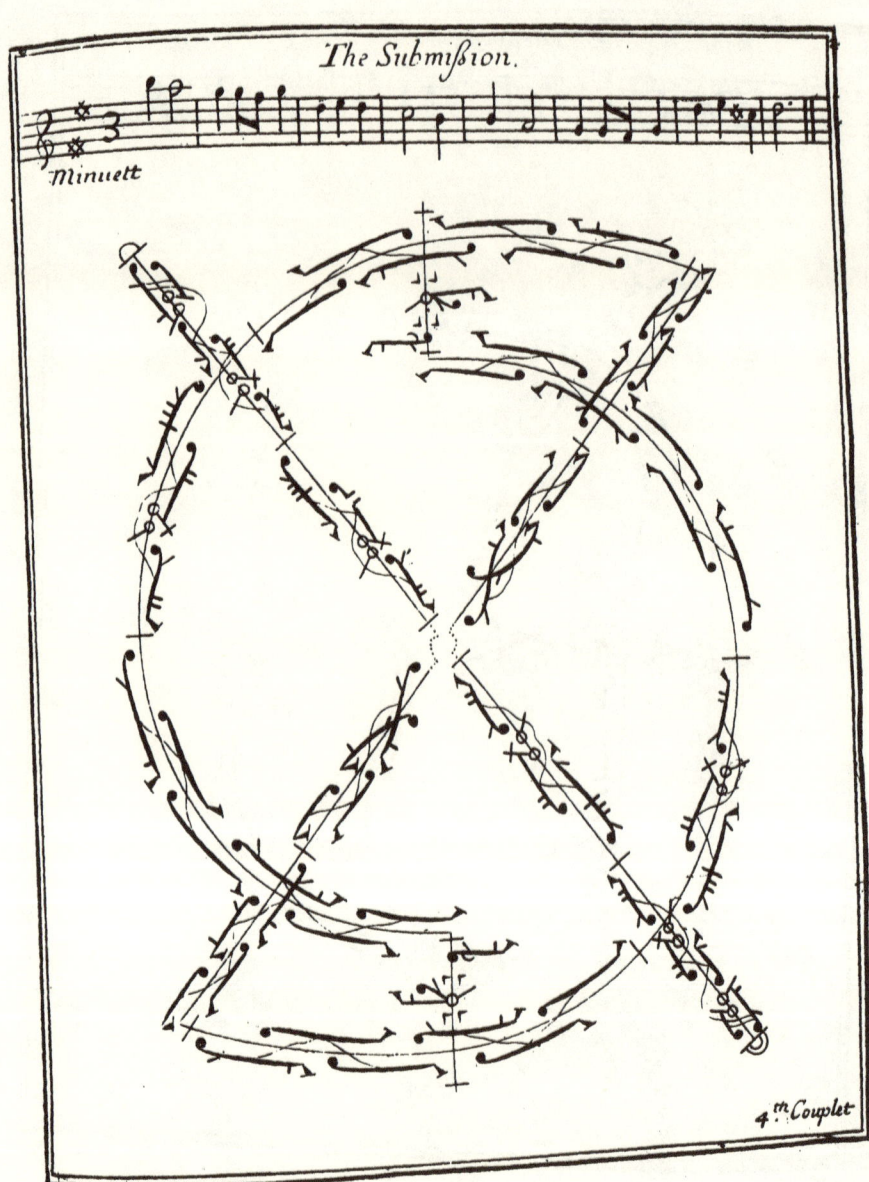

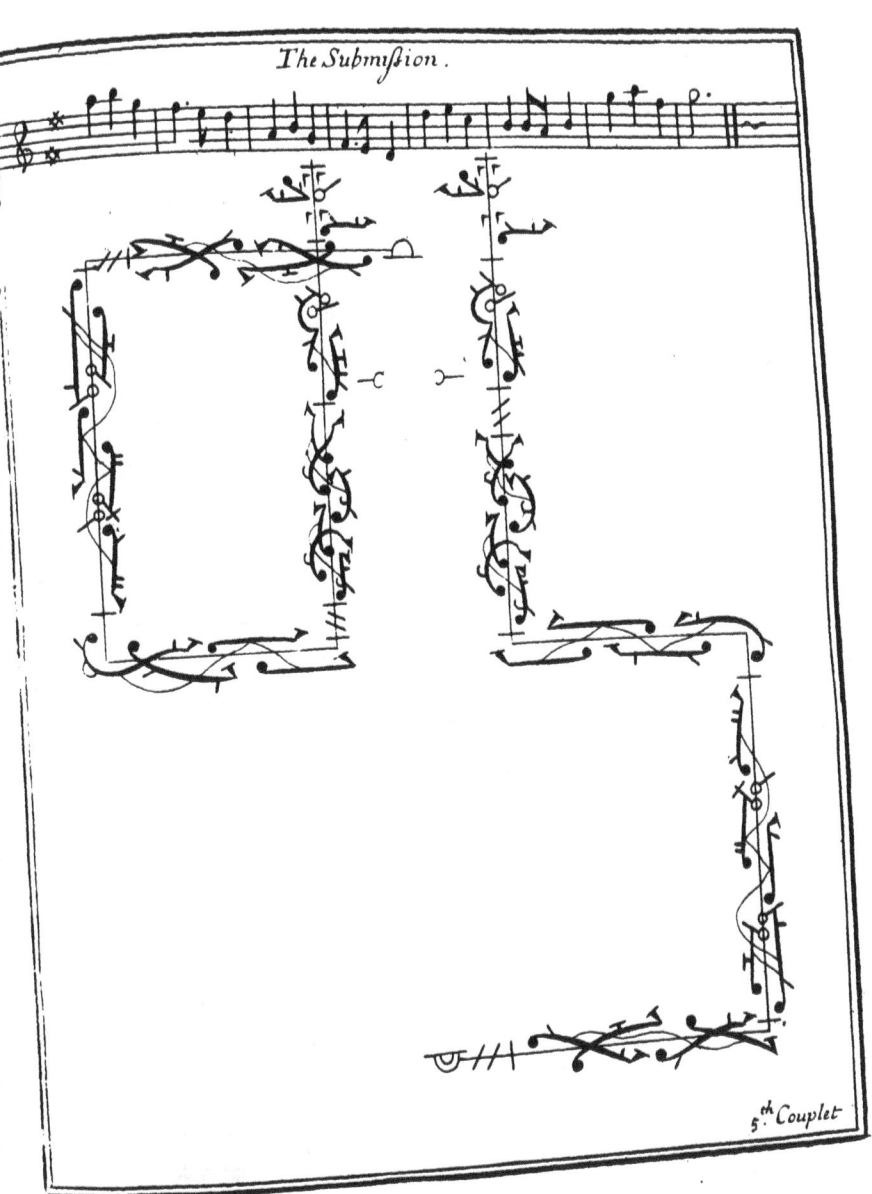

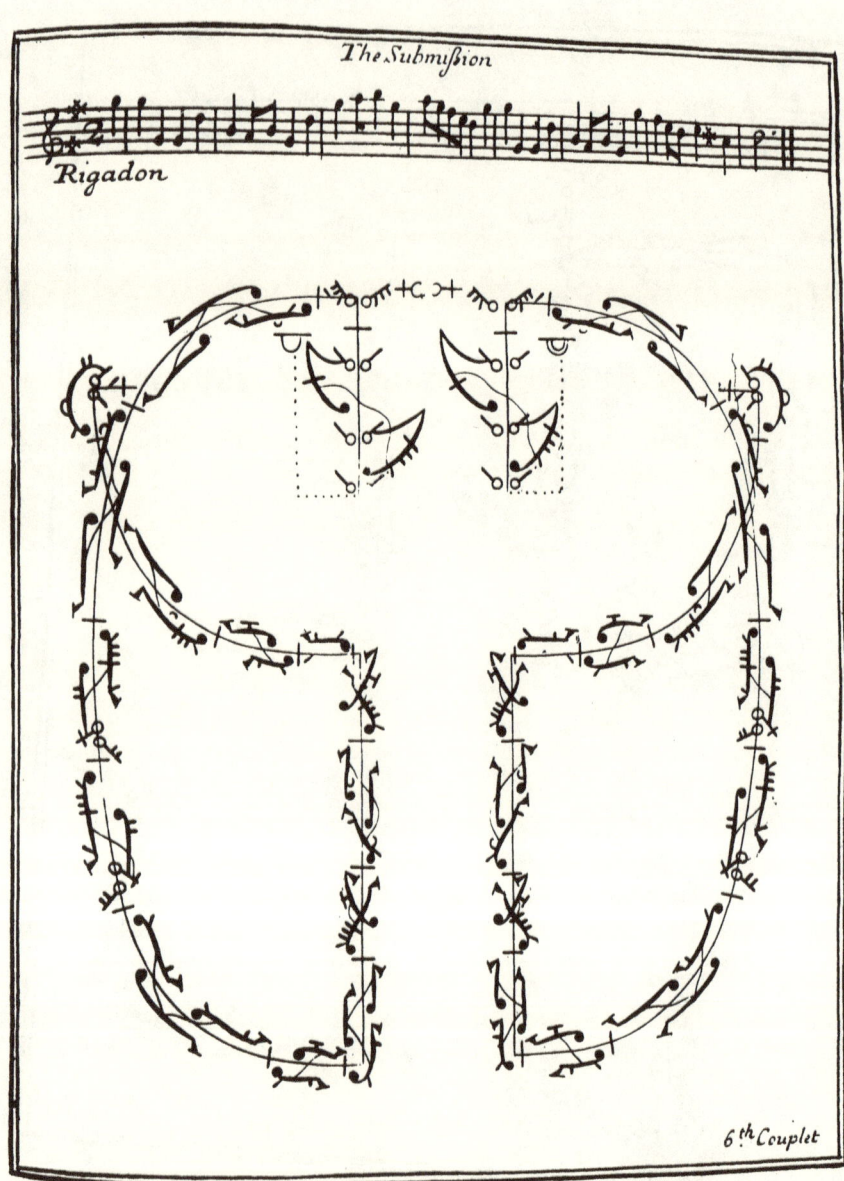

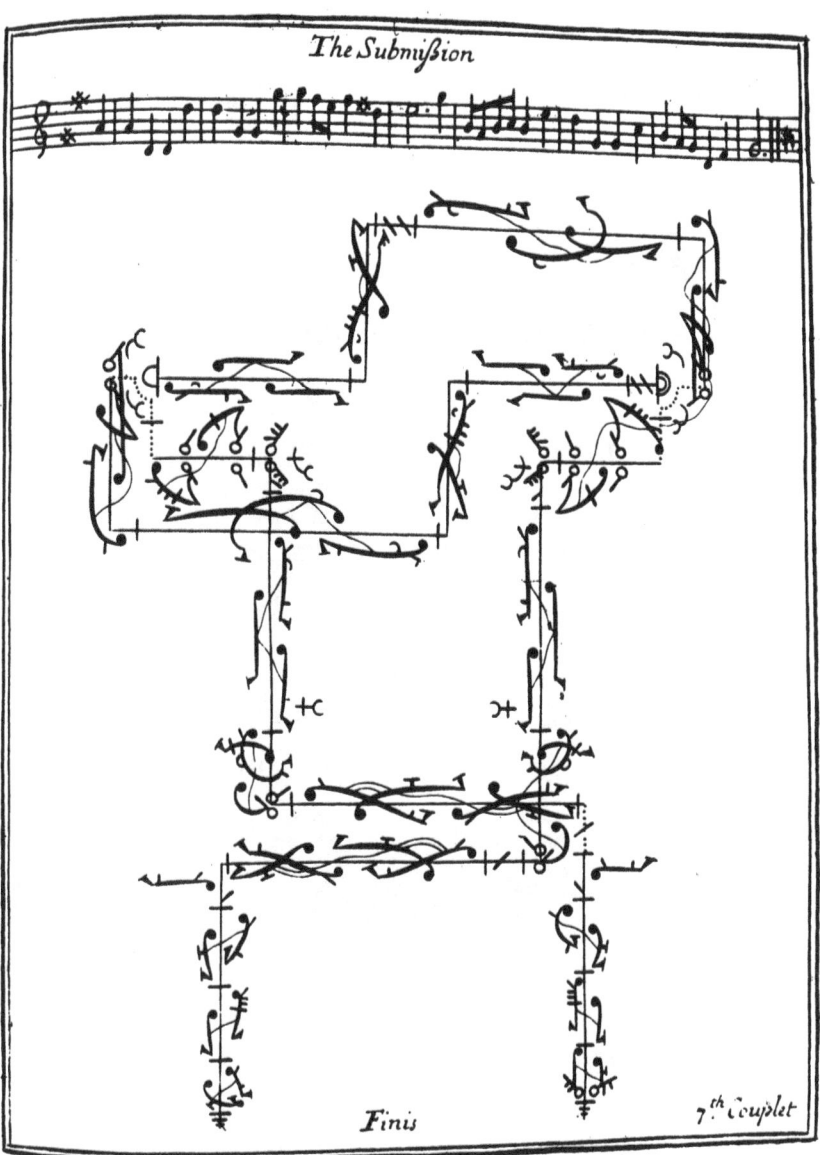

THE SHEPHERDESS.
A NEW DANCE,

Compos'd and Written into Characters,

In the Year 1716,

By KELLOM TOMLINSON, Dancing-Master.

Engraven into CHARACTERS and FIGURES, for the farther Encouragement of

DANCING.

Note, The Paffepied Round O, by Mr. KELLOM, is likewife printed.

To be had at the Author's Lodgings at Mr. *Smith*'s, a Coach-maker the Corner of *King's-gate-ftreet, Holborn*; or at Mr. *Walfh*'s, at the Harp and Hautboy in *Catherine-ftreet* in the *Strand.* (Price Five Shillings.)

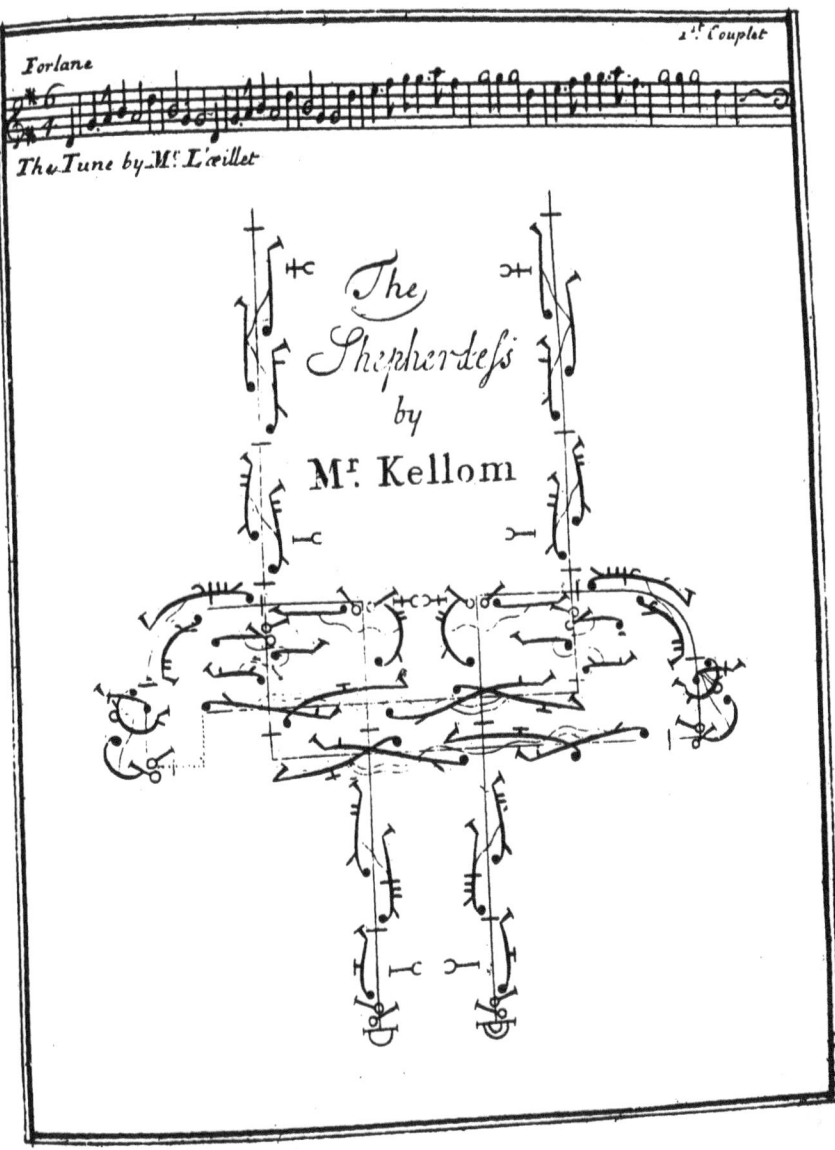

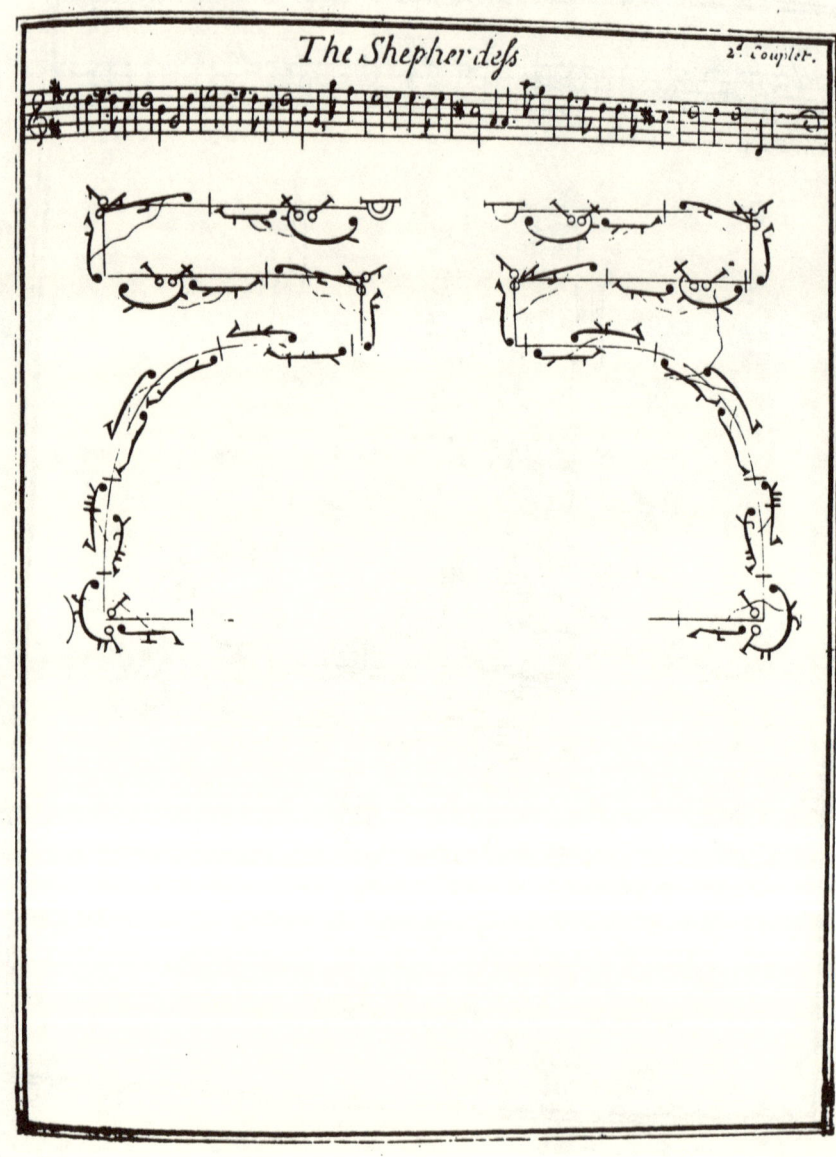

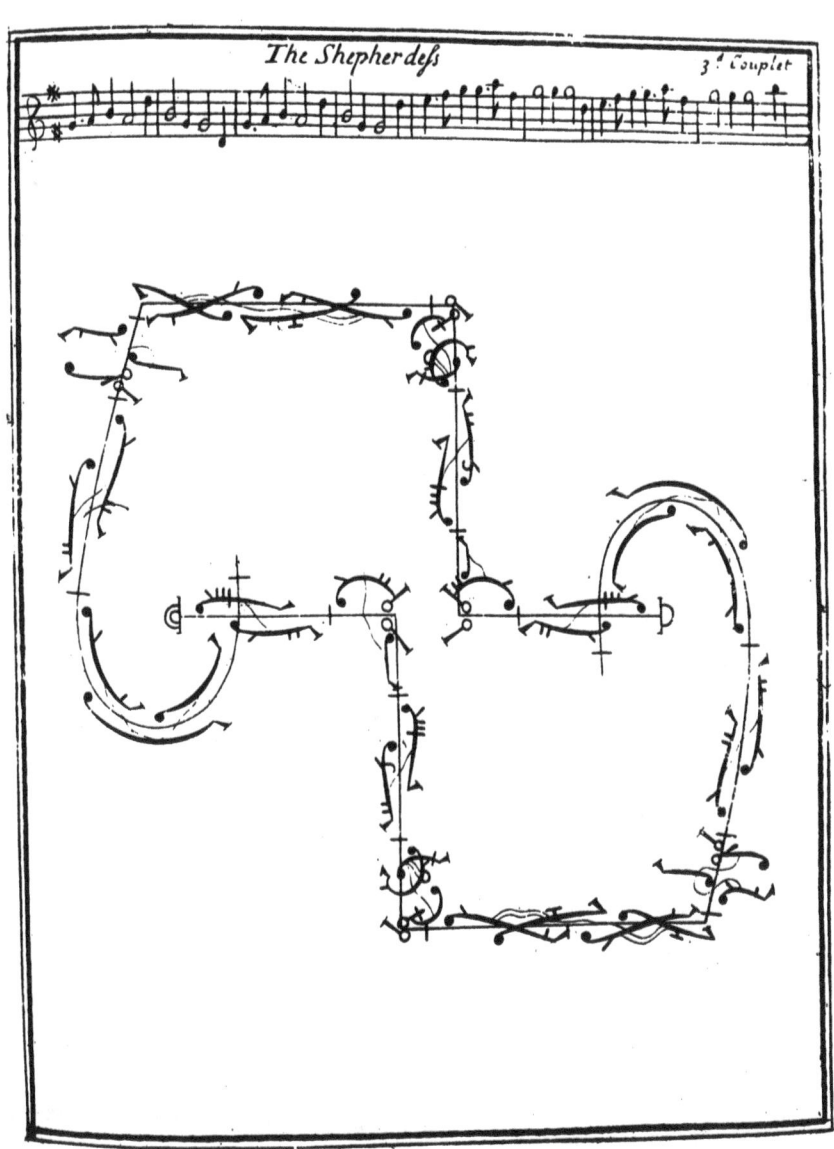

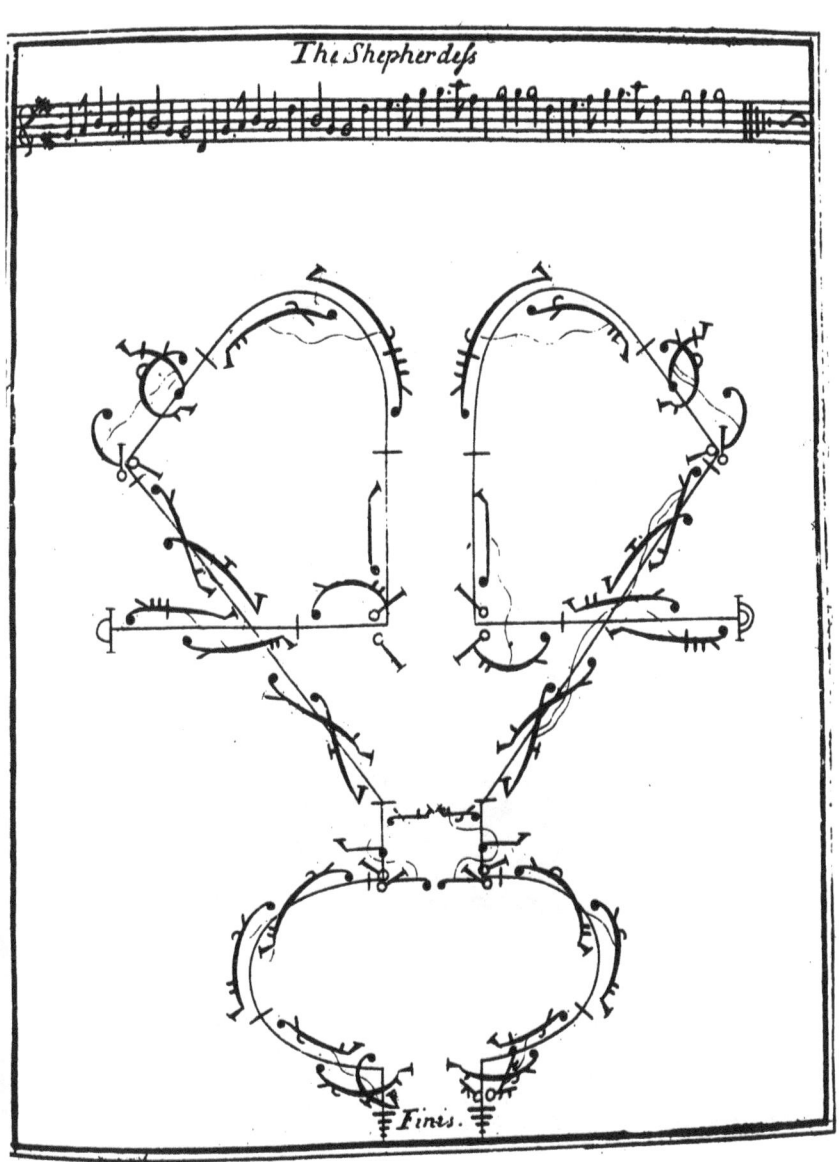

THE
Passepied Round O
A
NEW DANCE,
Compos'd and Written into Characters,

In the Year, 1715.

By *Kellom Tomlinson*, Dancing Master.

Engraven into CHARACTERS *and* FIGURES, *for the* Use *of* MASTERS.

To be had at Mr. *Walsh*'s at the Sign of the *Harp and Hautboy* in *Katherine Street*, or the Author's Lodgings, at Mr. *Smith*s a Coach-maker, the Corner of *King's Gate Street* in *Holbourn*
(Price Two Shillings and Six Pence.)

Passepeid Round

The tune by Mr. L'œillet

The passepeid Round O
Mr Kellom's new Dance
In the Year 1715

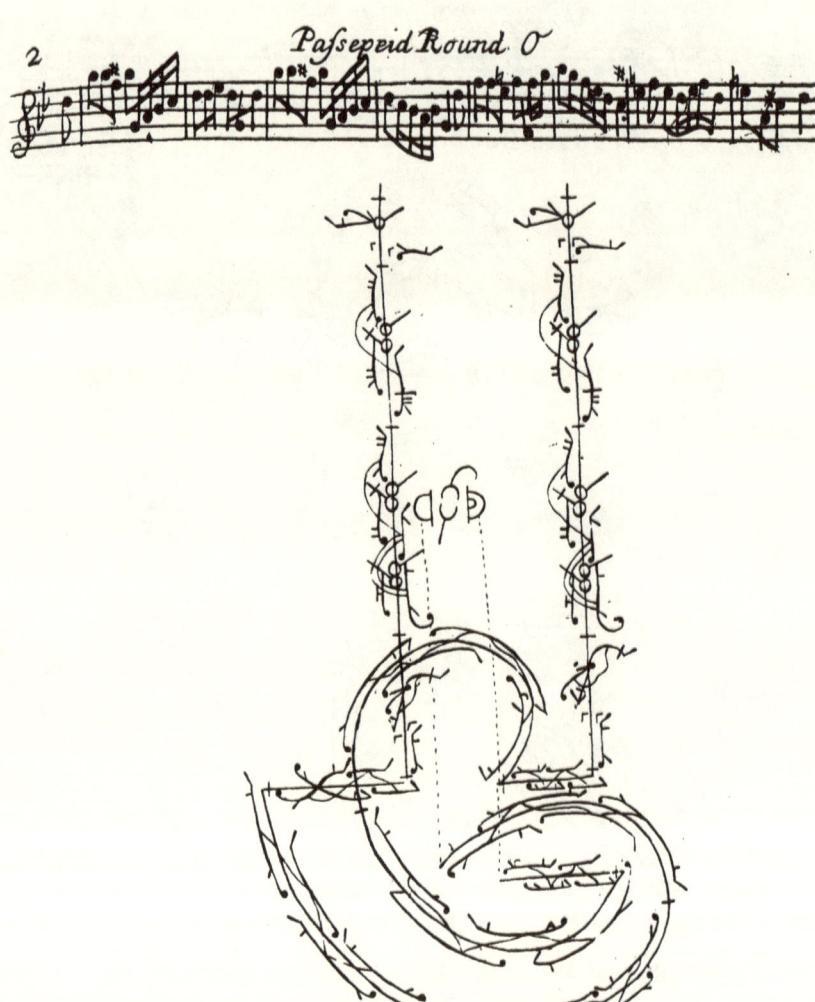

Passepeid Round O

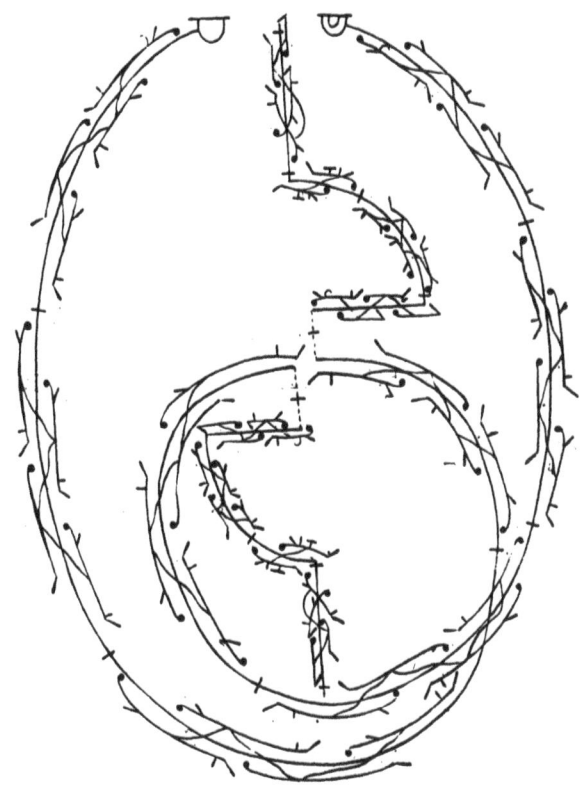

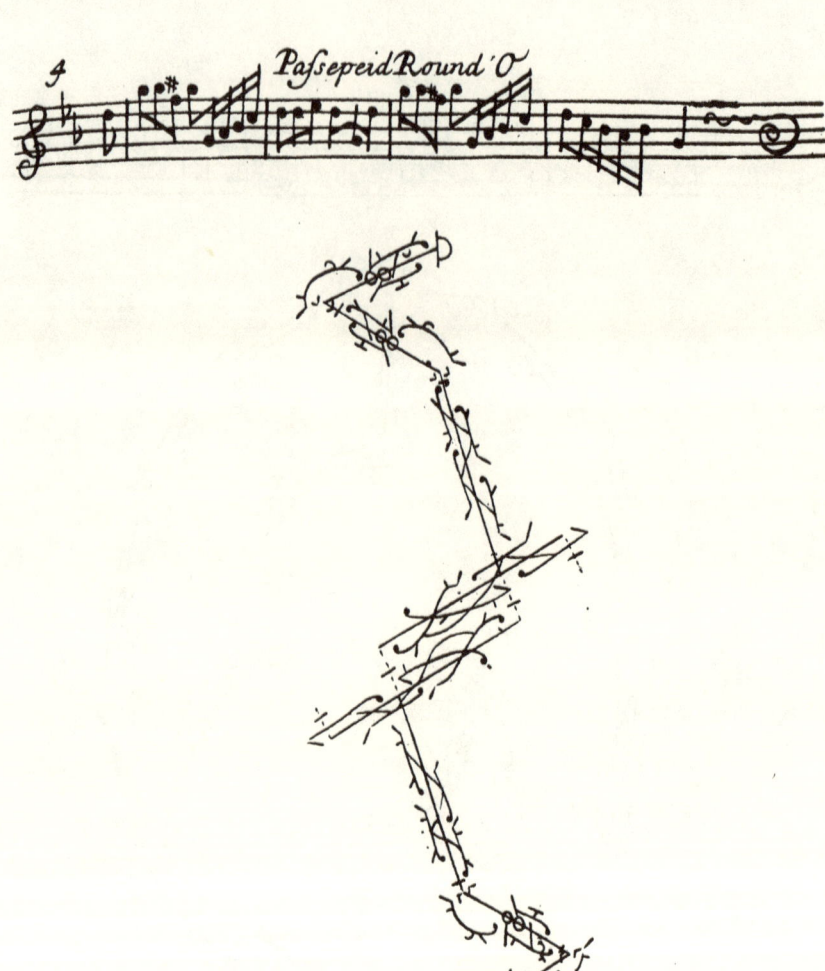

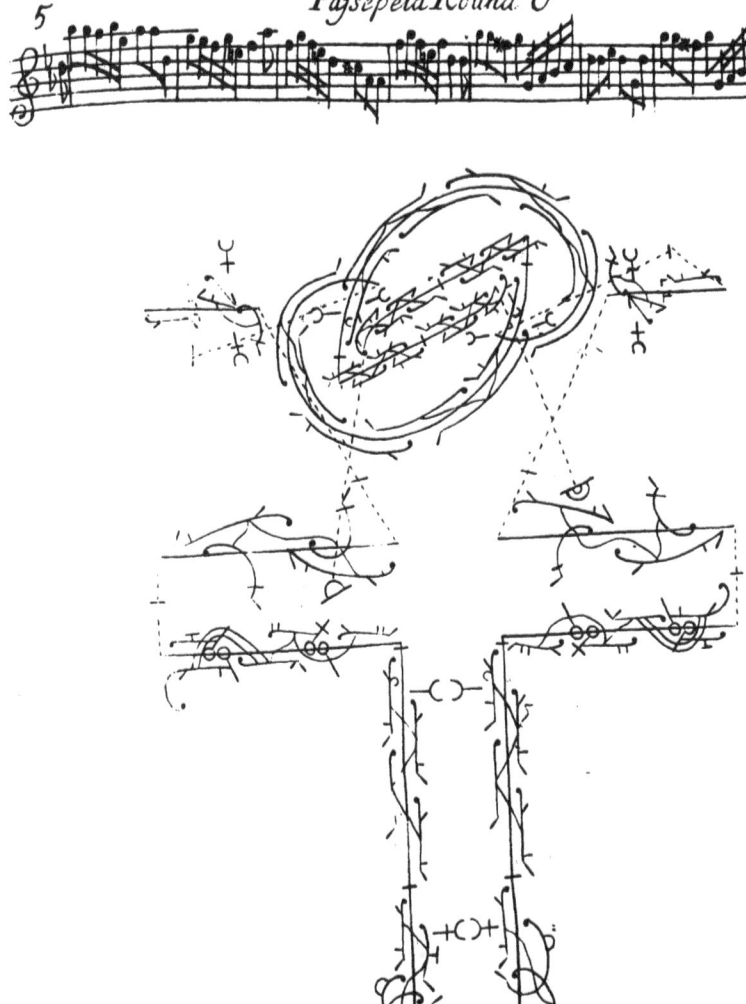

www.ingramcontent.com/pod-product-compliance
Lightning Source LLC
Chambersburg PA
CBHW032106280426
43661CB00105B/1316